PACE COLLEGE
OPPORTVNITAS
ARS COMMERCIVM CIVITAS
MCMVI
NEW YORK

D1247538

THE COMMUNIST MENACE IN MALAYA

GENERAL SIR GERALD TEMPLER, G.C.M.G., K.C.B., K.B.E., D.S.O.

High Commissioner of the Federation of Malaya from January 1952 to June 1954.

Photo "Straits Times"

Fr.

HARRY MILLER

THE COMMUNIST MENACE IN MALAYA

FREDERICK A. PRAEGER
NEW YORK

BOOKS THAT MATTER

First published in the United States of America in 1954 by Frederick A. Praeger, Inc., Publishers, 105 West 40th Street, New York, 18, N.Y.

Reprinted 1955

Composed in Granjon type and printed at the St Ann's Press Park Road, Altrincham. Made in Great Britain

DEDICATED

to the European women in the Federation of Malaya—particularly the wives of planters and police officers—who have quietly and courageously stood with their husbands against Communist terrorism

to the Asian women who have also suffered much with Eastern impassiveness

to the widows whose husbands met harsh deaths

and to my wife, Catherine, who encouraged me to write this book

Preface

THIS is not a political book; I leave such a task to others more competent than myself. This is presented as a newspaperman's report of the reasons behind, and the progress and implications of, the most difficult small war that British, Malay, Gurkha, and other Commonwealth troops, the Federation Police, and the Government have had to fight in British Colonial history. It must be admitted that the first three years of the war were largely three years of failure in the field; hence it has not been easy to write without underestimating the occasional successes of the troops and the Government and over-emphasizing those of the terrorists.

British troops have gone through far worse ordeals in Malaya than their predecessors did in the jungles of Burma; Gurkha warriors have enhanced their reputations as jungle fighters; young Malay soldiers have asked only to be well led to show their prowess in the field; the police, in the forefront from the very beginning, have done an exceptional job in their unaccustomed rôle. It has not been possible, of course, to relate every gallant episode by every battalion or each group of policemen, or to tell of all fine work by individuals —such as that of the engine-drivers, who kept the Malayan railways running in spite of derailments and other acts of sabotage.

The canvas of the Malayan war is a tremendous one, and my difficulty has been to select the highlights and the murky and deep black patches to give a fair picture. If I succeed in giving readers a good impression of what the war is all about, how it reached heights and dropped to depths, and how it clarified the problems that confront a country which craves only for peace, so that it can build itself up to become the most progressive in South-east Asia and receive independence in a tranquil atmosphere internally, then I shall be satisfied. I feel that too little is known in Great Britain and the United States of this war, which closely affects those two countries.

The conquest of the Communists and their eradication from Malaya for good and all are of the greatest importance to the democratic world. I do not think the peoples of Britain and the United States have sufficiently realized this; neither have they appreciated, I think, that time is not on our side anywhere in South-east Asia where Communists are waging war.

Much of my task on this book would have been impossible but for the considerable help I received from the police forces of Singapore and the Federation of Malaya. They gave me access to confidential documents, particularly those relating to the history of the Malayan Communist Party, the enemy of the country. I have to thank, too, many personal friends in both police forces, in the Federation Government, and in the planting and other worlds for the time and trouble they spent in telling me everything. As far as my police friends are particularly concerned, Malaya cannot be told too often how much it owes to the police force in the Federation. Whatever their deficiencies might be, they carried out a tremendous task, for which they were poorly equipped for at least three years.

Finally, I wish to thank my employers, the Straits Times Press, Ltd, in Singapore, for permission to use material and to reproduce photographs which appeared in their group of newspapers. Part of the material in this book was gathered while I was, for five years, their Chief Correspondent in the Federation, based in Kuala Lumpur. They were interesting years, and when the Emergency occurred they were not without danger. That made the job all the more exhilarating.

HARRY MILLER

NOTE

In the first part of the book I call the enemy Communists 'bandits,' which was their popular name in the early years. They are known now as 'terrorists,' the official term.

I have also taken the liberty of saying 'Malaya' instead of 'Federation of Malaya.' In the country itself the general geographical description 'Malaya' is taken to mean Singapore and the Federation of Malaya.

H. M.

Contents

Illustrations

Maps

Introduction

WITH the end of World War II there were signs that Russia had high hopes for expansion in the Far East. Stalin had spoken both before and after the War. He urged Communists the world over not to worry about " capitalist strongholds " in the West, but to look to the Far East, to the peoples " coming to nationhood " and awaiting " leadership."

China was the first to be engulfed in the maw of Communism. Korea would have been too, but for the intervention of the United Nations. To-day a great part of Viet Nam, one of the Associated States of Indo-China, is torn by a war launched by Communist zealots headed by a Moscow-trained Annamite, Ho Chi-Minh. Burma is attempting to destroy Communism. So is Malaya.

Of the South-east Asian countries on the mainland of the great continent of Asia, only Thailand is relatively free from internal Communist strife. Thailand has declared itself absolutely anti-Communist, but most close observers believe that if Indo-China was overrun and Red armies moved still farther southward Thailand would submit to Communism instead of waging war against it.

It was not until the middle of June 1948 that Malaya became the scene of conflict with Communists as represented by the Malayan Communist Party. This party had lived illegally from its birth in the nineteen-twenties until the Japanese declared war on Britain in 1941, when, in view of Russia's alliance with Britain in Europe, it offered its members as a guerrilla force against the new enemy.

After the surrender of Japan and the liberation of Malaya the services of the Party were recognized, as was Russia's status as one of the four Great Powers, and Communism in Malaya was no longer illegal. For the next two years the Party inspired industrial strife, published and uttered inflammable propaganda, and finally provoked terrorism and murder, which it hoped would turn Malaya upside down and force the British to quit.

In June 1948, only after strong public demand in Malaya and London, the Government of the Federation of Malaya declared the existence of an "Emergency," banned the Malayan Communist Party, and pitched British, Malay, and Gurkha troops and police against a Communist army which had been secretly built up and trained from the day the Japanese laid down their arms.

The British Government in London and the Federation Government at its capital in Kuala Lumpur, in the centre of Malaya, were confident that the Emergency would be over in a few months. They ignored the warnings of the experts in Malaya—the police and intelligence officers and civil servants, who knew the thoughts and ways of Chinese and the Communists among them—that, once the Red revolt broke, it would take years to defeat.

The Malayan war developed into the most complex and expensive small war in the history of the British Commonwealth. (It has cost the British and Federation Governments over £1,000,000 a month, apart from millions of dollars in property destroyed by the Communists.)

Malaya had a very narrow escape. It could have lost territory to the Communists in the first few desperate weeks after the declaration of an Emergency. The country was unprepared for war—for that is what it amounted to. Its police force was untrained and ill-equipped to combat large-scale internal hostilities.

The Communists possessed every initial advantage an army could desire. Its total strength was unknown. It could launch attacks on any rubber-estate, tin-mine, police station, village, or town at any time it liked, and with disastrous effect. Unlike the defenders, it had plenty of weapons and ammunition. A number of its leaders were experienced guerrillas.

Fortunately for Britain and Malaya, the Communists' plan of campaign went off at half-cock. The Party had far too complicated a military and political set-up throughout the length and breadth of the country for its war to be conducted effectively. Its forces lacked the equipment for successful modern guerrilla warfare, such as radio communications and transport.

Also terrorism and murder alienated the people whose open support would have won greater victories for the Communists. Another important reason for the Party's failure was the gallant stand of the producers of rubber and tin, who did not close their estates, mines, and factories as the enemy thought they would.

AN ALREADY-FAMOUS PICTURE OF CHILDREN'S LIFE ON A RUBBER-ESTATE

Twins in their sand-bagged nursery with a Special Constable on duty outside.

Photo "Straits Times"

Barbed Wire surrounding the Factory Area on a Rubber-estate

The Kind of Armoured Vehicle used by Planters in Malaya

Under the bonnet steel plating shields vulnerable parts of the engine.

So the war developed into a war without a front line, a war with no military threat to the country in which it was being waged.

This campaign must be considered as part of a preconceived, world-wide Russian plan to establish Soviet republics in the Far East. In Malaya they were trying for the first time to conquer British territory, although until now Russia and Communist China have given only lip support to the "struggle" by the Malayan Communists.

Despite this, a Communist invasion or infiltration via Indo-China and Thailand or Burma is still Malaya's greatest danger—and the Malayan Communists live in hopes of receiving such aid.

Malaya is one of the loveliest countries in South-east Asia. It is a country which knew peace and harmony from the days when it came under British rule in the nineteenth century right up to the beginning of the war with Japan.

With 50,600 square miles of mountain, jungle, and plain, it is a little larger than England without Wales, a little smaller than Florida, in the United States.

The country is always green. Rice-fields, rubber-estates, and tin-mines have been cut out of the jungle, which, however, still encompasses three-quarters of the country.

In the jungle there are elephant, tiger, rhinoceros, wild bison, deer, and a murderous bearded pig, 130 varieties of snakes, and more than 800 species of butterflies and 200 dragon-flies.

A mountain range down the spine of the country forms an effective economic barrier between the western and eastern coasts. In spite of more than a hundred years of progress, only the western half of the peninsula has been developed, and here are to be found almost all the 720 tin-mines and most of the three million acres of rubber-estates. The eastern half of the country still contains backward territory.

The population of the Federation of Malaya is about 5,300,000. The Malays number 2,600,000, the Chinese 2,040,000. The next largest groups are the Indians and the Pakistanis, who total 578,000. There are only about 12,000 British and other Europeans.

No Malay State on the west coast has remained predominantly Malay. Chinese preponderate, and control most of the business.

Only Kelantan and Trengganu, 'lost' on the isolated east coast, with limitations to economic expansion, have absolute Malay majorities in population. It is significant, therefore, that they have never really been sorely troubled by the Malayan Communists.

Politically this small country is divided into eleven separate governments. Each of the nine Malay States—Johore, Pahang, Negri Sembilan, Selangor, Perak, Kedah, Perlis, Kelantan, and Trengganu—has a Ruler who is head of his Government and possesses a certain autonomy. Each is assisted by a Malay Mentri Besar (Prime Minister) and a Malay State Secretary. Each State Council has a majority of Malay members.

The two remaining territories, the Settlements of Penang and Province Wellesley and of Malacca, are headed by British officers of the Malayan Civil Service.

The supreme authority in the country is the Federation Government. The Chief Executive is a British High Commissioner appointed by Her Majesty. He is advised by an Executive Council. A Legislative Council of seventy-four men and women endeavours to mould the country for self-government.

That briefly is the unique system of government in Malaya. It strives hard, but efficiency is retarded because the Federation Government has to consult each little entity before being able to introduce a measure important for the whole country.

This long process is aggravated by a lack of unity among the Malay States themselves.

Perplexing political problems have developed in post-war Malaya, and they mainly concern the two predominant races, the Malays and the Chinese, who are as unlike in character and ways of living and thought as a gazelle and a leopard.

The Malays are open, smiling, easygoing people, who are peace-loving. Despite the changing scene and the problems and dangers around him, the Malay outside the towns still lives from day to day. If he has enough money and rice to feed himself and his family for the next day he is content, and he relaxes in the pleasant company of his fellow-men under the fruit-trees in the tranquil kampongs.

A Chinese bends his back to labour, works most of the day, if need be, to make money. His ambition is to make enough to live comfortably in old age, in his own house which stands on his own land—properties he can pass on to his family. Even in Malaya a Chinese likes to follow the ancient national tradition of land-ownership. He only has a sense of permanent ownership when he can transfer property to his children. He has a proverb which says: "A land title is the hoop that holds the barrel together."

The Chinese have long been associated with the progress of Malaya. This association goes back to the early sixth century, when Malaya was the heart of the powerful Malay Kingdom. The Chinese came into the country to trade. When the British instituted government and quelled civil strife, the Chinese provided the industry and the wealth that helped to develop the land. However, despite this long connexion with Malaya, the Chinese remained aliens. Their loyalty was to China. From China they brought their women, customs, religion, and secret societies.

Sitting between the Malays and the Chinese are British civil servants, industrialists, commercial magnates, planters, miners, and other professional men—the mere 12,000, whose prestige has declined considerably in post-war years, but whose advice and guidance are continually sought, principally by the Malays. In pre-war days the British in Malaya led luxurious and comfortable but insular lives.

After the Japanese war the British woke from a dream world. The complete awakening was slow, though, and it took the Emergency to prove to them that their post-war function was to assist the Malays and the Chinese to come together and work out a fairly equitable life which would ensure internal peace and prosperity after independence had been achieved.

Of them all, the British government officer in the field is to-day the hardest-working man in the country, growing old before his time to save the country from Communism and to teach the people how to govern themselves.

That, briefly, is the background of Malaya.

The war against the Communist guerrillas has lasted six years. There are large armed forces in the field. Besides British, Malay, and Gurkha troops, there are other men from the Commonwealth—East Africans, Rhodesians, and Fijians.

In the air British Sunderlands, Spitfires, and Meteor jets, and Lincoln bombers from Australia, attack terrorist hide-outs. The Royal Navy patrols Malayan waters.

The six years of war have cost Malaya alone at least £90,000,000.

Why did the " Emergency " happen? To understand it all it is necessary to review the history of Communism in Malaya.

COMMUNIST AGGRESSION IN SOUTH-EAST ASIA

1

Birth of Malayan Communism

IT was as far back as March 1919 that the newly formed Third Internationale of the Soviet Republic laid down its future aim of establishing Communism throughout the world, if necessary by armed insurrection. Four years later it had the satisfaction of seeing a Communist Party formed in China which became strong in number and thorough in organization. By 1949, twenty-six years afterwards, the Chinese Communist Party had achieved its ultimate aim. It had overrun Nationalist China and had enslaved the minds and bodies of 400,000,000 people. Communist China has become Russia's biggest and most powerful satellite.

In 1924 the Chinese Communists sent agents to Malaya and other parts of the Far East to infect "overseas Chinese" with the germ of Marxism. Their political rival in Malaya was the "Kuomintang," a Nationalist Party, which had been born in China in 1911 after the successful revolution against the Manchu. The Kuomintang had progressed in China and by 1919 it had spread overseas. In Malaya it had struck deep roots, although the local Government had declared it an illegal society—a policy which was not modified until 1930.

While the Kuomintang thrived the early Communists achieved little success in Malaya. There were no downtrodden peasants or oppressed labouring class to succour. The Malays were too indolent to worry about politics. They saw no reason why they should conspire or revolt against the peacefulness of their padi-lands and the pleasantries they found with friends in the country coffee-shops. Conservative in thought, word, and deed, they were courteous, good-mannered people, who loved pleasure and hated hard work, and they made government easy for the British, who, in any case, had by treaty given them preferential treatment over other races. The Malays were impervious to Communist propaganda.

The agents worked on tough ground even among their own race. Chinese labourers were too intent building a comfortable life. Malaya after the First World War was the El Dorado of the Far East. Labour was well paid and, according to the means test of the time, lived well.

This lack of interest by labour had the effect, however, of encouraging the agents to look round for more susceptible individuals among the Chinese. They found two races ready to listen to their promises of vague sorts of ' freedoms ' in the future.

Their new and more gullible customers were the Hailams, who come from the south-western Chinese island of Hainan, and the Khehs, or Hakkas, who are popularly known as the gipsies of China. In those days the Hailams were despised by the more cultured Chinese classes, who considered them people of poor mentality. However, they held a monopoly of certain trades and professions in Malaya. They ran restaurants, lodging-houses, and businesses concerned with food. They made excellent silent-footed domestic servants and worked in all the hotels of the country. There were Hailam cooks and boys in all the foremost British homes from Government House and the homes of the Service chiefs down to the messes run by mercantile assistants. As a clan, and also because they in turn despised other Chinese, the Hailams were a close clique. Their independence of mind, their secretiveness, and finally their resentment of the treatment accorded them by their fellow-countrymen, made them most promising pupils to Communism. Years later Hakkas and Hailams who had been servants to top British Army, Navy, and Air Force officers, merchant princes, and rubber planters became important men in the Malayan Communist Party and its fighting arm. To quote one example, the commander of a battalion in the Malayan Races Liberation Army, now at war in the jungles of Malaya, was once a " boy " in the house of a leading British rubber planter in Johore.

Authorities on the subject of Malayan Communism are never able to say definitely whether the choice of the Hailam race as the first pupils of the Chinese Communist propagandists was accidental or deliberate. One authority, remarking on the fact that the Hailams have a good deal of aboriginal blood in their veins, considers that there was a potent psychological reason for it—perhaps they fell for Communism, he says, "to increase their prestige with the other Chinese by drawing attention to themselves."

What is positive, though, is that if the Hailams had not been so resentful of their treatment by other Chinese, Communism might not have found root in Malaya for many years. The Hailams did not really understand the creed they were being taught, but they took it up universally and they spread the words of Marx in night-schools, illegal trade unions, and craft guilds—small organizations that spring up wherever there are working Chinese.

These organizations proved such good cloaks that the real nature of their nocturnal activities was not discovered for some time by the Government. Swift action then followed, and many night-schools were closed; but Hailam schoolmasters had done their secret work efficiently. Propaganda had permeated the minds of a large number of young Chinese, who developed into ardent Communists.

Very soon afterwards the Singapore Government learned that Russia had backed the establishment in Singapore of a "South Seas Centre" to co-ordinate activities in Malaya. This centre was under the control of the Central Committee of the Chinese Communist Party, which had headquarters in Shanghai.

If documentary proof is required of Russia's part in this early movement it can be found in a Russian report dated October-November 1925 which said, "The English secret service has succeeded in getting on the track of the work in China and on the centre in Singapore, but no facts will be found to compromise the Soviet Republic publicly."

Between November 1927 and January 1928 five top-flight representatives of the Chinese Communist Party arrived in Singapore to organize the Nanyang (South Seas) Communist Party, which eventually became the "Malayan Communist Party." Shanghai posted to Singapore Communist journals with such stark names as *Blood Light*, *Red Rule*, and *Propertyless Youth*, and these were distributed to the "peasants and workers" who were expected to form the principal members of the new Party.

How determined, unscrupulous, and dangerous those early Communists could be was demonstrated in 1928 when they participated in a purely economic strike by shoemakers in Singapore. It was the first taste of things to come.

Communists planted many primitive bombs in cobblers' shops in the town. One night eleven bombs were flung into the streets. These did little material damage, but they showed the lengths to which the Communists were prepared to go. They also had considerable effect on the morale of the Chinese population.

The same year Communists were also behind an attempt in Singapore to kill Dr C. C. Wu, an important personality in the Nationalist Chinese Government, who was visiting the Colony. The assassin failed in his job, was caught, and sent to prison. The revolver he used, it was found, had been stolen from a planter in Johore. The Communists were also held responsible for several murders and for attempting to launch an anti-Japanese boycott. By the end of 1928 the police had succeeded in arresting most of the leaders.

Meanwhile Communist organization was spreading in the Far East. Chinese seamen on British, Dutch, French, and American ships formed the couriers of the Chinese Communist Party. All members of the Communist-inspired Nanyang Seamen's Labour Union carried Red literature and correspondence over the South-east Asian seas.

Even though Communism had arrived in British possessions in the Far East, the British Government were sceptical of its strength, and of its connexion and co-ordination with Shanghai. Mr R. H. de S. Onraet, who spent half his Singapore police career fighting the Communists and retired as Inspector-General of Police, records in his book *Singapore Police Background* that " Those in high places judged the potential menace of revolutionary Communism not by the brains that organized the movement but by the poor quality of the coolie masses used to implement it."

Ceaseless raids by the police on secretariats, printing-presses, and, on two occasions, bomb-making centres in Singapore, helped to keep the strength of the Party in check. It was inevitable that the Communists decided to reorganize. Their " Third Representatives' Conference " met secretly in Singapore in April 1930. This meeting made Communist history.

The Nanyang Communist Party and all its adjuncts were dissolved. The Malayan Communist Party was formed " to establish a republic in Malaya." It came under the control, not of the Chinese Communist Party, but of the more potent Far Eastern Bureau in

Shanghai, the Comintern for the Far East. The Communist parties in Thailand and the Netherlands East Indies were to be attached to the Malayan Communist Party until they were able to stand alone.

Among those who attended this historic conference was a Moscow-trained Annamite named Nguen Ai Quoc. To-day he is better known as Ho Chi-Minh, leader of the revolt in Indo-China. Even at that time Ho had a reputation. After launching unsuccessful rebellions in Indo-China, he had fled to Hong Kong. He had come to Singapore as the representative of the Russian Third Internationale.

The conference was acrimonious, with Ho Chi-Minh successfully leading criticism of the policy that local Parties should concentrate on Chinese only and forget other races. The conference formed a Southern Bureau which was to be established in Hong Kong to disseminate propaganda throughout the Far East. This bureau, however, had a short life. Within a few months the Hong Kong police had located and raided its headquarters.

Communism, however, seemed able to take a lot of knocks. The death of the Southern Bureau was discouraging, but Moscow sent out orders to establish a new and more powerful organization called the Pan-Pacific Trade Union Secretariat. Its primary object was to promote Communism in Malaya, the Philippines, Indo-China, Thailand, Burma, Netherlands East Indies, and Australia. Ho Chi-Minh was appointed to be the liaison between Moscow and the Communist parties in the Far East. In command as secretary in Shanghai was a Polish Jew, Hilaire Noulens.

In 1931 the Singapore police struck the first blow, which crippled this Far Eastern Bureau and disrupted the entire "South Seas" Communist organization for many years.

The Special Branch of the Singapore Police Force had by then become a first-class department. Its agents were growing in number and quality. It was ceaseless in action against Communist cells and Chinese secret societies. Its work naturally was secret.

As a reporter, I was welcome in the offices of its head, Mr René Onraet, and his officers, but I was rarely told anything. Mr Onraet and his men took Communism seriously, more seriously than did the Colonial Office in Whitehall. The same complacency and unwillingness to accept signs and portents were to be exhibited after the war with Japan by the Governments of Singapore and the Feder-

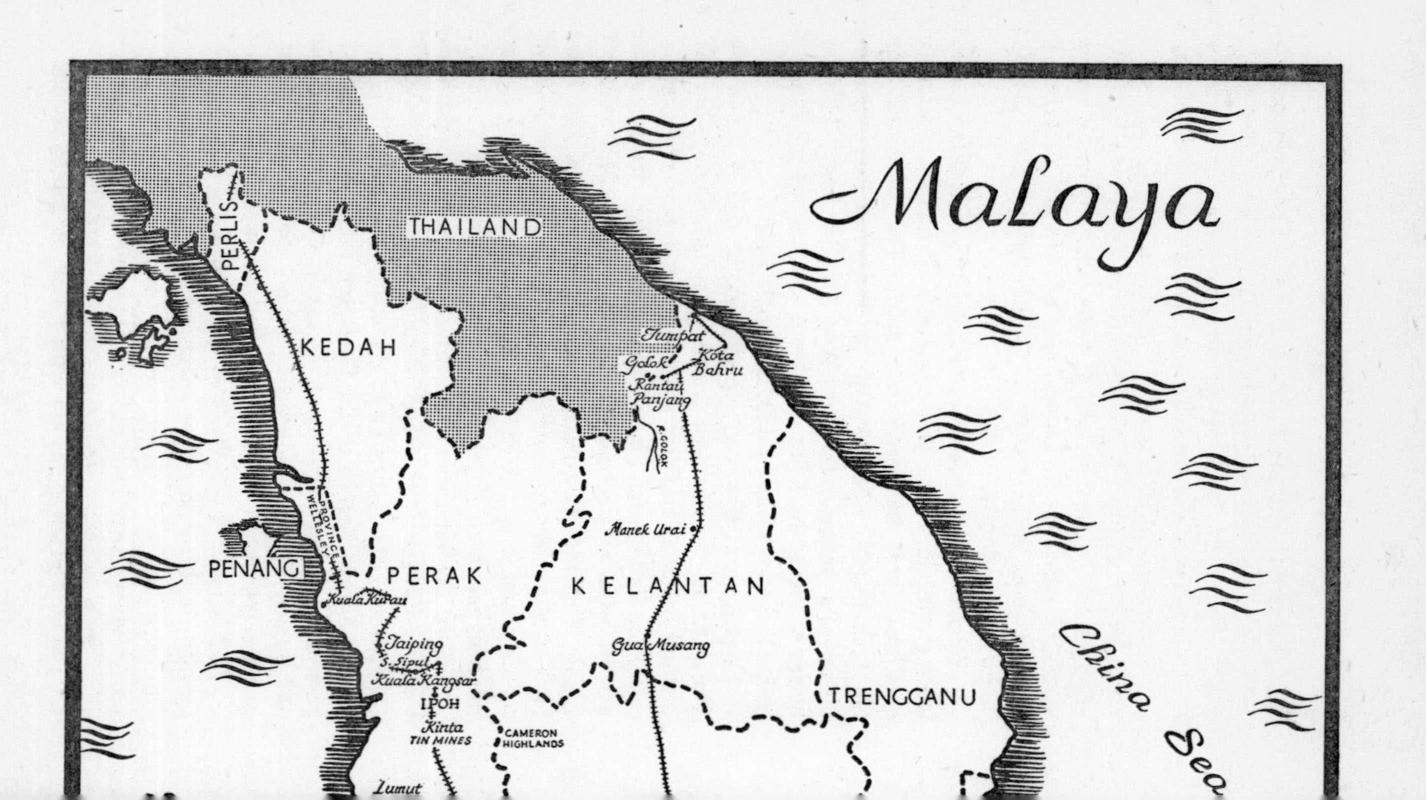
Malaya
THAILAND
PERLIS
KEDAH
PENANG
PROVINCE WELLESLEY
PERAK
Kuala Kurau
Taiping
S. Siput
Kuala Kangsar
IPOH
Kinta
TIN MINES
Lumut
CAMERON HIGHLANDS
KELANTAN
Tumpat
Kota Bahru
Golok
Rantau Panjang
R. GOLOK
Manek Urai
Gua Musang
TRENGGANU
China Sea

of Malacca
PAHANG
Tanjong Malim
K. Kubu Bahru
KUALA SELANGOR
SELANGOR
Rawang
Batu Arang
Batu Caves
KUALA LUMPUR
Ampang
KLANG
Kajang
Bentong
Karak
Mukim Songsang
Sanggang
Mentakab
Bangau
Bukit Segumpal
Jemerloh
Mengkarak
Triang
Manchis
Kemayan
Jasek Bera
JELEBU
Broga
Bahau
Kampong Baapa
NEGRI SEMBILAN
Kuala Pilah
Seremban
Gemas
MALACCA
SEGAMAT
MUAR
Bukit Kepong
JOHORE
BATU PAHAT
Rengam
Wessyngton
Layang Layang
Sedenak
G. Pulai
JOHORE BAHRU
Johore Strait
SINGAPORE
Main Straits
Straits of Singapore
SUMATRA
N
Main Railway
0
25
50
Scale of Miles

ation of Malaya, and by Whitehall, and they led to unpreparedness for the present "Emergency." The first steps to this 'revolution' had, it will be noted, been taken in 1930 at the Third Representatives' Conference in Singapore when it decided to "establish a republic in Malaya."

In 1931 the Special Branch surmised that the reorganization of the South Seas Group might mean the dispatch to Singapore of a high Party official to implement the decision. This, in fact, did happen, and when it did the Special Branch acted with a swiftness which did not give even the Pan-Pacific Trade Union Secretariat in far-away Shanghai any opportunity to break up and lie low.

On April 27, 1931, a Frenchman named Serge Lefranc landed in Singapore off a ship from Hong Kong. He told Immigration officers that he was a commercial traveller for a firm in Paris.

He opened an office in a block of buildings called Winchester House which fronted the busy harbour. He furnished it, and employed an Indian peon who only worked for three and a half hours until noon every day. Lefranc escaped police notice for about three weeks. When it was learned he was already at work in Singapore he was watched.

Onraet rented an office in Winchester House opposite to that of Lefranc. From it detectives watched the Frenchman's movements and trailed his visitors. His letters and his waste-paper basket were intercepted and their contents scanned. His letters were partly in French and partly in cipher. They were addressed to Shanghai, Hong Kong, and France.

Lefranc never realized until later that the Englishman who travelled up and down in the office lift with him several times was Onraet himself. In fact, he never suspected that his real identity—Joseph Ducroux, a French Communist of some repute—was known. The Special Branch, anxious to learn all about Lefranc's visit and, more important, his visitors, took great pains not to give him cause for the slightest suspicion until they had all the information they wanted.

They arrested Lefranc on June 1. Onraet was at the head of the raiding-party which burst into Lefranc's office. Simultaneously lightning raids were carried out by other Special Branch groups at houses in the Singapore suburbs.

Lefranc was surprised with two Chinese visitors who later proved to be leading members of the Malayan Communist Party. Onraet recognized one as a man he himself had arrested three years previously in a Communist bomb factory in Singapore. This man had been banished after serving imprisonment. He had somehow slipped back into Singapore.

In Lefranc's hip-pocket was a booklet, *Workers of the World, Unite.* His diary had addresses in Shanghai and Hong Kong. In his room in a boarding house in suburbia the police found more than 12,000 American dollars in travellers' cheques. It was learned later that Lefranc had been given 50,000 American dollars by the Pan-Pacific Trade Union Secretariat for Communist work in Malaya and Burma.

In all, apart from Lefranc, eighteen Chinese, including a nineteen-year-old Cantonese girl, were arrested that day. A large printing-press was found in a house in Sims Avenue, on the east coast of Singapore.

It was as " Joseph Ducroux, alias Lefranc " that the Frenchman was charged in court, accused of " assisting in the management of the Malayan Communist Party, an unlawful organization for the spreading of subversive propaganda." Most of his associates were accused of the same offence.

The public in Singapore and the rest of the world were given no inkling from the court proceedings of the importance of Ducroux' arrest. Ducroux stuck to his disguise as a commercial traveller, although, significantly, he would not go into the witness-box to be cross-examined. From the dock, he said he had arrived in Singapore to find a firm which would represent his own employers in Malaya; one large Belgian firm had agreed to do so, and he had waited in Singapore until his employers confirmed the arrangement. He had planned to leave Singapore about July 1, he continued, adding naïvely, " I spent a lot of time in my office studying local business conditions."

As for the booklet *Workers of the World, Unite*, he had found it in a parcel placed outside his office door. As he had " some writing to do " at the time, he had not looked at it but had slipped it into his trouser pocket. He denied being a Communist, or that he knew anything about the Malayan Communist Party. He was convicted and sentenced to eighteen months' imprisonment.

Ducroux had been a militant Communist since 1923. In the

following year he had started a Leninist school at Marseilles. He had then tried to come out to the Far East, but the French Foreign Office had issued a circular to all French provinces forbidding a visa to him. However, by underground means he obtained a passport in the name of "Serge Lefranc."

Ducroux had been sent to Singapore to make a thorough survey of the Communist position in Malaya. His orders were to establish direct communication with the Pan-Pacific Trade Union Secretariat in Shanghai, to reorganize Red labour unions, and settle the payment of subsidies to the Malayan Communist Party, to the Malayan trade unions (although there were none in existence then), and to the Malayan Communist Youth.

He had extensive contacts in India, Burma, and French Indo-China. From Singapore he had written to Communist centres in Paris, Brussels, and Berlin.

Onraet cabled the addresses in Ducroux' little book to the Shanghai police. Noulens and his wife were arrested at the Pan-Pacific Trade Union Secretariat headquarters. Ho Chi-Minh was arrested in Hong Kong.

The archives of the Secretariat disclosed the amazing extent of Soviet activity in the Far East. Japan, Korea, the Philippines, Formosa, Indo-China, Thailand, Malaya, the Netherlands East Indies, Burma, and trade unions in India were all in the Communist scheme of revolution. Expenditure had been on a huge scale, keeping in mind the value of sterling in those days. More than £80,000 had been distributed in a few months. Noulens had accounts in several Shanghai banks. He also had five local and four telegraphic addresses and eight post-office boxes.

A network of Communist groups had been formed in China, with cells throughout the Nationalist Army and in the Government arsenals. There were detailed plans for creating labour strife in China, particularly in Shanghai.

Noulens himself was an eminent member of the executive of the Third Internationale. He had seven aliases and an equivalent number of passports, including British. Outwardly his profession in Shanghai was that of teacher of languages in the famous Nanking Road. After a year on remand Noulens and his wife were convicted by a Chinese court and sentenced to death. This was later commuted to life imprisonment.

Ducroux later gave Onraet some enlightening figures of the strength of the Communist Party in Malaya. There were, he said, about 1500 members of the Party, 10,000 Communist Labour Unionists, about fifty active women supporters, and 200 people in a satellite organization known as the Anti-Imperialist League.

All these people did not represent a strong group in a population of two and a half million Chinese, but it was a dangerous one, which could—and eventually did—exercise considerable influence over the illiterate working classes.

With the break-up of the Far East Soviet headquarters in Shanghai, Malayan and other Communist organizations became bereft of guidance. They lacked funds and were in a bad way, but they were kept alive by resourceful local groups. The Malayan Communist Party in fact, expressed its own determination to carry on, but, as it had no plans and no money, it could not do any field work.

In 1933 Moscow succeeded in re-establishing the Far Eastern Bureau in Shanghai, and quickly sent directives to local Communist Parties to resume work. The Malayan Communist Party was 'granted' a subsidy of 300 dollars (£35) a month towards its expenses. It had to wait a year before it received the first month's grant.

Working on instructions, the Party set out to draw into its fold in the shortest possible time the Malay, Chinese, and Indian 'proletariat' in Malaya. The directive it received emphasized the need to establish cells in the Federated Malay States Railways workshops in Kuala Lumpur, on rubber-estates and in tin-mines, in factories, in the shipping docks in Singapore, Malacca, and Penang, and in the Naval Base in Singapore, which at that time was being extended, and was employing thousands of labourers.

It took the Party the next three years to bring its secret work to fruition. By 1936 it had organized itself sufficiently to promote strikes. In that year and the next the Federated Malay States suffered severe labour troubles. The Communists nearly gained control. Just how serious the situation was can be gauged from an extract from a report of the Inspector-General of Police in the Federated Malay States. "The Federated Malay States passed through the most serious crisis of its history. It was within an ace of dissolving into temporary chaos as a result of Communist intrigue."

The most serious strikes occurred in rubber-estates. Chinese tappers downed tools suddenly, which was a phenomenon, because they had always shown themselves ready in the past to discuss a situation and work out a settlement with a good deal of give and take.

The Chinese strikers were well-organized. Bicycles and buses were used by the Communists to send instructions over a wide area. The organizers maintained a high standard of discipline, and managed to restrain unruly elements almost completely. By the end of March more than 10,000 men and women in estates, rubber factories, and pineapple canneries were idle. The focal point of the strikes was, however, at the country's only coal-mine at Batu Arang, in Selangor, situated about twenty-six miles north-west of Kuala Lumpur.

This mine supplied fuel to the railways and to electric power-plants. The Communists organized a strike of 6000 labourers, who then took possession of the property. They set up an internal government, which included an elaborate defence scheme, and a court to deal with " criminal offences " and settle " civil disputes." The Europeans on the mine were defied but not molested. The situation was serious. Three hundred police and men of the 1st Malay Regiment and of the 2/2 Punjab Regiment who were stationed at Taiping, 180 miles away, were rushed to the mine.

They made a surprise night attack, shot their way through the defences, and regained possession of the mine. It was incomprehensible to the country that such a thing could happen: what it did not realize was—to quote the Inspector-General again—that Batu Arang had been " the trial of strength between the Communist Party and the Government."

Had the Communists in the mine not been crushed quickly there would not only have been a general strike but, in the words of the official report, the Federated Malay States " with its European women and children living in scattered bungalows or in estates, would have been in very serious danger of being overrun by angry and desperate Chinese mobs."

History has an unfortunate knack of repeating itself. Eleven years later the same mine was again the centre of Communist activity (but in a more vicious form), and this time men were killed and European women armed themselves in defence.

Parallel with the strikes in 1937 an anti-Japanese movement was developed by the Communists under the cloak of patriotism. They formed the Singapore Oversea Chinese Anti-Japanese National Salvation Association, which received considerable support from Chinese who were not Communist-minded but wished to indulge in some form of nationalism to display their feelings against Japan, which had begun a war in China. There was, of course, a deeper significance behind this Communist movement. They wanted more members, and it was not coincidence that the majority of the early supporters of the National Salvation Association were schoolmasters, students, and newsmen from vernacular newspapers—they were to be used for spreading propaganda.

As Japan's war against China progressed, the Malayan Communist Party multiplied its activities. In the Federated Malay States individual Communist-inspired ' patriotic ' societies with such fantastic names as The Hot-Blooded Corps, The Traitor's Elimination Corps, and The Dare-to-Die Corps merged into one Anti-Enemy Backing-up Society. With a membership of about 30,000, it succeeded in establishing itself throughout the social strata of local Chinese. Through the whole of Malaya the A.E.B.U.S. began an era of persecution against suspected Japanese sympathizers among the Chinese. It also organized violent demonstrations.

Rowdies broke into shops to ' examine ' whether Japanese goods were being sold. Looting followed as a matter of course. There were riots, the most serious being in Penang, where for forty-eight hours the town " looked like a city being sacked," according to the description given by a high police officer. The local police were outwitted and exhausted until Onraet, who had become Inspector-General of Police, went up from Singapore and instituted determined action.

There was no doubt that the anti-Japanese activities of the A.E.B.U.S. gave Communism a fillip. The police forces throughout the country raided headquarters of groups and cells in order to break the hold of the Party but without great success. Leaders who were arrested were banished, but by 1939 and the eve of the outbreak of the Second World War, the Malayan Communist Party had many useful substitutes.

The Party's strength had trebled from Ducroux' figures to 37,000. Singapore led with 18,820 members and adherents. The rest were grouped, strangely enough, in only four other areas —Selangor with 9880, Penang with 4410, the Batu Pahat district in North Johore with 1570, and the Muar district, just north of this, with 2530.

Russia's non-aggression pact with Germany resulted in a violent anti-British campaign in Malaya. Communist agitators went into action, especially after the Russian invasion of Finland, when they began spreading anti-British, anti-Imperialist, and anti-war propaganda. In Singapore they fomented serious strikes. They organized a special propaganda squad, sent out trained speakers to meetings of workers, and provided leadership in many trades where the employees were either unorganized or badly organized. Strikes were frequently 'lightning' ones. In many instances, the strikers did not know what some of their 'demands' meant. In most, the employers found it hard to get representatives of the workers to come forward for discussions.

The anti-British campaign was conducted principally in the Party's two most important newspapers, *Emancipation News* and *Vanguard News,* both of which had a fair circulation. The object of the campaign and the strikes was to cripple Malaya's contribution to the Imperial war effort.

Despite the attempts of the Government to counteract it, the Communists succeeded in accelerating their campaign. In 1940 they tested the strength of the authorities again, this time in Singapore. After a wave of strikes, the chief of which affected mechanics working in the docks, they called for a giant meeting of supporters on Labour Day. The European war was still in the doldrums, but it was imperative that the Communists should not be allowed to hold public sway in case Russia moved actively into war on the side of Germany, as much of the world thought she would. The Singapore Government banned the meeting planned for Labour Day and issued warnings against its being held.

Attempts by the Party to organize the mass meeting continued, however. On Labour Day hundreds of police were placed at strategic points. They prevented workers reaching the rendezvous of the meeting, but there was one serious clash and two people were shot. The meeting was not held.

The Communists launched another wave of strikes, which reached its peak when the valuable rubber and pineapple-packing industries were brought to a standstill. It must be remembered that all this was done under the cloak of Chinese patriotism by the Chinese National Salvation Association.

Suddenly the anti-British activities of the Malayan Communist Party were denounced by the Nationalist Chinese Government in Chungking. This denunciation had repercussions among the conservative Chinese in Malaya who had supported the Chinese National Salvation movement. They withdrew their support, called upon all other Chinese to dissociate themselves from the anti-British activities of the Communists as these had been " carried out under false colours," and urged that information about the Communists should be given to the Malayan Governments.

On June 22, 1941, Germany suddenly attacked Russia, who thus immediately became the Ally of Great Britain as she stood alone against Hitler's mighty forces. The Malayan Communist Party immediately toned down its activities. Its Central Executive Committee held a secret meeting in Singapore in July and decided to " co-operate " with the Malayan Governments, although, significantly, they stressed the determination not to veer one iota from the declared policy to " expel the British from Malaya " and to institute " a dictatorship of the proletariat." In due course Labour was instructed to " co-operate " with Capital so that Russia might continue to receive economic assistance from Britain via the enormous contribution of raw materials from Malaya.

Finally came the Japanese attack on Malaya in December 1941. The policy of the Malayan Communist Party changed immediately. It came down on the side of the Malayan Government. Within a few days of the Japanese landings along the north-eastern coast of Malaya and the bombing of Singapore, the Party sent a message to the Governor, Sir Shenton Thomas, offering all-out co-operation against " the enemy." After a great deal of consideration in Whitehall this was accepted, and so the Communist Party and the other Chinese political party, the Kuomintang, joined hands on a common war front.

At the end of December a Chinese Mobilization Committee was formed to assist the Government in every way possible. The Communist Party offered to mobilize its ranks into a resistance corps to attack the Japanese behind the lines.

After a little hesitation this offer was accepted by the War Office.

A meeting was arranged between British officers and Communists. For the first time since the inception of the Party, its Secretary-General, Loi Tak, emerged into the public eyes. He was to be one of the two Communist delegates.

2

The First Jungle War

IT was a singular commentary on Communist leadership of the period in the Far East that the Party bosses in two different countries should be Annamites. One of them, Loi Tak, was the Secretary-General of the Malayan Communist Party, a young man who used about thirty aliases, including the Western one of "Mr Wright." The other was, of course, Ho Chi-Minh, of Indo-China.

Loi Tak was not a prepossessing-looking fellow. A Britisher who met him described him to me as having a "rat-like face." He was a shrewd, clever man, with no high intellectual attainments, "a strange person altogether." He had charm, a fact which is confirmed by Colonel Spencer Chapman in his book, *The Jungle is Neutral*,[1] when he describes a meeting in the jungle with a Communist known as "The Plen" (Plenipotentiary)—no less than Loi Tak, craftily conducting his own affairs. Spencer Chapman says he was "a young-middle-aged Chinese of great charm, considerable intelligence, and quiet efficiency." He had a "large mouth, perfect, even teeth, and when he became animated his eyes grew round and his eyebrows rose about an inch and a half."

Loi Tak's pleasant manner had been developed over the years. He was artful as well as skilful. He had a contriving, intriguing brain. He was unscrupulous and could be ruthless. He showed much later that he was a man without nerves.

Above all, he was a tremendous organizer. He built the Malayan Communist Party into an edifice over which he reigned supreme. He was a boss whose identity was known only to a handful of men. He constructed an organization which could only be powerful as

[1] Chatto and Windus, 1952.

long as he was in control, because he manufactured an illusion about himself.

In reality Loi Tak was never a true Communist. He worked for his own ends. He was a fake—but a fake who got away with it for years.

There are no records of Loi Tak's early life. Who and what his parents were in the unknown village in which he was born are mysteries. It is probable that he never completed his education in a local school, although he later became fluent in French, English, and two or three Chinese dialects.

When he was Secretary-General of the Malayan Communist Party he claimed he had travelled to France and Russia, where he had studied Communism; but, in the light of later events, it is unlikely that he ever sailed west out of Malaya at any time in his life.

Undoubtedly he developed an early passion for politics, and in this direction his early history runs somewhat similar to that of Ho Chi-Minh, who picked up Communism in his home district as a youth and became inspired by it.

The paths of these two men crossed several times. It is unlikely that Loi Tak was in Singapore in April 1930, when the new Malayan Communist Party was set up. Ho Chi-Minh, then known as Nguen Ai Quoc, was present, and after this historic occasion he returned to his base in Hong Kong. It was then that the wiry, youthful figure of Loi Tak first came into focus. He was in Hong Kong when Ho Chi-Minh began stirring up interest in a Vietnamese Communist Party.

Loi Tak became an ardent worker in this cause, but when the Hong Kong police struck at Communist hide-outs on that island he fled to Shanghai. He claimed later that he had been an important member of the Shanghai Town Committee, but no Malayan or Chinese Communist could confirm this.

The Malayan Communist Party first came to know him about the end of 1934, when he arrived unheralded in Singapore from Hong Kong. He was a quiet, mild young man, apparently filled with zeal for Communism and all it promised. He astounded the untravelled local Communist ' yokels ' with his knowledge of the theory of Marxism. Loi Tak had undoubtedly made a deep study of this new Eastern religion, and he hoodwinked Party members with his facile descriptions of Communist life in France and Russia.

Cleverly he showed his opportunism by taking advantage of the drifting, confused state of mind of the leading Communists in Singapore, who had had little enough contact with big-time Communists. Fourteen years later, when the Central Executive Committee of the Party attempted to justify their failure to discover early enough the true calibre of Loi Tak, they muttered plaintively in a document they called " The Loi Tak Case," that he had " wormed his way " into the Party, and that, once in, he had " seized hold of the opportunity afforded by the unprepared state of thought, and employing to advantage various tactics, emerged as the representative of the Third Internationale, thereby raising his personal status."

This is precisely what happened, but no credit was given in that document to Loi Tak's organizing genius. He whipped enthusiasm for the cause into existing members of the Party, and inspired them to establish cells all over the country. By the time the Sixth Central Extended Conference was held in 1939, Loi Tak had established such a reputation that there was no opposition to his ' election ' as the first proper Secretary-General of the Malayan Communist Party.

Strangely, he had survived every police raid on the haunts of Communists in Singapore and on the mainland. Whereas other important Party men found themselves cornered and arrested, Loi Tak seemed to bear a charmed life. By the time the Japanese war broke out Loi Tak was firmly established as a remarkable leader.

This, then, was the man whose hand the uncomfortable British were clasping as a questionable ally against the Japanese in Malaya. At that time it seemed a justifiable risk to take.

All the elements of mystery and intrigue surrounded the meeting between the Communists and the British officers. The rendezvous was a dingy Chinese cubicle in the heart of Singapore's Chinatown. The British officers reached it by a circuitous route.

The two Communists sidled into the room after them. Both men were disguised behind dark sun-glasses. As if worried that they had been followed by Japanese spies, and so had to leave early, Loi Tak and his companion got down to discussion immediately.

Loi Tak did not do much talking, but he eventually agreed that the Party should select the men who were to be trained as guerrillas at No. 101 Special Training School in Singapore and used against the Japanese in any way thought fit by the British Army. The first fifteen students were to be sent to a secret rendezvous in two days. Three days after the meeting Colonel Spencer Chapman, who commanded the school, gave the opening lecture on guerrilla warfare to these eager young men.

No. 101 Special Training School had been secretly set up in Singapore early in 1941 to train British and local troops and civilians in irregular warfare in Far Eastern countries in the eventuality of a war with Japan. The School was really begun too late to be altogether successful, but it produced men who eventually fought behind the Japanese lines in China, Hong Kong, Burma, French Indo-China, and South Thailand. The Malayan Communists were destined to be its last pupils, and Spencer Chapman considered them " probably the best material we ever had at the School."

Altogether 200 Communists received some form of training before Singapore fell on February 15, 1942. As each group finished its course the men were placed in the jungle on the mainland as 'stay-behind' parties. The Japanese were leaping southward faster than the British experts had considered they would, and there was little time to plan properly and to equip each group with suitable radio and sufficient explosives to blow up bridges, railway lines, and roads. Isolated groups did succeed in ambushing Japanese convoys and in blowing up railways, but after Singapore fell and the war was over the guerrillas were forced to hide themselves, for the Japanese began searching for them. In the depths of the jungle, therefore, these 'stay-behind' parties began carving out a new life while they waited for leadership and more war-material with which to fight. With them was Spencer Chapman.

In Singapore itself the Japanese launched a reign of terror against their enemies, the Chinese. It was all done in the name of " anti-Communism." They herded Chinese into lorries, drove them to lonely parts of the island, forced them to dig trenches, then shot them into these graves with machine-guns. Communists, or suspected Communists, were tortured first to disclose the hiding-places of comrades. Afterwards they were beheaded. The Japanese killed thousands of Chinese who were innocent of any knowledge of the Communists. A failure to give information was not taken as a sign of innocence but rather as a refusal to betray. The Japanese were being tough because they feared the potentialities of the guerrillas. They were determined to find the leaders.

In August 1942, six months after the conquest of Malaya, most of the top men of the Malayan Communist Party in Singapore were suddenly arrested and killed. There seemed little doubt they had been betrayed—but by whom? There was panic among the rest of the executives, who went into hiding; but the Japanese were so well informed that in another seven months they had killed or imprisoned a great number of these men. By March 1943 Communist activities on Singapore island had ceased entirely.

On the mainland the Party leadership had also been decimated. The Central Executive Committee had summoned leaders and other officials to a meeting on September 1, 1942, to discuss a plan of campaign against the Japanese. The rendezvous was one of the innumerable caves which pitted a great limestone outcrop just outside Batu Caves village, eight miles north of Kuala Lumpur. It seemed a perfect place for a meeting. The approaches could be watched from many points. The Japanese would have required a large body of troops to surround and search every cave.

Yet the meeting had hardly begun when Japanese troops, already in hiding, burst among the Communists with guns blazing. There was a massacre. After a short battle, twenty Communists, including some of the most experienced leaders, were killed. About seventy others were captured. Only a few men escaped. Among them again was Loi Tak, the Secretary-General.

Once more there was little doubt that the Party had been betrayed. The Batu Caves massacre proved the most severe blow the M.C.P. suffered in the three and a half years of the Japanese occupation. After the war the Party declared September 1 a local anniversary to commemorate the 'martyrs.' Indeed, later, as their own war against the British progressed, they fashioned an oath to be chanted by all comrades on each anniversary. The oath was all-embracing—and a morale-booster. It ran:

> We members of the Party and members of the Party's force do hereby sincerely and solemnly affirm before the '91' martyrs[1] that, in

[1] Called the " '91' martyrs " because they were killed on the first day of the ninth month.

the course of the present gigantic anti-British National Liberation War, we will fight to the end to drive the British Imperialists out of Malaya and liberate the people completely in accordance with the outline for the formation of a Peoples' Democratic Republic State.

We shall be ever decided and firm in our struggle and shall not compromise or surrender. We shall strive to overcome all difficulties with our revolutionary spirit.

We further affirm before the '91' martyrs that we shall follow your bloodstained footpaths to defeat the enemy in order to establish a Peoples' New Democratic Republic State.

We members of the Party and the forces shall not submit, surrender, or compromise with the enemy. We shall continue to serve the people to the end.

It took a long time for the Party to recover from its disasters in Singapore and Selangor. Slowly, though, new secret organizations were born in all the western States and Settlements of the mainland. Theoretically these consisted of State, District, and Section Committees. Each State was responsible for its own affairs, subject only to directives from the Central Executive Committee. Loi Tak, as Secretary-General, kept in touch with each State Committee through an underground network of communications.

The reasons for this independence by States was the difficulty of communications between each of them and the Central Executive Committee. As the Japanese were on the *qui vive* in towns and villages, road and river journeys for Communist couriers were dangerous. They were forced to find routes through the jungle, and they assiduously began to blaze trails. A great number of these were never found by the Japanese. In time to come these tracks gave the Malayan Communist Party a great initial advantage over the next 'enemy,' the British. After they had begun their rebellion they took secret routes to kill and plunder.

The Communist guerrillas in the jungle, including those trained at No. 101, were formed into compact groups. Slowly, there developed in each State independent 'regiments' of a new guerrilla force named The Malayan Peoples' Anti-Japanese Army.

Those 'regiments' were formed on Communist lines. Each had a headquarters consisting of the Party representative, who invariably was liaison officer with the State Committee, a commander, a deputy commander, and an administrative officer. The

Party representative was also the political leader and had absolute power in the ' regiment.' The military commander, who did not have to be a member of the Party, was his junior.

The original No. 101 group formed the nuclei of the M.P.A.J.A., but, as news of its formation seeped out of the jungle, hundreds of young Chinese who wanted to fight the Japanese became recruits. They were armed with weapons picked up from recent battlefields, but they had little ammunition and less explosives for continuous warfare. The guerrillas were never, therefore, a real menace to the Japanese, but—as was the case many years later—they had a considerable nuisance value, which necessitated Japanese troops being held in readiness to repulse their attacks.

The guerrillas descended on small Japanese units and isolated police stations. They kidnapped and assassinated Japanese supporters or informers. They had what they called " Traitor-killing Camps " dotted throughout the country. Each held not more than twenty men, who systematically and ruthlessly eliminated traitors, informers, and spies, and Japanese. They sought out and killed Chinese, Sikh, Malay, Tamil, and Japanese men and women. Their weapons ranged from tommy-guns and grenades to the wooden handles of changkols (the local hoe) and their bare hands. Spencer Chapman, visiting one such camp which was situated five miles east-south-east of Ipoh, found its armament " prodigious." Twenty men had four tommy-guns, twelve rifles, six shot-guns, ten pistols, including two Mausers, a Luger, and three .45 automatics, and plenty of grenades and reliable ammunition.

The M.P.A.J.A. was a force of young men, most of them under twenty-five years of age. They were rubber-tappers, tin-mining coolies, vegetable gardeners, squatters, woodcutters, barbers, shop-assistants, and house-servants.

Women guerrillas taught the Mandarin language or singing, helped in the kitchens, or were nurses or seamstresses. Few women carried weapons or fought actively against the Japanese—a situation which changed in the next war, when they became fanatical ' gun-molls ' and either shot at British troops or flung grenades at them.

The M.P.A.J.A. possessed no uniform. When troops went into a town or a village for food, or on a job, they dressed smartly because ragged, unkempt men were always suspected by the Japanese of being guerrillas. The M.P.A.J.A. received tremendous backing from the Chinese of the country, even though they were Communists. This was because they were fighting a common enemy. There was no doubt that an element of fear also compelled co-operation.

The Chinese, although hostile towards the Japanese, also lived in fear of Communist reprisals. The Communists had formed such organizations as an Anti-Japanese Resistance League, an Anti-Japanese Self-Protection Society, the Friends of Guerrilla Warfare, youth associations, and Farmers' Unions, through which they collected or extorted supplies and funds. These also gave them considerable underground control over districts. Under a guise of nationalism again they built up terrorism.

The most successful arm of the M.P.A.J.A. was the Malayan Peoples' Anti-Japanese Union, a vast army of supporters, who fed the guerrillas, found them money, clothes, and fighting material, spied for them, arranged guides to take patrols through unknown territory, and formed corps of couriers. Without the help of this Union the M.P.A.J.A. could not have existed.

Here too history has repeated itself. In the present campaign, the Union has been given the Chinese name Min Yuen, meaning Peoples' Movement, or Mobilization of the People. They number hundreds of thousands and they are sought diligently. Once the Min Yuen is crushed, the fighters cannot live.

The personality of Loi Tak kept this vast organization alive and vibrant. His visits from Singapore—his headquarters—were inspiring but infrequent. His comrades marvelled at his courage in travelling through dangerous Japanese territory in a high-powered motor-car. He motored frequently to Kuala Lumpur, where he had a secret contact spot, and also an Annamite mistress.

Loi Tak was thorough in his organization. He hand-picked women as his couriers, and none ever fell into Japanese hands. Through them he sent directives and messages to the State Committees. They personally brought messages to him, which they concealed either in a rubber contraceptive worked into the heels of their shoes or in sanitary towels which they wore. It was all very crude but effective.

It was in these days that Loi Tak could have stood comparison with Ho Chi-Minh in his later hey day when he launched the Viet Minh rebellion which pushed the French troops back perilously close to Saigon. Loi Tak then really had more power than Ho Chi-Minh ever had; he was, indeed, an absolute dictator, because anything he said in the days when it was difficult to summon a Central Executive Committee meeting hastily was law, and was obeyed.

Amid the alarms by, and excursions against, the Japanese, Loi Tak and his Central Executive Committee settled down to the business of planning the future of the Malayan Communist Party. The Party may have become 'allies' of the British through the chances of war, but it had never for a moment given up its plan of driving these 'Imperialists' out of Malaya.

In 1943, therefore, the Central Executive Committee met in the depths of the jungle—this time far enough from the nearest Japanese soldiery to prevent another surprise ambush—and, after considerable discussion, drew up the following nine-point, long-term programme:

1. Drive the Japanese Fascists out of Malaya and establish the Malayan Republic.
2. Establish a National Organization composed of representatives universally elected from the different nationalities to govern and protect our Motherland. Practise peoples' sovereignty. Improve civilians' living conditions and develop industry, agriculture, and commerce, in order to build up Malaya as a harmonious, free, and felicitous country.
3. Give freedom of speech, publication, organization, and thought. Abolish all the old oppressive laws and release all prisoners and anti-Japanese captives.
4. Improve peoples' living conditions, relieve the unemployed and the refugees, increase wages and salaries. Abolish high and unnecessary taxation and money-lending at high interest.
5. Alter and reorganize the Malayan Anti-Japanese Guerrillas into a National Army of Defence which will defend our territory. Bestow special care upon the anti-Japanese soldiers and assist the families of those warriors who died for the liberty of Malaya. Relieve wounded and disabled soldiers.
6. Free education will be practised universally in the various national languages by the different nationalities in order to develop National Culture.
7. Confiscate the properties of the German, Italian, and Japanese Fascists and traitors. These will become national property. Return the properties confiscated by the Japanese to their original owners provided they are people in Malaya or our friendly nations.

8. Practise autonomy of tariff. Sign friendly agreements and establish commercial relations with friendly countries.
9. Combine with Russia and China and support the struggles for independence of the oppressed nations in the Far East. Give help to the Japanese people to fight against Fascists.

This programme indicates the low intellectual level of the Communist executive, but the serious and significant parts of their design are in the first, fifth, and ninth points. The Party in the previous two years had not altered its intention of creating a republic, but it had realized the value of its possession of a new and powerful weapon with which it could carry out its purpose when the time came.

That weapon was the M.P.A.J.A., whose potential became all the greater as the next few years passed.

Meanwhile reports of the existence of this Communist resistance corps had reached India, the headquarters of the Allied South-east Asia Command. Lord Louis Mountbatten, the Supreme Allied Commander, decided to send an advance party to Malaya to assess the situation, and, if possible, come to a working agreement with the Communists to carry on the war until an invasion of Malaya had opened.

Mountbatten possibly had no illusions about the probable political aims of the Malayan Communist Party. But, as in Yugoslavia, where the Allies were supporting an avowed Communist, Marshal Tito, against the Nazi occupation forces, so, in Malaya, Mountbatten probably considered it would be to the ultimate advantage of South-east Asia Command to aid, and co-operate with, local Communists.

In May 1943, therefore, a submarine from India landed a party near Lumut, on the west coast. Captain (later Colonel) John L. H. Davis, who had been in the Malayan police, landed and led his five Chinese agents inland. Two months later he was joined by Richard Broome, another Malayan officer, who brought a wireless transmitting set. Both men were members of Force 136, the new Allied guerrilla organization that had been formed to fight behind Japanese lines in South-east Asia. They eventually found Spencer Chapman in Perak, and they began the difficult task of getting in touch with the executive of the Malayan Communist Party.

The whereabouts of the Secretary-General appeared to be a

close secret among the Communists; so was the location of Party headquarters. However, one of the first men Davis and Broome met was Chen Ping, a pleasant-faced little Hakka fighter who knew English but preferred to speak Cantonese. He proved to be Loi Tak's right-hand man.

In the light of later events, when he became Secretary-General and launched the revolt against the British, it would be useful here to know a little more about Chen Ping. His real name is Wong Man-Wa. He is a Malayan Chinese by birth; that is, he was born in the small coastal town of Sitiawan, in South Perak, where his father ran a small but successful bicycle-selling and repairing business.

After an early education in Chinese in Sitiawan, Chen Ping went to an English school. He was a good scholar, an intelligent boy who picked up things rapidly. He developed a quick-thinking and orderly brain.

However, while he was still in school he came under the influence of members of the Malayan Communist Party, who were establishing cells all over the country. Young Chen Ping became engrossed in Marxism. In 1940, when he was eighteen years of age, he was accepted as a member of the Party. He started his new life in a lowly but nevertheless important job: he cut stencils for propagandists.

He was in Sitiawan when the Japanese war broke out. When it became necessary to organize the members of the Party State by State the ardent Chen Ping was appointed a member of the Perak State Committee, which became one of the most powerful in the Communist set-up.

After the formation of the Malayan Peoples' Anti-Japanese Army Perak developed a formidable corps of guerrillas, who collected a considerable supply of weapons, ammunition, and explosives, and used them on the Japanese despite their own lack of training. Chen Ping was not a fighter; he never has been. His forte was administration and organization, and it was not surprising that very soon he was promoted to the important position of Perak State Secretary. This made him the Number One Communist in the State.

He rapidly organized his guerrillas and his supply units into one of the finest corps in the country. The majority of his men were under twenty years of age; a few were over twenty-five years. Chen Ping, believing in seeing things for himself, travelled quite a lot in Japanese-occupied Perak, and he became familiar with the guerrilla routes. Spencer Chapman in his book mentions the food lines in Perak " so efficiently laid on " by Chen Ping.

When Davis arrived in Perak to negotiate with the Chinese guerrillas Chen Ping proved a tower of strength. He opened up new food lines for British camps; he made himself personally responsible for the safety of Davis, Broome, and Chapman, the trio who laid the foundation for guerrilla reinforcements and activities in Japanese-occupied Malaya. He fell sick with typhoid, but he still kept on working for Force 136.

His appearances in the Davis-Broome-Chapman camp at Blantan, 2000 feet above sea-level in South Perak, always lifted the morale of the three men, who had come to look on Chen Ping as the only man in the Party executive who would—or could—get anything done. The other leaders they met seemed terrified of doing anything that might be regarded as wrong.

In quiet moments in the jungle, when Davis, Broome, and Chapman talked in Cantonese with him, they found Chen Ping to be " a sincere Communist." He was straightforward enough to tell them what he thought of ' British Imperialism ' and he made it plain—he was never given to lying—that one day, after the Japanese war, the Communists would rebel against British administration and ' liberate ' the country.

Broome told me once that one day Chen Ping said to him: " We are fighting together now because we both have a common objective—the destruction of the Japanese. But, of course, you understand that our ultimate objective is different from yours—we are aiming to establish a Communist republic in Malaya."

As politics was a forbidden subject for Force 136 officers to discuss with the Communists, the three men could not argue with Chen Ping. It is diverting to wonder whether they could have converted him had they been permitted to have political discussions.

Chen Ping also warned Davis and Broome that if Force 136 dropped any revolvers or pistols for the M.P.A.J.A. these would not be returned, although rifles and other weapons would. It was a strange and apparently ingenuous statement, but Chen Ping proved right. Neither revolvers nor pistols were returned when the

M.P.A.J.A. surrendered their weapons after the War; they became the badge of rank for officers in the next war.

Chen Ping agreed to try and arrange a meeting between Davis and a plenipotentiary of the Party. However, it was not until January 1, 1944, that this man—no less than Loi Tak himself—came to Davis' camp at Blantan.

Broome told me that neither Davis, Chapman, nor he knew the true identity of the plenipotentiary until long afterwards, but he was a man who certainly "exuded an aura of power." By comparison, Chen Ping was a mere subordinate

The conference began round a jungle-built table. Davis presided, with Broome and Chapman supporting him. Loi Tak and Chen Ping were the only Communists. Davis had the authority to act as the representative in Malaya of Lord Louis Mountbatten, and he produced these credentials, which Loi Tak accepted.

It was agreed from the beginning that no questions of post-war policy were to be discussed, as Davis' mission was purely military. Broome told me, and Chapman agrees, that the talks progressed in an atmosphere of caution—even cynicism—on both sides. Loi Tak took meticulous care in getting a clear-cut decision on every point after the most detailed discussion.

Two days later an agreement was signed in which the Communists consented to help the Allied Command to defeat the Japanese, and also—a point of some significance—assist during the period of Allied military reoccupation afterwards. In return, if and when contacts were established with India and transport was available, the Allies would supply the M.P.A.J.A. with new weapons, ammunition, and explosives, and British liaison teams would be sent to train the Chinese guerrillas. In addition, the British would finance the M.P.A.J.A. with about £3000 a month. "We were all very pleased with the results of this conference," says Chapman.

The Communists undoubtedly could not have been anything but delighted. As it was learned much later, the Party Executive had decided to maintain the M.P.A.J.A. as its permanent armed force. They had issued a secret directive to all M.P.A.J.A. leaders, ordering that 'secret,' as well as 'open,' units of the Army should be formed. They stressed that they were fighting for racial liberty, and consequently they had to develop and expand their fighting force so that it might be ready to become the ' Army of Malaya ' which would ' liberate ' the people of the country.

Therefore a tight force of long-tried members, including most of the important Party leaders, began to be built. It remained incognito. It collected or ' confiscated ' as many arms as possible as supplementary weapons to be used not only against the Japanese but also against the British later should the British Government not introduce a ' Peoples' Republic ' to the liking of the Malayan Communist Party. Thus the Party prepared itself for its inevitable ' direct action ' against the British.

In Kandy, in Ceylon, the Allied plans for the liberation of Malaya slowly moved to their climax. Allied submarines began sinking Japanese ships in the Straits of Malacca. Liberator aircraft laid mines in the Strait of Johore. British officers, non-commissioned officers, and wireless operators of Force 136 were parachuted into the country, or were landed by submarine to join forces with the M.P.A.J.A.

Large quantities of arms and ammunition were dropped to the guerrillas. Most of the containers were picked up, but the guerrilla recovery teams declared a large number ' lost.' Davis and company were aware that the ' lost ' consignments were being painstakingly concealed in secret places for the revolution foreshadowed by Chen Ping, but they could do nothing about it. Protests at the frequency of these ' losses ' received bland shrugs and impassive references to the difficulties of finding the drops in the thick jungle.

In March 1945, fourteen months after the first agreement had been signed, Davis arranged another meeting with Loi Tak. Once more he came to Blantan, and Chapman records that the atmosphere on this second occasion was " one of complete understanding and cordiality." There was no bargaining. While no further papers were signed, ways and means of implementing the first agreement were discussed.

Davis asked to be attached to central headquarters of the Party, or alternatively that a representative from Party headquarters should be attached to him. Loi Tak promised to take this point up with the Central Executive Committee. However, weeks went by without a reply. It looked as if the Committee were not anxious that a British officer should be among them. It was also suspected that the leaders wished to retain their anonymity for subversive activity after the reoccupation. Eventually, however, Davis was told that Chen Ping had been selected as the M.C.P. representative at the British headquarters, and that his appointment was being confirmed at a meeting to be held " in South Malaya " on August 12.

By the beginning of August, when President Truman, in Washington, was planning to use an atom bomb on Hiroshima, in Japan, over 2000 weapons had been handed out to the M.P.A.J.A., which had grown to about 7000 strong. The guerrillas had been given a function similar to that allotted by the Allies to the Maquis in the invasion of France.

They had received training in jungle camps strategically established near the main road and rail communications. Force 136 teams, consisting of a British officer and Asian radio-operators, were with seven of the eight M.P.A.J.A. 'Regiments.' Thirty patrol liaison teams, each with two British officers, radio-operators, and interpreters, were with a similar number of Communist patrols. In the jungles of the mainland were a total of three hundred and eight men, including eighty-eight British officers, from Force 136, ready for guerrilla warfare.

Then Japan surrendered, and the active services of the Chinese guerrillas were not wanted. It was a bitter disappointment to them and to the British teams who had spent months training them.

After the surrender Mountbatten declared that by August, when his great seaborne invasion force was on its way to Malaya, the guerrillas could have stopped all rail movement and could have created havoc behind the Japanese lines. Three years later these trained Chinese guerrillas played havoc with British lives and property.

3

Road to the Emergency

THE liberation of Malaya was greeted with warmth by its peoples. Three and a half years of oppression were forgotten in the wild moments of jubilation in town and country. In Singapore, the welcome to the fine, fighting-fit men of the Allied Navy, Army, and Air Force, who had fought all the way down through Burma, was tumultuous. In Chinese homes bottles of Scotch whisky, hidden through the years of occupation for just this occasion, were opened, and they gave added stimulus to the toasts to " Victory," " Churchill," and the " Allied Forces."

The celebrations north of Singapore were no less jubilant, but, significantly, most of them were directed to the men of the Malayan Peoples' Anti-Japanese Army. This was understandable in a way. Singapore had heard of the resistance army, but had never seen any of the guerrillas until liberation day, when groups from Johore came into the city in lorries and gave the crowds their sign of victory—raised clenched fists.

In the towns and villages north of Singapore the guerrillas had always been among the people, who had helped them and who had been killed for them. But, added to all this, the delay in sending British and Indian troops into the hinterland until several weeks had passed since the day of Japan's surrender, had helped to focus the glory on the M.P.A.J.A. themselves—they who were on the spot first.

As they emerged from the jungle in their green British uniforms, which had been dropped to them from the air, and as they took over control from dejected Japanese military and civil groups, the Chinese guerrillas received the adulation of the population. Triumphal arches, festooned with frangipani and hibiscus, with coconut-palm and banana-tree leaves, spanned the streets of tiny villages. Each carried Chinese inscriptions paying tribute not to the Allies but to the "glorious Anti-Japanese Army." In Ipoh, the capital of Perak, the decorations and celebrations were exclusively in honour of the redoubtable 5th Regiment.

The M.P.A.J.A. were quick to turn all this to their own advantage. They told admiring villagers that they, the Chinese Anti-Japanese Army, had beaten the Japanese. They lorded it over the populace. In most instances the M.P.A.J.A. maintained reasonable discipline, but in places along the east coast, and in the interior, their men began their own little reign of terror. They requisitioned buildings for their 'headquarters' and 'offices,' and collected funds and supplies at the muzzles of the sten-guns they had never used against the Japanese. It was in these little pockets in Pahang, Perak, and Kelantan—in the out-of-the-way places—that the British Military Administration, when they eventually arrived, found the guerrillas overbearing, arrogant, insolent, and insulting. They had to be dealt with firmly.

Brigadier L. H. O. Pugh, who in 1950 came to Johore from Hong Kong with the 26th Gurkha Infantry Brigade to fight the terrorists, told me that after he had landed in Malaya in 1945 with Mountbatten's 'Operation Zipper' force he was sent to Pahang to take control of the State. He found the towns of Bentong, Raub, Kuala Lipis, and Jerantut virtually in the hands of the Chinese guerrillas. In Raub they flew the hammer and sickle flag above the Union Jack. "I refused to let them participate in the Victory Parade in the town unless the positions of those flags were reversed," said Pugh. The Communist flag soon fluttered below the Union Jack.

In Kota Bahru, in Kelantan, the Chinese guerrillas occupied the town and proclaimed themselves masters. They terrorized the local peoples, robbed them, and looted their homes. They put up road blocks, examined every vehicle and all passengers, and stopped every pedestrian. They exacted a toll and a salute. Only firm handling by British forces when they arrived put an end to M.P.A.J.A. terrorism.

It is necessary here to pause a while and take stock of the physical, moral, and political situation existing in the country soon after its liberation from the miserable three and a half years of Japanese domination. Pre-war and post-war Malaya were vastly different.

Physically, the country was like a beaten boxer wavering on his knees who is saved by the bell. It had taken terrific punishment. The body-blows of Japanese maladministration, the foul kidney punches of Japanese barbarities, the uppercuts of undernourishment, had all given Malaya a severe beating. It was a country of refugees and displaced persons, victims of a vicious régime which had forced people away from the towns so as to ease the burden of feeding them. Growing food had become the most important thing in life. A little vegetable plot was far more valuable to a man than the possession of hundreds of Japanese Government dollars, because these could not buy what the mind and body craved—food. Even golf-links were dug up and the ground cultivated.

Malaya was a country of physically weak people, and, in consequence, of mentally weak ones also. Malnutrition opened the doors to dysentery, typhoid, and other killing diseases. Malaria was the greatest killer of them all, because all health measures had ceased months before.

Malaya was a country of violent crime unparalleled in its history. Armed robbery and murder were rife. The principal criminal types were young men of eighteen to twenty-four years who had been deprived during the occupation of parental or school influence. They used tommy-guns, stens, rifles, bayonets, revolvers, automatics, and hand-grenades which they had acquired in quantity after the surrender of the Japanese. These criminals had a free run because the police force was, comparatively, without sufficient arms of any sort, depleted in strength, and undermined in morale—a state of mind that was aggravated by a lack of uniforms. It was but a patchwork police force.

Malaya was a country of growing labour unrest. This unsettled condition developed out of the strain of living under the barbarities of the Japanese occupation, which had left labour emaciated and so undernourished that it was months before men were fit for normal output of work. Their homes on estates and mines had been neglected, and the fairly decent standards of sanitation and hygiene which had existed pre-war had deteriorated to the low level of primitive civilization.

Malaya was a country in which the white man had lost his prestige. His failure to hold the Japanese at bay had been the first blow to his standing. His degradation as the prisoner of war had been another. Normandy and the atom-bomb on Hiroshima were too remote to help balance the situation. Mountbatten's great liberating force was admired, but its influence was diminished by the unfortunate behaviour of many officers of the British Military Administration. If these were the type of men who represented the Raj, could not Malaya fall again to another foe, thought the weary people of the country.

Malaya was a country with a new and growing national spirit among the Malays and the Malaya-born Chinese. The influence of India was there. So was the determined effort of Indonesia to achieve independence from the Dutch. But, contrary to what had happened in India and what was going to happen in Indonesia and Burma, the Malays (except for some Indonesian elements) and the Chinese (except for the Malayan Communist Party) desired nothing but orderly transition to independence.

But this pleasant prospect was given a near-mortal blow immediately after the reoccupation by the tactics of an unthinking British Government which had 'planned' Malaya's future without consulting its peoples or those latently powerful individuals, the Malay rulers.

The joy and eagerness with which the people had hailed the return of the British in September 1945 was short-lived. For the Malays, the fond expectation of a return to the pre-war political state was rudely shattered by the arrival of the British treaty-maker, Sir Harold MacMichael. While an unimaginative Military Administration which was insensitive to the growing feelings of nationalism in the country set to work to try to restore order out of Japanese chaos—and, in doing so, created further chaos—Sir Harold made a quick trip to each of the Malay Rulers with proposals for a new political set-up to be called the Malayan Union.

Some Rulers wanted time to consider the plan and an opportunity to consult their councils according to their pre-war practice and constitution. This was refused, and, because they still trusted the British, these Sultans signed the treaty, albeit hesitantly and almost unwillingly. One Sultan, who refused to put his name to the treaty at first, was warned, it was alleged in knowledgeable Malay circles, that if he did not sign it he would be deposed. Within a fortnight all the Rulers had signed.

The treaties had been planned in Whitehall during the stresses of World War II. They established a united Malaya working under one Government instead of nine, as had been the case before the War, but they were regarded as depriving the Malay Rulers of their sovereignty. This was completely contrary to all previous treaties, the first of which dated back to the 1870's. Here it may be worth recalling that after Singapore had been founded in 1819 the British Government immersed itself in the development of the three Settlements of Singapore, Penang, and Malacca. It showed no interest in the civil wars that were being fought in the Malay hinterland between rival Sultans and chiefs.

Eventually, however, as Sir Frank Swettenham, an historian of Malaya, puts it, " The British Government was invited, pushed, and persuaded into helping the Rulers of certain States to introduce order into their disorderly, penniless, and distracted households." Trained British civil servants were sent to advise the Rulers and to organize a system of government which would " secure justice, freedom, safety for all."

Right up to the outbreak of the Japanese war the Malay States were never British territory. Their Rulers had only placed themselves, their peoples, and their lands under the benign protection of the British, who were strictly enjoined not to interfere in any way with the Mohammedan religion and ancient Malay custom. The position and authority of the Rulers were never questioned, even though as the years passed they were slowly denuded of more and more power until, in some States, the chief British official, the Resident, held more authority than the Sultan. He was in fact a little king.

The proposed ' Malayan Union ' planned to convert the nine protected States into a single British Colony. This reconstitution may have been intended to make life pleasanter and government less complicated, but the methods adopted for achieving ' agreement ' did nothing but alienate the Malays and discredit the name of Britain still further.

An immediate—and most serious—aftermath of the MacMichael " treaties " was unequivocal distrust of the British, which reached a climax when a Civil Government took over from the Military

Administration in April 1946. The Malays boycotted every aspect of the new Government. No Ruler or Malay Government servant —in fact, no Malay—attended the ceremonial installation of Sir Edward Gent as first Governor of the Malayan Union. The insult to the British protecting Power was intentional. It had been planned that way.

Sir Edward, a man who ardently desired friendship between the Malays and Britain, went out of his way to try to ease the strain. His task was made doubly difficult, however, because reports pointed to him as having been one of the architects of the Malayan Union plan.

Before he landed in Kuala Lumpur, the capital of the country, on April 1, 1946, Sir Edward had been a Colonial Office expert on Malaya. The Malayan Union was his first governorship—and was thought by many to be a 'plum' handed him by a grateful Labour Government for his hard work in planning a new era for the country.

Sir Edward must have noticed the political agitation in the pool of Malay languor. The first pebble to ruffle the calm had been the conquest of the country by Japan. The next had been the self-confident and overbearing conduct of the Chinese guerrillas, coupled with some serious Sino-Malay clashes in parts of Malaya. To the Malays, some obvious signs about the future were already there—the Chinese were dominating the field, and unless they, the Malays, recouped the situation, they would find themselves a people without a country.

The third pebble was the agitation of Indonesian independence across the waters of the Java Sea and the adjoining Straits of Malacca. By nature indolent, easy-going, by preference peace-loving, the Malays had felt the cold breezes of nationalism blowing from Indonesia not long before the Japanese surrender.

Groups of hot-blooded Javanese and Boyanese had sneaked into the country, trying to win support for the establishment at the end of the Japanese war of a great Malay republic embracing all the territories of the Netherlands Indies, and Malaya.

Living quietly in his home in Johore Bahru was a middle-aged Malay, Onn bin Ja'afar, born of a Circassian mother. Onn had had a varied career in Johore and Singapore before the War, but the next few years were destined to see him become the acknowledged leader of two-and-a-half million Malays in the country.

To him went these emissaries from the Indies. He showed the shrewdness which characterized the first few years of his power in Malaya. He wanted independence for the Malays but not at the price of bloodshed—except as a last resort. He gently told his visitors to achieve their own independence first, and then, perhaps, in the course of time when Malaya had become independent itself, the opportunity for discussing their fusion into a strong Malay republic would arise.

Onn had long determined that the Malays had to 'wake up' and take cognizance of the dangers surrounding them. One, he saw, was that of being swept away by the industrious and powerful Chinese.

MacMichael heaved into the pool the boulder which brought Onn into action and Malays straight into the world of politics.

Onn toured the country from end to end rallying the Malays to the banner he had unfurled by forming the United Malays National Organization. The primary aim of this Party was the abolition of the Malayan Union, and after that the political, social, and economic progress of the Malays towards the self-government which was in the foreseeable future.

To look ahead for a moment, U.M.N.O. was fated never to become what Onn had planned for it, because after four years as its unchallenged president he resigned and formed a rival all-communities organization named the Independence of Malaya Party. Whatever might have been the internal dissensions that disrupted U.M.N.O. and reduced its importance as a powerful political party, it did succeed in developing among the Malays the realization that they had to learn to stand on their own feet and fight against an already politically conscious Indian community and an ambitious and rich Chinese community.

The post-war Malaya saw a radical change also occurring among the non-Communist Chinese. They were no longer immigrants wanting to make money and then return to their villages in China to die. Conditions in Nationalist China did not attract them any more. They wanted to stay in Malaya, be domiciled in it. They wanted a secure footing in the country. They wanted to be brought within the administration, not just be controlled by it.

One-quarter of the Chinese population had by force of Japanese treatment moved out of towns and villages and was 'squatting' in the country. By the time of the reoccupation these rural Chinese had become a group outside the law. Many of them who had been boys of thirteen or fourteen in 1941 were young men of seventeen and eighteen in 1945. They had never known any Government except the hated Japanese.

The return of civil government to Malaya in April 1946 brought the disliked and feared Malayan Communist Party into the political and economic scenes. Its malignant influence began to reach out to all Chinese workers. The M.C.P. flouted the authority of the Government. Thinking Chinese were bewildered by the attitude of *laissez-faire* adopted by the British to this Communist freedom. Some Chinese had a fair idea of democratic principles, but many of them could not clearly distinguish the differences between Communism and Socialism. Liberty they could understand, but they felt in those months after the return of the civil government that they were living in a period of licence rather than liberty. The British had failed to stop the Japanese. They claimed that they had defeated the dictators, but, instead of asserting their authority and protecting law-abiding citizens in the old tradition, they were now permitting Communists to have their sway and say in Malaya.

The Malayan Union had been acceptable to the more educated Chinese as it promised racial equality. To look ahead again so as not to break the continuity of this little dissertation on the Chinese: the Malayan Union was eventually scrapped—Onn and U.M.N.O. won—and a new Federal Agreement established the Federation of Malaya, a protectorate of nine Malay States, each retaining the sovereignty of its Ruler, and including the two Settlements of Penang and Malacca. This began a controversy between Malays and non-Malays over the question of citizenship.

The Chinese saw all sorts of perplexing and ingenuous legal restrictions devised specially for them. They protested at the implications of Federal citizenship. They dubbed it 'second class' citizenship, and began a struggle to have this situation changed.

Then came the Emergency. The police, many famous units of the British Army, the Gurkhas, the Malay Regiment, and the Royal Air Force were unable to defeat the handful of Communists.

A hatred of the Chinese—the race from which had come the

terrorists—began to develop. The Malay Governments felt that the Chinese were nothing but saboteurs of the Federal Agreement and unworthy of consideration or sympathy. Even some senior British Civil Service officers, steeped in the pro-Malay tradition, developed a dislike of the Chinese. This feeling remains among some of them to this day.

The recognition of Communist China by the British Labour Government had a very serious effect on the Chinese. They became a collection of individuals paralysed by fear—fear of the present and fear of the future. Was Britain really trying against the Communists in Malaya? Was she going to slide out and leave Malaya to the same fate as Burma? Was she going to let the Malays have full sway and turn the Emergency into an anti-Chinese war? How safe could they be from the machinations of the Communists if Red consuls operated in the country?

With all these questions passing through their perplexed and frightened minds, the Chinese adopted a rôle they did not relish—that of fence-sitters. They did not know what the British were going to do, and they feared the Communists.

There was a great gap between the wealthy and middle-class Chinese. Many of them desired to assist the Government, but they were afraid of the future. They decided to organize themselves, and they formed the Malayan Chinese Association. As a political body it has not been an unqualified success, but its formation had a marked effect on the Communists, who feared that it would present them with a united front among the Chinese who were opposed to them.

Therefore in all respects after the Japanese war Malaya was in a maelstrom. The Government was an unhappy one. The Malays and Chinese were full of distrust of each other. Nationalism was spreading. The country was near bankruptcy. Overwhelming problems concerning the rehabilitation of the vital rubber and tin industries had to be faced. Rice, the staple food, was scarce. Living costs were soaring. Labour was restless. The only people jubilant about the situation were the Communists. It was against this background—distrust of the British, a dismal lack of foresight by Whitehall, a failure to accept the signs by the King's Representative in Kuala Lumpur, and a growing political turmoil throughout the country—that the Communists began spreading their influence until they opened their 'revolt' in June 1948.

From October 1945, the Malayan Communist Party made a determined bid for attention. They publicly announced an 'Eight-point' programme. This differed from the original 'Nine points' in only one aspect: this was the silent omission of their ninth decision to establish a Malayan Republic.

To the British officers who had worked among the Communist leaders this omission merely meant that the project had been temporarily shelved. They warned the Supreme Commander, Lord Louis Mountbatten, of the dangers that faced a continued alliance with the Malayan Communist Party, which was beginning to convert its supply arm, the Anti-Japanese Union, into the People's Democratic Movement, with a membership that might run into thousands, and these members could be put into action again without much preparation.

The Party had also formed a Communist youth organization known as the New Democratic Youth Corps. They held rallies in towns and villages, and their propagandists began to stir up discontent by referring to the serious food situation and the mounting cost of living. There were rice riots in Perak that October, and British troops had to fire to disperse the crowds.

The Party was in a dangerous mood, and would have taken advantage of the situation by launching their revolt then had it not been for the presence of more than three divisions of highly-trained troops. Loi Tak is believed to have wielded his considerable influence by urging the more hot-headed members of his executive to hold their hand until these Allied armed forces had left.

Those were tense days, and there was a sigh of relief when the Communist Party accepted with outward good grace the British decision that the Chinese guerrillas should be disbanded. This meant the disarming of a potentially dangerous force. The disbandment of the M.P.A.J.A. began on December 1, and everywhere it was made an occasion for pageant and circumstance. Local British commanders paid lip tribute to the courage and resource of the guerrillas and their "contribution to the victory in Malaya," before each man handed in his gun.

Lieutenant-General Sir Frank Messervy, General Officer Commanding-in-Chief, Malaya Command, himself took the salute at an impressive central parade in Kuala Lumpur. He thanked the guerrillas for their "gallantry and determination in resisting the evil foe we have been fighting together." He said it needed both moral and physical courage to take up arms against a ruthless and powerful enemy in a country firmly occupied by his troops and full of his spies. A copy of this speech, the Burma Star, and the 1939–45 Star ribbons, and a gratuity of 350 dollars (about £45) were presented to every guerrilla in the country. The Royal Air Force sent Thunderbolts and Spitfires to fly low in salute at all disbandment parades.

It is a strange fact that the guerrillas handed back all the arms supplied to them by Force 136 for which receipts had been given—plus 700 other Service rifles and more than 1000 shot-guns. It was a disarming gesture, which had the effect of reassuring high military administrators but did not fool the few who knew the Communists well. To these few it indicated that the M.C.P. was satisfied it had enough weapons to equip its 'secret' army.

Mountbatten himself paid tribute to the guerrilla leaders in a final great parade that was held on the green padang in Singapore. It was all well staged. Fifteen jungle guerrillas, three of them Malays, the others Chinese, led by Chen Ping, were driven through the streets in four open cars. They were escorted by British Military Police outriders. On the padang a guard of honour from the 1st Battalion the Cameronians (Scottish Rifles) received them at attention. The band of the Royal Marines played.

As his name was called out in Mandarin each Chinese hero stepped forward to Mountbatten, saluted, and was decorated with the war ribbons. It was noted that eleven Chinese gave the Communist clenched fist salute. Within seventeen months of this splendid decorative but ironical occasion every one of the Chinese heroes was to be back at his old jungle headquarters, directing a campaign against his former allies.

The Communist Party immediately formed an M.P.A.J.A. Ex-Services Comrades' Association. Branches were established in almost every town and fair-sized village in the country. All demobilized guerrillas—except those who were to form the secret army—were instructed to register as members, a step which ensured that when the day of revolution came every former trained Anti-Japanese fighter could be found and called to instant arms.

The secret army was fed, clothed, sustained, and kept contented by contributions from the Ex-Services Comrades' Association. Demobbed guerrillas were forced to contribute a great portion of their gratuity towards the expenses of this secret force, which by the end of 1945 numbered about 4000 according to information given to the Federation Government.

The Malayan Communist Party was astute in another direction. The British Military Administration offered employment to the demobbed guerrillas, but the Party declined on their behalf. It wanted to keep a tight control on its members, and it refused to allow them to work in Government employment, not only out of fear that they would be scattered, but—much more important—that they would become content with life in employment.

The Party, however, accepted invitations from the British Military Administration to appoint representatives to serve on the Advisory Councils being set up throughout the country. These Councils were completely informal and met irregularly; they were advisory in their functions and were intended to enable the Administration " to discuss frankly " the problems of each territory with " leading and responsible " representatives of all schools of thought. Unfortunately, several of the Councils met in secret, which gave the Communists the opportunity of asserting the undemocratic nature of these bodies.

The Party, however, enjoyed having men on the Councils, for this gave it a standing in the public eye, even though it was generally known that its representatives on the Councils were unimportant members of the Party.

Meanwhile the Party formed a secret central organization under the chairmanship of Loi Tak. It existed alongside the open and known Central Executive Committee, but it was more important and its work more significant to the cause. Loi Tak was assisted by Chen Ping and two other men, Yeung Kwo and Chan Wing. These three men had been his principal lieutenants during the Japanese occupation. The Japanese had listed them as the most dangerous Communists in the country.

Chen Ping we know. Yeung Kwo, secretary of the Selangor State Committee, had been Loi Tak's right-hand man in dealings with the Negri Sembilan and Pahang committees. Chan Wing was the Party representative in the 4th Independent Regiment in Johore.

Loi Tak sent out directives calling for the formation of labour, youth, and women's Communist organizations. The staff work was good. These associations rapidly mushroomed in the country. There were the General Labour Unions and there were the New Democratic Youth Leagues, which marked the culmination of the Party's efforts to reorganize their pre-war Communist Youth League. These began to build up a formidable membership.

Everything seemed to be going well with the Communist Party and particularly with Loi Tak, but he was scheduled for a fright in September that year when a Chinese newspaper in Penang denounced him as having been a traitor to the Party during the Japanese occupation. The denunciation came from a man named Wong Yeh Lo, who had been the Party representative on the Chinese Mobilization Committee, formed in Singapore in 1941, when the Japanese were advancing down the Peninsula and the Communists had already offered an alliance with Britain.

This attack was, however, ignored by the Central Executive Committee. The reason for their reaction was simple: Wong Yeh Lo had been a known agent of the hated Japanese Military Police during the occupation, and they classed his allegation as the rantings of an enemy. Once again Loi Tak was hailed as having been the Party's deliverer and preserver from the Japanese, and when the Central Executive Committee met in January 1946 he was re-elected Secretary-General.

That meeting of the Committee was important for other reasons. For one thing, it took stock of the situation in Malaya and in the Far East. It found that cells had been established in a tremendous number of labour organizations in Malaya, and that, with deft handling, these could probably obtain control of the workers. Communism was still admittedly not very popular with the masses, but intense propaganda in the cells and in the coffee-shops, theatres, and parks might assist in bringing more members.

The Committee made some important decisions. It laid down a definite anti-British policy, which aimed at overthrowing the Government, if necessary by violence—although the word violence was carefully not used—and establishing a Peoples' Republic. The Committee decided to contact Communist parties in Thailand, India, Indonesia, Indo-China, and Britain. It accepted an invitation from the British Communist Party to attend an Empire Communist conference in London in February, 1947. It also decided to write to the Communist Party in India, expressing the hope that it would be able to send experienced men to Malaya to organize cells among Indians. In Malaya itself the Party would appeal to a newly formed Malay Nationalist Party to accelerate Communist work among the Malays. Propaganda was to be launched on a considerable scale throughout the country. The final decision was to launch strikes in industries—the first active step towards the chief objective.

Within a few days of this decision the Party achieved a sweeping success. Its General Labour Unions called a general strike throughout Singapore and the mainland. This caught the Administration napping. In Singapore alone 173,000 men stopped work. Business and transport were paralysed. The British Military Administration was surprised, not by the suddenness of the strike, but by this revelation of the extent of Communist control over labour. It peevishly declared that the strike had nothing to do with wages or conditions of labour, but was an attempt by " a foreign body " to subvert law.

The Communists called off the strike on the second day, before the troubles could reach monster proportions on the Malayan mainland. The Party had had its taste of power. It was essential, however, for the Administration to act quickly to show who was master. The Communist Party had become much too powerful. Banishment was still a very powerful weapon. No Chinese, let alone Communists, wished to be sent in handcuffs to China, where Generalissimo Chiang Kai-shek, still in power, dealt forcibly with such men. The Administration arrested ten labour leaders and propagandists in Singapore and banished them. A few other arrests were made in Singapore in a tense atmosphere.

These steps, insignificant as they may appear, had a remarkable effect on the Communists. Loi Tak himself called off more widespread operations.

In between staging Malaya's troubles, Loi Tak took long trips to Thailand, Indonesia, Indo-China, and China to foster Communist relations. In Hong Kong he was known to have met General Fong Feng, an important member of the Central Committee of Mao Tse-tung's Party. Information which reached British Intelligence circles later indicated that the General had told Loi Tak not to expect financial aid from Mao Tse-tung.

Loi Tak was advised to organize a united front in Malaya, but not to embark on an armed insurrection. General Fong Feng suggested that, as long as the British Labour Government remained in power, the Malayan Communist Party should work for self-government by constitutional means.

By the time Loi Tak returned from his trips in January 1947 the Malayan Communist Party considered it had achieved control over labour. Once again orders for widespread strikes went out. It was at this juncture that Loi Tak again found himself in a dangerous position. During a meeting of the Central Executive Committee a member accused him of being " a dictator " and " a bad leader." The irate member characterized the Committee itself as incompetent, afraid of Loi Tak, and—a terrible accusation for the Party—of " adopting a right-wing policy " which, he said, was taking the Party on the road to ruin. The meeting broke into an uproar and had to be postponed for a fortnight.

Loi Tak was in a difficult position. This was the second time he had been criticized and had allegations made against him. He was now expected to reply to the charges. A showdown was near. There appeared to be two camps in the Executive—the pro- and the anti-Loi Tak.

The next meeting of the Executive was fixed for March 6. The rendezvous was a place five miles outside Kuala Lumpur. That day the members of the Committee arrived one by one—but Loi Tak did not turn up. The Committee waited several hours for him. It never saw him again.

A few days later it learned that Loi Tak had disappeared with most of the Party's funds, a sizeable figure running into thousands of dollars. He has never been seen since.

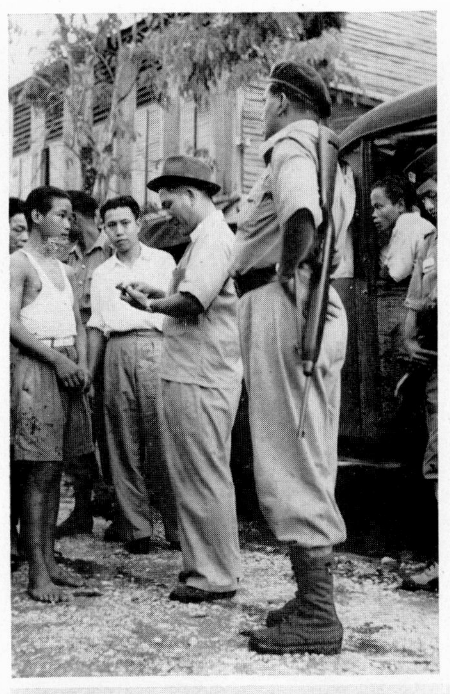

A Common Scene in Malaya To-day
Checking identity-cards in village and town.

Behind these Gates is One of Several Camps used for the Detention of Thousands of Suspects
Photo "Straits Times"

CHEN PING, SECRETARY-GENERAL OF THE MALAYAN COMMUNIST PARTY

The most wanted man in Malaya to-day.

A SURRENDERED INDIAN TERRORIST TELLS RUBBER LABOURERS THAT COMMUNISM WAS HIS DOWNFALL

4

A New Party Boss

LOI TAK'S personality, prestige, and power had been so remarkable that even Party executives who had disliked him found it difficult to accept the repugnant meaning behind his disappearance. Fear of dissension and revolt breaking out in the lower ranks of the Party caused the Committee to decide that, for its own security of position, it should not allow news of the vanishing of Loi Tak to seep out beyond its own close circle. If it succeeded in finding evidence which would expose him it could then justify its secrecy with the statement that it had been for the good of the Party generally. The Committee fully appreciated the quicksands of their own predicament.

" Central " constituted itself into "an Examination Committee" and unanimously appointed Chen Ping to find Loi Tak if possible, or, at the very least, to unearth everything possible about his private life, his finances, his activities during the Japanese occupation, and to trace him to wherever he was. They had picked the right man for the job. Chen Ping had been Loi Tak's boon companion; he knew his haunts and his friends. All the same, it was an unpleasant task for Chen Ping, who had looked upon Loi Tak with a great deal of respect and admiration.

Chen Ping himself had never deviated from being an honest man, and it is possible, therefore, to look on the results of his inquiries with a certain amount of confidence. One can accept Chen Ping's two most startling discoveries: that during the Japanese occupation Loi Tak had been a catspaw of the Japanese and had betrayed most of the leaders of the Central Executive Committee who had lost their lives, and that immediately afterwards he appeared to have assisted the British Intelligence. It was a fantastic story of cross and double-cross by a clever man who had apparently tossed aside Communism for the attraction of power and money.

No British source, either Government or police, would officially admit to me that Loi Tak had been a star informer on the Malayan Communist Party both before the Japanese war and immediately after it. It has proved impossible for me to confirm officially the indiscretion I heard somewhere in Malaya that Loi Tak had been brought from Hong Kong in the early nineteen-thirties by a British police officer from Singapore and planted in the Malayan Communist Party to act as an agent. The fact that he rose to be Secretary-General by sheer personality and competence, coupled, as Chen Ping found, with a dexterous ability to distort the truth, may be considered a tribute to the man who chose him originally as a British agent—if the story is true.

One cannot, however, overlook the fact, in trying to find evidence of Loi Tak's connexion with the police in Singapore, that he was never once arrested and that he always happened to get away just before a police raid on an address used by important Communist leaders.

Loi Tak must have been a very clever actor, too, because he did his work as Secretary-General so well that he must have given his British paymasters some very anxious moments, particularly in the critical days of 1946.

Chen Ping's investigations lasted until the end of 1947, and when he produced his evidence before the Central Executive Committee the enormity of Loi Tak's ' treachery,' and more particularly the facile way in which he had fooled the Party from the nineteen-thirties onward, so appalled them that they kept everything a dead secret for several months.

It was not until March 1948 that they allowed the news to leak out slowly, first to the State Secretaries, then to the members of State Committees, and then down to the district committees. Finally the rank and file received a fulsome cyclostyled pamphlet called the *Loi Tak Exposure Document,* which in simple language told them the story. The document was dated May 28, 1948. Copies of it fell into the hands of the police within the next two months, and what follows has been culled from it and from evidence obtained by the police from other sources.

The document began:

Dear Comrades of the entire Party,

In 1930 our Party held its first National Representatives' Conference and formally set up the Malayan Communist Party. Not long after the British Imperialists began to intensify their efforts to disrupt it, and in 1934 they conducted actual raids on it, resulting in the arrest of all comrades in Central. The Party's relations with the Third Internationale (in Shanghai) were then cut off, and its internal organization thrown into confusion.

It was under these circumstances that at the end of 1934, or during 1935, Loi Tak wormed his way into the Party. Once he got in he seized hold of the opportunity afforded by the unprepared state of thought and the lack of centralization in the organization of the Party, and, employing to advantage various tactics, emerged as the representative of the Third Internationale, thereby raising his personal status. He was accordingly elected as the Secretary in Central at the 6th Central Extended Conference held in 1939.

During the pre-war period, through his craftiness he gained a complete mastery over the working personnel to deceive others while increasing and maintaining his own status. By this means he managed to win the confidence of comrades. He has had a lot to do with the losses and defeats of our Party through successive terms.

During the period of resistance against the Japanese he took upon himself to direct the various activities of the Party on the strength of his pre-war prestige and on the strength of high power conferred on him by the Central Plenary Conference held on December 1, 1941, at the outbreak of war. Thus, following a well-calculated plan, he posed as a sacrosanct 'hero,' as a person of unusual capability transcending all others in the various organs of the Party. He also set out to make all comrades develop a subconscious attitude of looking upon him as being supreme in everything and of following him blindly. He was thus trusted and believed beyond any of the various Party organs. . . .

Let us now follow the saga of Loi Tak during the Japanese occupation as garnered from the 'Document' and from what the police learned by interrogating officers of the Japanese military police for whom Loi Tak had worked.

Within a few weeks of their beginning a reign of terror in Singapore to sift the Communists from among the Chinese, the Japanese military police found a prize in their hands—no less than Loi Tak. He never allowed the Japanese the opportunity of torturing him to get what they wanted: he disliked pain; he loved life better. He offered to give them information about his Party.

The Japanese wanted proof of his sincerity, so he gave them the names and addresses of many of the Singapore members of the Central Executive Committee. That was how these men found themselves rounded up, tortured, and killed. Loi Tak provided a few more addresses, until within six months of the fall of Singapore there was only one important Communist left in Singapore—himself.

Loi Tak had gone out of his way to make certain that there would be no comrade of any importance left in Singapore capable of betraying him to the Party. He protected himself in this way so well that, from March 1943 up to the time of the surrender, the Japanese in Singapore were not troubled by a single Communist. Those who had succeeded in evading the Japanese round-up had vanished into the jungles north of Singapore.

The Japanese military police then made a deal with Loi Tak. They allowed him to carry out his job of Secretary-General as long as he fed them with information. Loi Tak was clever enough to keep them satisfied. He went north and passed on the dreaded news of the fate of the Singapore Committee. He summoned a meeting of the rest of the Central Executive at Batu Caves, outside Kuala Lumpur. And so the 'Batu Caves Massacre' was arranged. . . .

To his comrades, however, Loi Tak bore the most charmed life they had ever known. He seemed invulnerable.

Loi Tak made Singapore his headquarters. The Japanese military police set him up in a house. They gave him a car. In it, he had free passage over the causeway from Singapore to Johore, which the military police controlled with grim efficiency. It was no wonder that comrades in the jungle marvelled at his brazenness in crossing the Japanese barriers so openly and getting away with it every time, right under the Japanese noses.

Once across the causeway Loi Tak became again the 'ardent Communist.' His organization was superb, but he occasionally deviated from the path of Communist duty to betray the odd comrade.

It may be recalled that when Davis established a headquarters in Perak and asked for a message to be sent to the Secretary-General, it took weeks before he got a reply. The reason for this delay was, of course, not that Loi Tak was at a secret and remote headquarters in the jungle, but that he was in Singapore, and guerrilla leaders had to wait for him to turn up before they could get any business done.

It was unlikely that Loi Tak considered betraying any British guerrillas, because he realized his future safety lay with them. He had no scruples, however, about exposing Asian ones.

The only people whom Loi Tak could fear were Communists of his own black type—men who had become secret agents of the Japanese; but he depended upon his own histrionic abilities to refute their allegations should these ever arise. As the 'Document' said quite correctly, "Very few comrades had any idea of his mode of living, for he was really a 'mysterious person.'"

Among the other facts unearthed by Chen Ping during his prolonged inquiries was that Loi Tak had never been a representative of the Third Internationale. Neither had he studied in the Soviet Union, nor visited France, nor had he held a position on the Shanghai Town Committee of the China Communist Party, nor had he helped the Vietnamese Communist Party to form a strategy to resist the Japanese.

"All this," commented the 'Document' wryly, "was only to raise his own status so that comrades not only had nothing to suspect him of but trusted and revered him."

Turning to the period after the Japanese surrender, the 'Document' accused the Party policy fixed by Loi Tak of being essentially "a running dog" one, "traitorous to the cause of the revolution."

"It can be clearly seen that he had been in league with the Imperialists to sabotage the revolution," said the Committee, and it went on to make the significant allegation, "Although for the moment there is no means of investigating his pre-war activities, yet it is estimated that the possibility of his having conspired with the Imperialists is very great."

Undoubtedly Loi Tak's post-war efforts to postpone the revolution to overthrow the British in Malaya led to his own betrayal. The 'Document' says: "His directing policy gave rise to dissatisfaction by his comrades, and at two meetings he was severely criticized."

"He was forced to escape," concludes the 'Document,' "because post-war environment no longer afforded him the opportunity of putting his deceptive and traitorous tactics into effect."

It is intriguing to wonder whether Loi Tak would have reached the position and authority he had achieved over the Malayan Communist Party if there had been no Japanese war.

Loi Tak was solemnly dismissed from membership of the Party as a traitor. The Central Committee had ranked him as "the greatest culprit in the history of our Party." The inevitable sentence of death as a traitor was passed on him.

I have learned that Loi Tak hid himself in Malaya, probably Singapore, for some months before he left for Hong Kong and then Thailand. The last report of him, and it was merely a rumour, was that in Thailand he was 'liquidated' by Chinese Communists put on to him by the Malayan Communist Party. This, though, has never been confirmed.

The Malayan Communist Party had to find another Secretary-General. Because he had done so much for it and had had such a large hand in extending the ramifications of Communism in Malaya after the Japanese war, the Central Executive Committee unanimously elected Chen Ping to the position. It was as Secretary-General, in fact, that Chen Ping had followed the trail of his predecessor. It is safe to assume that he was, and has since been, most carefully watched by the members of his own Executive, for they must have been determined that there should not be another Loi Tak among them.

It would probably be useful at this juncture to take another look at the new Secretary-General who was to declare war on his former friends the British, who, in their turn, were eventually to offer the incredible reward of £30,000 for his capture alive.

When he became Secretary-General in 1947 Chen Ping was only twenty-six years of age. He is five feet seven inches in height, with a fair skin, and a slight limp. His soft voice can speak six languages—four Chinese dialects, Malay, and English. He has a quiet and gentle manner.

I have already remarked on the terrific impression he created on Davis, Broome, Chapman, and other British officers who met him. Indeed, after the war, these men had had hopes that Chen Ping would give up active Communism and go into the bicycle business with his father, who had prospered and had established a branch in Penang. Chen Ping had married, and there had seemed a possibility in the early days of 1947 that he was interested in settling down. Loi Tak's defection, however, put an end to these hopes.

Chen Ping had been a sincere chief assistant for the British when the Military Administration was immersed with the problems of disarming the M.P.A.J.A. He accepted an invitation to go to London with other M.P.A.J.A. men for the great Victory Parade past King George VI.

However, when he returned to Malaya he received what he must have considered a greater reward; he was appointed a member of the Party's Central Executive Committee. He was the youngest man ever to have been brought into that tight Red circle, and Loi Tak, the worshipped Secretary-General, immediately made Chen Ping his trusted lieutenant.

Loi Tak had, of course, his two other trusted assistants, Yeung Kwo and Chan Wing. These three had been his main links in communication work during the occupation. Chen Ping operated in Perak, Yeung Kwo, as secretary of the Selangor State Committee, had held sway in Kuala Lumpur and was in touch with Negri Sembilan and Pahang units, and Chan Wing, as the Party representative on the 4th Independent Regiment, had been the link with Johore.

Loi Tak sent Chen Ping outside Malaya to sound Communists in neighbouring countries about co-operation from them in the revolt to come. He received no satisfaction, and he may have been slightly disillusioned about the great brotherhood of Communism when even the Chinese Communist Party remained unreceptive to his approaches.

Meanwhile a grateful British Government—despite the warnings that Chen Ping would be a dangerous enemy in a short time—had appointed him an Officer of the Order of the British Empire. Chen Ping never received the decoration, because it arrived in Malaya for presentation to him by the High Commissioner, after the Party had begun its revolt. The award was cancelled after the outbreak of the conflict.

Only a handful of Communists know where Chen Ping is to-day. It is generally believed he is in the jungles of Pahang, where experienced British soldiers think he and his Central Executive Committee members have gone to hide in comparative safety. But he might also be in his home State of Perak—or even in Singapore.

His wife is in the jungle, not with him, but working for him. She is a prominent member of a propaganda unit. They have two children, both about six years of age. The son is living with Chen Ping's mother in Sitiawan, the daughter with his wife's mother in Penang. It is possible that Chen Ping and his wife may have seen their children a few times in the last six years, but certainly not more often, for the homes of both families are carefully watched by men of the Special Branch.

Chen Ping, as Secretary-General, reorganized the direction and control of Communist affairs, and drafted a new set of objects for the Party. These again admitted that the Party " embraced Marxism and Leninism as its guiding principles," and that, while its ultimate goal in Malaya was the establishment of Communism among the masses, its immediate objective was self-government by people of various races in the country by whatever means was found necessary.

The Executive decided that it might be useful to make contact with other Communist parties in the world, so its delegates began to roam, at Party expense, through Europe, going to Prague, Paris, London, and Belgrade, among other cities. Boyishly enthusiastic about their own Party, and just as boyishly bursting with pride, they told Soviet officials in Paris and British Communists in London about their plans for a new Malaya—but found that these received a discouragingly lukewarm reception.

The patronizing Russians would give no promise of support in an armed struggle. The British, being thoroughly insular, patted them on the back and wished them luck. Indeed, so disappointed was one of the delegates who went to the Empire Communist Conference in London that he declared vehemently upon his return that the British Communist Party had tendencies to the right and was not sufficiently extreme in its views.

However, the large bright red banner which the British Communist Party presented to the Malayan Communist Party was given a place of honour on the walls of the headquarters in Kuala Lumpur. Its gold lettering proclaimed to the gratified rank and file:

BRITISH COMMUNISTS SEND FRATERNAL GREETINGS TO THEIR MALAYAN COMRADES AND PLEDGE SUPPORT IN THE STRUGGLE FOR FREEDOM

I sat under that flag one day talking to two of the brighter stars of the Party, a Malayan-born Chinese named Wu Tien Wang and a Jamaica-born Chinese named Liew Yit Fun, a very able propagandist and orator, whose mother had been English. A print of Stalin, a charcoal drawing of Mao Tse-tung, father of the Chinese Communist Republic, and a great hammer-and-sickle flag dominated the wall behind a stage.

Wu flowed with friendliness except during the moments when he lost his studied calm and spoke excitedly about Britain's "Imperialistic pretensions in South-East Asia." Once he struck the table between us with his fist as he said: "There is an Iron Curtain between the United Kingdom and the Colonies. The British people —even the Members of Parliament—seem ignorant of the developments in Malaya—the rise of trade unions and the demands among the workers for better treatment, higher wages, and better living conditions."

His friends in London, he said, were D. N. Pritt, Harold Davies, Zilliacus, and Gallacher (the then Communist Member of Parliament). He went on, "They have promised to fight in the Commons for the justifiable aspirations of the Malayan people." Wu to-day is among the hunted, while Liew is under detention after serving a sentence of eighteen months' rigorous imprisonment, which began in May 1948, for sedition.

5

The Emergency Declared

THE Communist Party began to put into effect its plans for industrial strife in 1947. It had already gained a disturbing control in a large number of trade unions, many of which had been formed on a regional basis, irrespective of trade distinctions. Party propagandists and strike leaders, however, were given excellent grist because wage rates had not kept pace with the rising cost of living.

In that year there were over 300 major strikes and industrial disputes in the country, most of them occurring on rubber estates. They caused a loss of 696,036 working-days—a prodigious figure. While the Communists admittedly did not play a part in many of the troubles, they were behind most of the serious ones, which invariably were accompanied by violent demonstrations.

But adding to the restiveness among the population caused by the industrial strife was the ugly birth of banditry, much of which really could not be laid at the doors of the 'secret army' of the Communist Party, as this had not yet decided to give itself shooting practice. The majority of the bandit gangs who plundered and killed, mostly in Perak, Kedah, and Pahang, comprised men of the Malayan Overseas Chinese Self-defence Army (M.O.C.S.D.A.), which had been formed by the Chinese nationalists for the express purpose of fighting the Communists—in a World War III! They were vicious groups, but many men later surrendered and in 1948 formed the nucleus of Chinese jungle squads in Perak which were sent out on the track of the Communist terrorists.

September 1947 was a particularly terrifying month in Johore. One British planter visited by a marauding party escaped with his life. Mr F. B. Pratt was manager of Wessyngton Estate, near

Rengam, in Central Johore, a lonely area. Like hundreds of other estates in the country, Wessyngton can be reached only by a branch road running off the main road.

On the night of September 21 Mr Pratt saw torches flashing outside his bungalow, where he and his wife were entertaining two friends. Labourers were running for the rubber-trees. "I knew bandits had come," said Mr Pratt later. "I tried to phone the police, but the line had been cut. We were isolated. The bandits had surrounded the house, but they never interfered with us." Pratt was unarmed and fortunately decided not to intervene.

Ten Chinese, all dressed in Japanese military uniforms and carrying British rifles, ransacked the homes of the labourers. They left three hours later with several hundred dollars in their pockets. This incident gave the impression that the bandits—and the general public were not then minded to distinguish between M.C.P. and M.O.C.S.D.A.—spared those who did not resist them.

Mr Pratt was luckier than Mr Archibald Nicholson, forty-year-old manager of Gunong Pulai Estate, in south-west Johore, who was motoring home with his wife after a visit to Singapore when he was ambushed at a corner. A rifle-shot punctured a tyre of his car, which overturned. A deep head-wound and a fractured skull killed Mr Nicholson.

His wife, in a daze, saw two armed Chinese emerge from the drain on the roadside. They took a gold ring from her husband's finger, then tried to force a diamond ring off her finger. When she resisted they clubbed her into unconsciousness with their rifle-butts. They were M.C.P. men.

Grim-looking planters from Johore stood at Mr Nicholson's grave the next day. They were worried men, but there was more than a grain of truth in some feelings they expressed, such as "There's no security in Johore now," or "We haven't even got arms to defend ourselves."

Theirs was only a small murmur in the rising crescendo of voices of planters and miners throughout the country, who were to say to the Governor of the Malayan Union, Sir Edward Gent: "Act on your own and stress to the Secretary of State for the Colonies the dangers to life and property in this country." The voices called for all troops to be moved into the gangster-ridden areas, for more troops to be dispatched from England—but long years were to pass before anything like a sufficient number of troops was to be in the field in battle.

It was not surprising, therefore, that by the end of the year 1947 Malaya was living in a state of nerves. The war between the Chinese Nationalist Government and the Chinese Communists had projected itself on Malaya. The Malayan Communist Party could take heart from the success being achieved by Mao Tse-tung's forces, and, despite previous assertions that it should not expect any assistance, it confidently expected that when China was overrun some Communist forces would be diverted to back up anything that might break out in Malaya. Communists in Burma, India, Indo-China, and Indonesia were restive. Moscow felt the time was ripe enough to do something.

In February 1948 Russia sponsored a meeting of Asian and Australian Communists in Calcutta to disclose its plan for South-east Asian countries. Experts in Communist affairs consider that from this conference stemmed the general strikes, agitations, and strifes that broke out afterwards in India and Burma, and that it inspired the Malayan Communist Party to switch to the armed struggle which it had been planning for so many years.

Russia considered the Calcutta conference so important that she sent sixteen delegates as observers. The Australian Communist Party was represented by its president, Lawrence Sharkey.

Upon the return of the Malayan delegate the Central Executive Committee lost no time in calling its Fourth Plenary Conference. This passed the fateful decision to embark on murder, arson, and general terrorism. This armed revolt would have taken place eventually anyway, but at this time it fitted neatly into Russia's policy of revolt which she had enunciated after the Second World War when she called upon all "anti-Imperialist" forces in South-east Asia "to unite to oppose oppression of Imperialism and reactionaries within each country."

It is necessary to digress for a moment to examine how the Party had fared in its own plan to dominate labour in Malaya. Its policy was to secure as many key positions in the trade unions as possible for its own adherents, and to concentrate its strength on the formation of larger unions or associations of unions, which would enable it to organize agitation and strikes involving the largest numbers of workers possible. At the same time it wanted to create the widest gap between the labourers and their union executives to ensure unquestioning obedience.

The Party had formed an all-embracing organization called the Pan-Malayan Federation of Trade Unions, which it completely dominated. Through it, the Party promoted strikes and labour unrest on trivial pretexts. In industry it resorted to violence, intimidation, and extortion to assert its authority. Technically, however, the Party lost this struggle.

By the beginning of 1948 many unions had become dissatisfied with Communist domination. Then the Government introduced legislation which enacted that office-bearers of trade unions must have had a minimum of three years' experience in the industry concerned; prevented men convicted of extortion, intimidation, and other crimes from holding office in unions; and finally prohibited any federation of trade unions, except on an industrial or occupational basis. This directly nullified the Communists' tactics, and when they realized that their labour-infiltration attempts had failed they resorted to their final weapon—violence.

In the first few months of 1948 there was a rising tide of resentment against the apparent disinclination of Sir Edward Gent, then the High Commissioner, to take stern action against the Party and its leaders. The Government had one powerful weapon of banishment, but neither the British Labour Government nor Sir Edward was prepared to use it unless they had irrefutable evidence that the Communist leaders were planning an uprising.

It was simple then to criticize Gent, who, admittedly, was not a very strong High Commissioner. He had achieved a certain popularity in Malaya through his approachability and affability. He was a good mixer. He did not seem, however, to take any decision without referring it first to the Colonial Office.

Gent was therefore faced with the kind of dilemma that occasionally faces a Governor. If he acted too soon without evidence he would have been branded locally and throughout the world as an "imperialist" ogre. If he waited until he had evidence then he was bound to be too late—which was precisely what happened.

The Government's Intelligence services had growing evidence that the Communists' plan for armed revolt was taking shape. There was already evidence that the Calcutta decision was being put into effect in other countries. The Communists in Burma had begun to harry a weak Burmese Government. The Indonesian Reds had started internal disorders. In Malaya the Intelligence experts looked on the rising number of ambushes and hold-ups and murders as 'practice' and 'rehearsals' for the secret army. But Gent would not take action without evidence.

On June 1 the Federal Legislative Council, the paramount legislative body, met in Kuala Lumpur in an atmosphere of tension. The Councillors were ready to use harsh words against Sir Edward. The question was, what form should the censure on Government inaction take?

Lobbying was thick, and when the time came the Indian representative on the Council, Mr V. M. N. Menon, a leading trade unionist, dramatically moved the "immediate adjournment" of the House to discuss "an urgent matter of public importance—the sudden recrudescence of industrial disputes and the causes thereof." Mr Menon spoke of the fact that "no regard was being given to the moral value of life" and chaos reigned on the industrial front. Wages had been increased, but peace and order had not been maintained. Violent crime accompanied industrial strife. Mr Menon wanted a commission of inquiry.

His seconder was a British businessman, Mr Aubrey W. Wallich, who did not mince his words. The unrest, he said, was not the manifestation of discontented and oppressed labour. It was a campaign organized and directed by forces "whose origin is outside Malaya," and by individuals who were not genuine labourers, and who had little, if any, interest in labour, except as medium for subversion and intrigue.

Labourers had been corrupted. Tens of thousands of honest workers had been deprived by threats, not only of work, but of the right to work. Property and goods had been wantonly destroyed. People had been injured. There had been brutal, cold-blooded murder of men whose offence was that they joined associations of employers to negotiate upon approved lines with corresponding associations of employees.

The instigators of trouble, Mr Wallich said, were the "professional sedition-mongers, who demonstrate under a foreign flag, whose speeches and pamphlets are one long incitement to violence and anarchy, whose salutation is the clenched fist." These people, emphasized Mr Wallich, represented " a tyranny as complete, as unscrupulous, as sinister as that of Nazi Germany."

The longest applause went to Dato Onn bin Ja'afar, then the Mentri Besar (Prime Minister) of the State of Johore. He asserted that it was the duty of the Federal Government to suppress the lawlessness. He said:

> As a unit of the Federation, the Government of Johore demands that peace and order be maintained. The time has come when the Federation Government should firmly show by its actions that it will have no truck with Communism in this country, that every power that this Council can give should be given to the police and to others to maintain law, and that Communism is eradicated and those responsible for its ideology in this country banished for ever.

The Commissioner of Police, Mr H. B. Langworthy, then made the first official admission that all the unrest was due to " subversive organizations, which were prepared to go to extreme lengths." What their intention was subsequently he did not know, but " we can rest assured that it will be very serious for this country's future."

Sir Edward Gent shrouded himself in words which only made the country feel that he was not admitting the seriousness of the situation. He described it as " a war of nerves by the forces of disorder," but " if there is evidence that the security of the country is being endangered by British subjects prostituting themselves to serve the ends of crime and violence then a remedy must be found in consultation with His Majesty's Government."

These were not the words to use to a country that was demanding immediate action, and not more " consultation with His Majesty's Government." Sir Edward failed to appreciate the feeling of the country that there should be no need to consult His Majesty's Government, that what was wanted was power to enable the police to round up and deport aliens who had anything to do with intimidation, violence, or assassination. What Malaya wanted was a house-cleaning with more drastic application of the banishment broom.

Outside the Council Chamber the situation was hotting up. A police squad killed seven labourers and wounded ten others during a riot on a Chinese rubber-estate near Segamat, in north Johore, after a magistrate had ordered the 200 labourers, armed with spears, stones, lead-piping, and bottles, to disperse quietly. His order was defied, so the police started shooting.

Then in three widely separated areas of Selangor Chinese gunmen shot and killed two labourers on a tin-mine, murdered a sleeping kepala (headman) on an oil-palm estate, and fought a battle with a police patrol near a remote sawmill. Round the tin-mine posters had been plastered warning labourers to continue their strike or suffer death by shooting. The two shot men had been in a group of labourers who had broken a strike on the mine. All the kepala had done had been to build an archway on his estate in honour of Generalissimo Chiang Kai-shek's birthday.

As the days moved on Gurkha troops were sent into Johore to help the police keep order in the troubled rubber-estates. One night posters were found on estates throughout Johore. These exhorted: " Destroy those who rob labour by underpaying men," " Destroy those who work for other races," " Destroy those who are running dogs of the police." All this seemed to be a signal for a fresh wave of lawlessness in the State.

The murders continued. At 10.30 A.M. on June 7 seven men with stens and tommy-guns surrounded the bungalow of Mr W. J. Wallace, of the Consolidated Eastern Plantations Estate, in Rengam, Central Johore. They asked a servant if the master was in. Strangely enough, it was the first morning for nearly two years that Mr Wallace had not returned from his rounds at that time. A new assistant, who was in the house, was warned by a Javanese maidservant, and he jumped out of a window. He was seen, had three shots fired at him, but escaped.

That same day, but on the other side of the mountain range in Pahang, a Chinese estate manager, a Nationalist, was killed as he walked across the main street of the little village of Triang. Also on the same day, in Perak, two Malay Government officials were murdered while on duty.

All these outrages had taken place within a week of the debate in the Legislative Council, and they seemed to be a deliberate challenge to the Government after the assurances of stern action by the Commissioner of Police and the High Commissioner. Everything seemed to point to a recrudescence of the guerrilla activity that had marked the Japanese occupation; it was being carried on by the same elements. Significantly, in Johore the worst troubles had

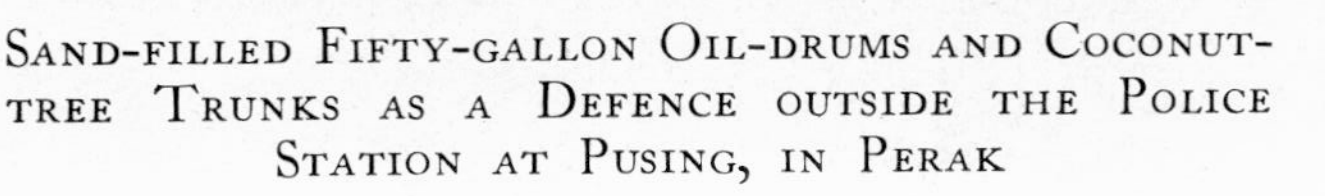

Sand-filled Fifty-gallon Oil-drums and Coconut-tree Trunks as a Defence outside the Police Station at Pusing, in Perak

Photo "Straits Times"

British Paratroopers' Jungle Camp

In the jungle in the Belum (North Perak) area.

Photo by Major D. C. B. Harvey, D.A.D.P.R., Malaya, who dropped with the troops

A Paratrooper of the Special Air Services Regiment crossing a River during an Operation in Belum, North Perak

Photo by Major D. C. B. Harvey, D.A.D.P.R., Malaya

One Type of Communist Camp

A 'basha' for about ten men.

Photo "Straits Times"

been experienced in districts that had been notorious for guerrilla activities during the occupation.

There were renewed demands that the Malayan Governments should ban the Malayan Communist Party. Once more the Federation Government was urged to give the police wider powers to round up all known toughs, thugs, and strong-arm elements; but still there was no action.

Planters said they could not carry on normal routine on their estates. Perak planters sent a telegram to Sir Edward Gent demanding immediate action in their State. "Managers," they said, "are appalled at the present general lawlessness. They are no longer able to maintain orderly routine on their estates. They demand that a state of emergency, martial law, or other appropriate action be instituted immediately. In our opinion the present deplorable conditions are entirely due to the weakness of civil government by its failure to implement police action and court judgments."

Farther north the Kedah Planters' Association called on the Government "to face facts and be positive in its action."

On June 9 the Selangor C.I.D. arrested Liew Yit Fun, who was then acting as manager of the *Min Sheng Pau* (*Voice of the People*), a Chinese-language newspaper owned by the Malayan Communist Party. He was charged with publishing seditious material.

The same morning Selangor police officers began to carry weapons not only while on duty but also off duty. The Chief Police Officer warned the people of surprise checks and of roadblocks. These were, he said, the initial step in a police campaign to rid the State of its "gangsters." He went one step further: he advised planters to buy firearms for their own protection. Unfortunately there were very few on sale in the shops of the country.

In Johore, planters in Rengam formed a 'mutual protection corps.' Many of them had received warnings from gangsters to leave the district.

As more murders were committed, the British Labour Cabinet finally met to discuss the Malayan situation. Questions were asked in the House of Commons. In Malaya Sir Edward Gent called a special meeting of his Executive Council. All Chief Police Officers in the Federation were summoned to Kuala Lumpur to be told the line of action that was to be taken. Was this the promised drastic action? But the Malayan Communist Party was still not banned—the British Labour Government for political reasons still said no.

However, one good thing eventuated out of all these talks in London and Kuala Lumpur. The police were given powers to banish any person connected in any way with intimidation and violence in the course of any industrial dispute.

The Communist gangsters retorted with more murders. They shot a Kuomintang Chinese conductor on an estate and burned a rubber smoke-house on a Malacca estate. Finally on June 16 they perpetrated three murders which forced Sir Edward Gent to declare an "Emergency."

Sungei Siput is a district in North Perak, on the northern fringe of Kinta, the tin-producing cradle of the British Commonwealth. The town of Sungei Siput is like many other little towns in the country. It straddles the trunk road north. Tin-mines stretch round the town, interspersed by rubber-estates. Two of the largest estates are Sungei Siput Estate and Elphil Estate. They lie on either side of one of the loneliest roads in the country, the Lintang Road, which turns north out of Sungei Siput town, runs for twenty miles, then comes to a dead end.

The managers of these two estates had been in the country for years. They were respected men, who treated their labourers well. Arthur Walker, aged fifty, was at Elphil Estate and John A. Allison, aged fifty-five, was at Sungei Siput, with a twenty-one-year-old assistant, I. D. Christian, who had been an officer in the Gurkhas.

At eight o'clock on the morning of June 16 Walker was in his office working before returning to his bungalow for breakfast. Because of the nature of their work, most planters have breakfast at about ten o'clock. Mrs Walker had left the estate half an hour before to go shopping in the Perak royal town of Kuala Kangsar, a few miles south-west. The only bright thing on the dark Malayan horizon for the Walkers was their impending holiday; they were due to go to England in July.

At half-past eight three young Chinese rode up to the office on bicycles, jumped off, parked their machines, and walked into Walker's room. His dog barked at them. Walker tried to pacify it. The estate clerk, A. H. Kumaran, an Indian in the next room, heard a Chinese voice greet Walker with "Tabek, Tuan [Salutation, sir]." He heard Walker return the greeting. Almost immediately afterwards there were two shots.

Kumaran saw the three Chinese mount their bicycles and ride away. It was significant of the times—and of the years that were to follow—that nobody made any attempt to stop the murderers. They disappeared down the road.

Walker was dead, shot through the head and chest. The key to the office safe was on the floor. The safe-door was shut and 2000 dollars inside had not been touched. It was believed that Walker, thinking the men were robbers, had flung the safe key at them. Months later it was confirmed that they had been members of a 'killer squad' of the 8th Regiment of the Malayan Peoples' Anti-British Army in Perak.

Half an hour later and a few miles away, on Sungei Siput estate, twelve Chinese, armed with a variety of weapons, surrounded the office. Christian, the conductor of the estate, K. N. Mudaly, a clerk, Tan Ah Joo, and another conductor, Cheah Lip Chong, were in a room discussing the day's work. Two Chinese entered and in English ordered them to put their hands up.

One asked Christian for his pistol. He replied he had not got one. The man took a piece of string from his coat pocket, walked up to Christian, and tied his hands behind his back.

Allison, the manager, was in the next room. He too was tied up. A Chinese took the keys of two safes from his pocket. The gunmen rifled the safes of 1000 dollars. Allison was then asked for his pistol. He said it was in his bungalow.

Allison, Christian, Tan, and Cheah were marched to the bungalow a hundred yards away. Tan and Cheah were halted outside. The two planters were taken inside. After ten minutes they were brought out and marched back to the office. A Malay-speaking gangster said to Tan and Cheah: "We are out only for Europeans," and added as Allison and Christian were being taken back to their office: "These men will surely die to-day; we will shoot all Europeans."

Allison and Christian were killed seated on chairs. After setting fire to a rubber store the twelve men disappeared. Soon afterwards a police officer arrived at the estate while on his way to Elphil Estate in response to a summons for murder.

Walker and Allison had been prisoners of war during the

Japanese occupation, the former in Singapore, the latter in Sumatra. Allison's wife was at Putney, in London; his son was at Northcliffe House School. Christian had arrived at Sungei Siput estate only a month before. The day he was killed he was to have gone to another estate near Ipoh to become manager.

I have dealt fully with the murders of these three men, because it was their deaths which roused the long-suffering planting industry to savage wrath and forced the Government to recognize that the country was at the mercy of extremists who were prepared to kill for control.

Horror and anger surged through Malaya after the murders. A delegation of planters in Kuala Lumpur demanded an interview with Sir Edward Gent. They spent an angry hour with him and spoke their minds. Their leader said afterwards, " We demanded immediate and ruthless action."

That same day there were two more murders—one on Senai Estate, near Johore Bahru in the south, where a Chinese head labourer was killed by fifteen bullets fired by ten men who were waiting for him, and the other on a Taiping estate, not far from Sungei Siput, where a Chinese contractor was killed.

That afternoon Sir Edward declared an Emergency to exist only in the Ipoh and Sungei Siput police districts of Perak, and in certain districts in Johore. The regulations he introduced were simple compared to the extensive powers that came much later. The police had special powers to arrest, detain, exclude people from particular areas; to impose curfews; to search people and their houses; to close roads, paths, and waterways; to requisition buildings, vehicles, and boats; and to seize seditious documents and any article which they thought could be used as an offensive weapon. Death was the penalty for the unauthorized possession of firearms, ammunition, or explosives.

Any person arrested under the Emergency Regulations could be detained for one year without a charge being brought, but he had every right to place his objections before a reviewing committee. No warrants were necessary for the police to enter and search premises, or to stop and search vehicles or individuals. These were measures which were completely foreign to ideas of British justice, but Malaya recognized the need for them.

They were, however, not enough for the country. It wanted

the police to be substantially strengthened, to be fully equipped with modern war weapons, to be mobile, to have wireless equipment. It wanted more troops. It wanted men with guts to handle the situation. It wanted the Secretary of State for the Colonies to remove obstacles which prevented the Federation Government banishing British-born subjects where it was necessary for public security. The threat that was developing in the Federation was as dangerous as the conquest of the country by the Japanese.

One newspaper, the *Straits Times,* in an editorial headed " Govern or Get Out " (" Our heading . . . is not aimed personally at the High Commissioner of the Federation ") said:

> We have no reason to believe that, whatever may have been the case last year, Sir Edward Gent has not done all in his power to act on the advice of his police and law officers in coping with the rapidly worsening situation of the last two months. Our heading to-day refers to the challenge that exists to the whole régime in this country —the régime which stands for peaceful industry and trade, law and order for all classes and communities, and ordered political progress along democratic lines. Is it to be constitutional and civilized government? Or is it to be a government by the gun and the knife? That is the choice which faces Malaya to-day.

In Kuala Lumpur the police made a rather belated raid on the two Communist-controlled newspaper offices, the *Min Sheng Pau* (whose manager they had already arrested), and the *Vanguard*, a weekly paper. They rounded up forty-six Communists who worked on them. They found, however, that most of the presses and machinery at the *Min Sheng Pau* had been dismantled.

By the night of June 16 managers of all estates in the Emergency areas of Perak and Johore had police or Gurkha escorts. Police squads had moved into strategic points.

Twenty-four hours later Sir Edward Gent extended the Emergency Regulations over the whole country. All leave for police officers was cancelled; those on holiday in England were recalled. The Army accepted the request to assist the civil power. They also agreed to issue a considerable number of sten-guns and ammunition to the police. Planters who knew how to handle stens were given them without any formality of permits or licences.

Singapore was watching events in the Federation closely. It

might become a bolt-hole for Communists, so it also gave itself emergency powers to cope with the situation.

In the succeeding days there was an air of bewilderment in the Federation. Outside the rubber-estates and certain Government offices and the police force, few civilians clearly understood what was happening or appreciated what faced them. It was difficult to understand why a white man, or a Chinese associated with the Kuomintang Party, or an ardent follower of trade unionism stood in danger of losing his life. People stared unbelievingly at planters who strode into the peaceful hotels in Kuala Lumpur with revolvers tucked in their waists or rifles firmly grasped in their hands. The traffic constable wore a revolver—a strange sight. Conversations were full of "The Emergency." There was some talk of an "enemy," mysterious men who had assisted the British guerrillas during the Japanese occupation, but who had now turned against their former comrades in arms.

Inevitably, life became confused, strained, and tense, and if you were living alone, even in the heart of the town, as I was in Kuala Lumpur, you half expected to be shot as you stepped out of your front door.

The planters were bitter men, so bitter that some of them in the worst districts of Perak ran a sweepstake on death. The winner was the one who guessed when, where, and against whom the terrorists would strike next. None of the dates picked went beyond forty-eight hours, and all those named as probable victims lived in those districts.

It was learned later that the Communist Party had a priority list of people to be murdered. High up on it were estate and mine managers and certain police officers. Next came district officers. Lower still, certain Government officers working in Kuala Lumpur.

6

Pattern for Murder

IN those first weeks of June 1948 the British Labour Government was forced to concede in the House of Commons that Malaya was faced with an armed revolt which aimed at terminating British rule in Malaya and substituting a soviet government.

In Malaya a rough guess was made that the Communists had between three thousand and four thousand armed fighters. This figure was later changed to five thousand men, where it stayed for nearly three years before it was officially admitted that there were "plenty of recruits." The Federation Government has never been willing to acknowledge that the force might have been augmented by dribbles of trained men infiltrated from China via either Thailand or the China Sea.

Set up against them were 10,223 police officers and men, and an Army garrison of two British Infantry battalions (the Seaforth Highlanders and the 1st King's Own Yorkshire Light Infantry), six Gurkha Rifle battalions, three battalions of the Malay Regiment, the 26th Field Regiment, R.A., and, in Singapore, a Malay coast artillery unit. All these battalions, however, were suffering from post-war demobilization of their most experienced personnel, so they were all below strength.

As the weeks passed the pattern of the Communist strategy became clearer. The terrorists were concentrating their attacks largely on estates and mines. It became imperative that these industries should be defended. With the regular police under strength, with the Army, called out in aid of the civil power, too small for a country-wide defence, and hamstrung by having to fight a war with gloved fists, it became necessary for the estates and mines to have their own static defence corps.

A Special Constabulary was formed, and plans were also made to strengthen the Regular force. Within three months 24,000 Malays had been enrolled into the Special Constabulary; within six months the figure was nearly 30,000. The great bulk of the men were untrained in the art of defence with weapons. They were raw countrymen from the kampongs and ne'er-do-wells from the towns. Too few of them were attracted to the Constabulary by a sense of loyalty. It was a means to an end, an easy way of earning a regular income. It was also a job which at that time did not promise much work.

An undisciplined rabble, however, met the requirements of the moment. Drafted to estates, mines, and other vulnerable points, they were given a beret, a uniform, and rubber shoes, and told they were to maintain guard. Because there were no instructors to spare, the Government placed the burden of teaching this motley army discipline, basic drill, and shooting on the planters and miners. They had to convert the special constables into a defence force if they wished to live.

Every morning after the early-morning muster of their labourers these gallant men, most of whom had been Japanese prisoners of war or internees, paraded their squads, sometimes patiently, sometimes irascibly, put them through elementary drill, showed them how to handle a rifle, how to take up defensive positions, and to obey orders. Apart from this the planters and miners could do nothing—not even give their men target practice, because there was not enough ammunition in the country. The most that could be set aside for this purpose was five bullets per man per month, and a monthly account had to be rendered for every bullet fired by the Specials. This was not a war, it was administrative red tape in action. It showed clearly how the authorities viewed the Communist campaign.

The planters and miners began throwing their hands up in desperation. Producing rubber and tin to keep exports up, defending their companies' properties, building defences with barbed wire (a material which remained scarce for at least two and a half years), keeping their ill-disciplined constables on the alert, all created a strain on them under which they almost cracked. They lived dangerous, hard-pressed lives. Their nerves were shot, and nobody would have blamed them had they quit, but they stubbornly hung on, refusing to allow " bastard Communists " to drive them away.

Two years later the Government admitted, " If it had not been for the indomitable determination of planters and miners to stand fast during the early months of the Emergency, and the loyal support they received from their staff and labourers, large areas of the country might have fallen under Communist control and so made possible the establishment of small Communist Republics—one of the terrorists' declared aims."

Fortunately, before they could break physically the strain was taken off the planters and miners by the arrival of several hundred British sergeants who were being demobilized from the Palestine Police Force. Many splendid young men were among them, but there were also some rough types and adventurers, who arrived in the country with fixed and rash ideas of how to treat the ' natives,' notions fostered in Palestine, where a heavy hand had been used on Jew and Arab without discrimination, and the butt-end of a rifle had more effect than an appeasing tongue.

To many of these sergeants every Chinese was a bandit or a potential bandit, and there was only one treatment for them, they were to be " bashed around." If they would not talk a sock on the jaw or a kick in the guts might have the desired result. I myself once saw a British sergeant encouraging a heavy-booted policeman to treat a suspect like a football. The young Chinese was kicked all round the room until a threat to report this treatment to headquarters brought the game to a stop.

On the other hand, the sergeants did the job expected of them—they trained those special constables; and in many instances were so enthusiastic about getting a crack at the enemy that they took their squads out on offensive patrols in search of bandits in their district. Many were to be killed, and many were to be decorated for gallantry. Three were to be awarded the George Medal. One of these three was killed within three months of his award. He never saw his medal.

Gradually in the estates and mines there grew up a static defence force operating behind barbed-wire fences which surrounded the factory and the dredge, and the managers' and assistants' houses. Strong arc-lights shone outward at night into the darkness, and booby-traps were rigged up to give warning of the approach of strangers.

The Communists had in the meantime shown their capabilities. On June 28, twelve days after the declaration of the Emergency, forty-two men descended on the isolated village of Kuala Krau, in Central Pahang, cut its telephone wires, surrounded the wooden police station, and poured a steady stream of bullets into it. A policeman's wife was killed.

The three constables in the station gallantly stood their ground and fired back. For some strange reason, probably the cowardice that showed in all their ' battles ' with men who fought back, the bandits never rushed the station. After half an hour they withdrew, leaving thick blood-trails, which indicated that several of them had been seriously wounded. The people of the village had stayed behind closed doors and shutters from the first sounds of shooting.

The next day men of the same gang captured the township of Jerantut, about 20 miles north of Kuala Krau. After burning down the police station and shooting people they moved back into the jungle-clad hills with a number of Chinese and Malay prisoners who were later released by them.

Farther south, in Johore, ten armed men attacked the police station at Sedenak, but were driven off after a stiff fight in which one of them was shot dead.

The country was perturbed at the devilry that the Communists were able to accomplish with ease. It was appalled at the thought of the greater destruction to life and property they could and might effect. Like diabolical swordsmen, the Communists appeared anywhere suddenly, thrust with deadly effect, and disappeared again with no fear of being found. They had the whole vast jungle to pop in and out of; they could move freely; they could plan their coup with deadly effect. The great advantage of surprise, which all armies in the field devoutly desire, was theirs and theirs alone.

The brutality of the Communists was intensified by the class doctrines and political hatreds which they introduced. These were entirely new features of the Malayan scene. The Communists completely dominated the ordinary labouring classes in every district in which they operated. For instance, in the large village of Layang Layang in Johore many people watched a Malay corporal battling single-handed with three Chinese gunmen, but not one man attempted to help him, or to volunteer afterwards to name the gunmen. There was a savagery and ferocity in the Malayan air which had never been known in the country before. It was a challenge to the régime.

On June 29, when Jerantut was burning, Sir Edward Gent left Malaya by air for London for what was officially described as "consultations in connexion with the state of Emergency in Malaya." Four days later he was killed in a collision between his aircraft and another over London. Whitehall did a disservice to Sir Edward when they failed to deny a report that the British Government had decided to relieve him of his post; the reasons for his recall were allowed to die with him.

Malaya mourned Gent for his untimely death and for the friendliness and open-heartedness that had made him the most approachable High Commissioner for years. The job, though, had become too big for him, and the wall of Whitehall too tough for him to break down.

Malaya wondered whether it would get a strong man as its next High Commissioner. It needed a forceful man. The British Government knew it had a fateful choice to make, and it took time over it. Not until September did it announce that Sir Henry Lovell Goldsworthy Gurney, aged fifty, former Chief Secretary to the Palestine Government, would succeed Sir Edward.

Sir Henry proved himself a good choice, but he was fated not to leave the Federation with the Emergency at an end and with due honours heaped on him for meritorious work for the country. Two years to the day after he was installed as High Commissioner he was assassinated by the Communists as he motored up to a hill-resort for a few days' holiday. In the meantime nothing could have been more admirable than the steady and clear-sighted manner in which the Federal Government, under Sir Henry's leadership, had pushed on with constructive programmes in the social, economic, and political fields, while not slackening in determined and ever-expanding measures to deal with the Communists. He saw, and declared, that Communism had to be fought with the weapons of social and political progress as well as with guns and men.

In the midst of tragedy and bloody strife Malaya suddenly perked up and laughed at the audacious exploit of my old policeman friend, William F. Stafford, then in the C.I.D., Selangor, who had posed as a Russian officer to unearth a Communist arms-dump.

This is Stafford's own story:

We knew there was a dump in the Kuala Selangor (North-west Selangor) area on the coast of Selangor, and we knew that if we arrested the man guarding it he would not tell us where it was. It was well known that only certain Communists knew the site of every arms-dump in each State. The Communists had been wise enough, when laying the caches during the Japanese occupation, not to spread around what they were doing.

My Chinese detectives and I planned a stunt which could have meant injury, if not death, to some of us. I dressed myself up in a Russian-like cap, khaki shirt and shorts, and jackboots. My detectives went on ahead to a hut in an isolated part of Kuala Selangor. A youthful Chinese Communist was inside. They said to him, "We have been sent from Communist headquarters to check your weapons." He was a clever little guy; he asked my detectives for their credentials. We had foreseen this, however, and they pulled out a couple of pieces of paper stamped with the hammer and sickle sign from a seal we had picked up in an earlier raid.

The bluff succeeded. My detectives told the young man that they had brought a Russian officer who had parachuted into Malaya. He became excited, and asked to meet me. On a signal, I duly appeared, and [here Bill splutters and laughs] over a cup of coffee in his hut, we spoke of Communism and the terrorist campaign. One of my detectives acted as interpreter. He was an eager and enthusiastic Communist, that young man. He asked if we were not frightened of the police. We showed our contempt for the 'running dogs' by spitting on the floor, and pointing to our weapons. He was delighted with such 'comrades.' Yes, he said, he would show us the weapons. He dug them out—and then we went into action. Before his horrified eyes this Russian officer comrade pointed a pistol at him, and a detective said to him, "We are police officers."

Two days later the General Officer Commanding, Malaya District, plucky little Major-General (later Sir) Charles Boucher, who had once fought Greek guerrillas, stood before the Federal Legislative Council, and said brightly of his campaign plans: "I can tell you this is by far the easiest problem I have ever tackled. In spite of the appalling country and ease with which he can hide, the enemy is far weaker in technique and courage than either the Greek or Indian Reds."

General Boucher sincerely believed that, and he worked himself sick planning the fight. He returned to England a few months later, a very sick man. He died not long afterwards. I am certain General Boucher did not for a moment believe that the fight against the Communists would last six years and more, that it would break the reputations of strong and tried men, and that eventually Britain would have to call on the Commonwealth nations and the United States for military and technical assistance.

The principles on which General Boucher worked were offensive action, mobility, flexibility, surprise, and co-operation, but there were still insufficient troops in the country to ensure even the minimum success in each of these fields, and the people of the country were showing that they would not co-operate unless they first received protection.

On July 12 Selangor Communists carried out an operation which showed what they were capable of. They attacked the country's only coal-mine at Batu Arang, twenty-six miles north-west of Kuala Lumpur, and occupied it for nearly an hour. They killed five men, assaulted the police station, confined more than fifty people in the mine's railway station for more than half an hour, and sabotaged three giant dragline excavators and eight trailers.

Batu Arang was a township of about 12,000 people, eight miles from Rawang, the nearest town with a large police force. Batu Arang had a small police station. By a system that had been instituted throughout the country, main police stations had to telephone isolated estates, mines, and police posts every hour. A line that was dead demanded investigation, for it might mean that bandits were in action. In the morning, the line from Rawang to Batu Arang went dead. The Rawang police sent a posse along the winding eight-mile road towards the coal-mine. Had not this precautionary move been taken Batu Arang would have been in the hands of the Communists for more than an hour.

A very senior police officer admitted to me later: "We had definitely underestimated the forces the Communists could bring to bear. Certainly we never expected such a really well-planned attack. It drove home to us that the Communists could make concerted and disastrous attacks on industry everywhere in the country." So the Government looked around to see what other vulnerable 'Batu Arangs' it had, and sent reinforcements to them post-haste. There was not, in fact, a second 'Batu Arang' in the years that followed, but there was the 'liberation' of a tiny area of country called Gua Musang, in the deep isolated jungles of South Kelantan.

On July 16 the Communists suffered a serious blow when their most important war-leader was killed by police in the grimmest short-range battle that had occurred up to that time. The man killed was Lau Yew, a thirty-year-old member of the Central Military Committee of the M.C.P. He was the commander of the fighting forces. He also led the contingent of Malayan guerrillas in the Victory Parade past the King and Queen in London.

It was Bill Stafford and his special assault squad of fourteen Chinese and Malay detectives who killed Lau Yew. They had not the slightest inkling as they drove out first to Kajang, a Communist-infested town, and then a mile beyond it across country, that anybody of the calibre of Lau Yew would be within shooting range. Their destination was a hut in which, informants told them, they would find two quite innocuous Communists, but still Communists who should either be dead or in prison.

They first climbed a 400-foot hill, then slid down into a little saucer-like valley. There stood the hut. Dawn had just broken, and they were seen by women outside the hut as they moved in. Three men rushed out, firing as they ran. They made for the hill. The police opened fire. A detective took a bead on one man as he was backing up the hill and shot him dead. It was Lau Yew. He had a hole as big as a fist in the middle of his forehead. A second Chinese was killed. The third man was captured.

The police closed in, searched the hut, and found a table strewn with opened maps of Kajang and of Klang, a town twenty-three miles south-west of Kuala Lumpur, and of the State of Selangor. There were also four rifles, three shot-guns, three pistols, and 2000 rounds of ammunition in a jute sack. Six women inside the hut were rounded up. One was Lau Yew s wife. She identified his dead body. Following the usual practice, the hut was set on fire to prevent the Communists using it again.

The police were packing up when the counter-attack came. The hut was burning beautifully by that time, but they were not interested in the sight. The Communists seemed to be firing from fifty yards' range, shooting down the hill. Stafford realized he was outnumbered. Earlier he had sent six men back to the road to bring a truck in for the women, the bodies, and the booty. That left him and thirteen detectives to fight between thirty and fifty men using bren-guns and stens.

Stafford withdrew his men up an opposite hill and continued the battle. Then he ordered a charge, and the terrorists scuttled away over their own hill. There was silence again. In the thick gunfire smoke drifting across the little valley, Stafford and his men quickly began to collect the exhibits again. They found that five of the women were dead, killed in the cross-fire.

Lau Yew's widow had disappeared. She must have slunk away during the battle. Suddenly shooting broke out again. The Communists were back. Bill rallied his detectives up the hill, and then down again. They charged shouting in Malay and Chinese: "The Gurkhas are here, the police are here." They shot two more bandits. The rest retreated over their hill again, and there was quiet again.

By this time the police had become dangerously short of ammunition and they lived anxious moments waiting for the third counter-attack, but there was only the sound of an approaching police truck. It took them out quickly after they had counted the bandit casualties, six men and five women killed. The one police casualty was a detective cut by barbed wire.

They returned with reinforcements in order to take the battle to the bandits this time. There was no sign of them. A search revealed that the bandits had taken away nine bodies, including those of the women. They always tried to prevent identification by the police on these occasions.

Some weeks after the battle the police confirmed the startling facts that Lau Yew had been presiding at a meeting of some of the most important men of the Central Executive Committee of the Party. They were planning to concentrate a very large force of Communist troops in order to capture Kajang town, occupy it, and make it the headquarters for the anti-British campaign. Reinforcements were to come from Negri Sembilan and Pahang. Every important member at this meeting had brought his bodyguard, groups of tough fighters numbering between five and ten for each of them. On the scene, too, were troops to protect the bodyguards and the Committee members. Stafford and his squad had walked straight into a hornet's nest.

It took months for the Communist Party to recover from the death of Lau Yew. They had to give up their optimistic plan of capturing Kajang. Had Lau Yew's meeting not been so fortuitously interrupted, the Communists would undoubtedly have attacked the town and would probably have occupied it. Just for how long they would have been able to stay there is a difficult question to answer, but the moral effect of such an exploit on the peoples of Malaya and beyond would have been disastrous. The killing of Lau Yew can still be considered the most important police coup of the campaign.

The police force was slowly being strengthened. Malaya drew on men of the former Palestine Police Force for many of the officers required. Foremost among these was Colonel William Nicol Gray, C.M.G., D.S.O, who had been Inspector-General in Palestine. He arrived as the new Commissioner of Police. Gray proved to be a strong man, possibly too strong. Unfortunately, the importation of a large number of ex-Palestine officers into the expanding Federation Police Force at this time, with consequent effect on the seniority of existing officers, caused some internal friction.

This raised a hatred against Gray, and the morale of tried and tested men dropped as they felt that they had no future under him. The discontent that arose among British, Malay, and Chinese officers and the rank and file grew to such an extent that eventually a Police Commission was sent out from England. Its report took a middle course, but it made recommendations which attempted to ensure that treatment would be equal between Malayans and ex-Palestinians.

The police force settled to an acceptance of the situation, but Gray, courageous, far-sighted, went on, absorbed in his determined task of producing a force which, he hoped, would eventually get the credit for breaking the Communists. It was not to be. Gray had roused such an antagonism against himself among the powerful planters and miners that when the Secretary of State for the Colonies, Mr Oliver Lyttelton, came to Malaya late in 1951 to see the situation for himself he received many requests for reorganization in the police force, part of which in effect meant "Gray must go."

Gray eventually resigned, but by that time even the Malayan officers who had cause to dislike him had come to recognize his value as the strong Commissioner which a serious internal situation demanded.

In the early days of his new job, in 1948, Gray sought and got weapons and equipment for the police. He called for an expert from the Home Office in Britain to plan and create a police radio network throughout the country to link State headquarters with districts, towns, villages, and remote kampongs. The Army lent Gray radio sets until special ones built to specifications arrived, and the Navy and R.A.F. supplied the first operators and initiated Malay policemen into the mysteries of radio reception and transmission.

Meanwhile the British Labour Government seemed slow to accept the fact that more troops were necessary in Malaya. The twelve battalions could not be spread effectively over the whole peninsula. In August a battalion of the Royal Inniskilling Fusiliers arrived from Hong Kong, and then the War Office announced that no less than a Guards brigade was to sail to Malaya. This created military history, for not even during World War II had any Guards battalions been sent out of Europe to fight. Britain was fastening on Malaya's armour.

The tall men of the 2nd Guards Brigade arrived in October. They were the Scots Guards, the Grenadier Guards, and the Coldstream Guards. They made a great reputation. They took to the jungles as easily as marching down The Mall. An American correspondent put it rather picturesquely in a dispatch saying, "Well, Britain's pride of the palaces are just one more bunch of boys in the basha-huts of Malaya."

Jungle, rain, and heat was their daily fare instead of the London fog, sleet, or summer sunshine. Instead of bearskins they wore floppy jungle-green hats. There was no spit and polish for them for eighteen months, but they never forgot their famous parade-ground drill. The Guards took their job of fighting the bandits more seriously than did some other British battalions. . . .

It was in the air on a flight somewhere between Kuala Lumpur and Kota Bahru that a group of enthusiastic ex-Force 136 officers planned a volunteer force to play the same guerrilla game as the bandits. It was called Ferret Force, and its job was precisely what its name implied. Volunteers were put through specially rigorous training. They entered the jungle and stayed in it for weeks with the dual purpose of spreading the gospel of the Government among the frightened jungle-dwellers, and trailing and killing groups of bandits. Ferret Force, however, was to have a short life. Jealousies between the police and the Army about its administration and its composition were reported to be behind its death; but whatever the real reasons, the disbandment of Ferret Force after a few months was regretted by experienced guerrilla fighters. Strange to say, the need for a fighting arm of this nature was realized again later, and no less a man than Colonel " Mike " Calvert, of Burma fame, was called in to form a Special Air Services Battalion for deep penetration tactics.

Troops, whatever their numbers, cannot fight unless they know where to find the enemy. The jungle was the bandits' home. It became essential for British battalions and for Ferret Force to have trackers, men who could read tales from a turned leaf, a bent twig, or a brushed-aside blade of grass. The Borneo Government agreed to send Dyaks to Malaya, and scions of the old head-hunting tribes arrived in their numbers, seeing the world beyond their placid rivers for the first time, flying from Borneo in giant ' birds ' which made a lot of noise but which dropped them gently on land hundreds of miles from their homes. The Dyaks, and later the Ibans, also from Sarawak, were invaluable. They established great friendship with the British troops with whom they worked. They were brave, too. One of them, Awang, won the George Cross in a jungle battle.

That was the picture on the ground. In the air the Royal Air Force played a big part, too, in those early days. An advanced Air Headquarters was established at Kuala Lumpur. From here Dakotas and Spitfires went out on reconnaissance. Their cameras took photographs which showed tiny clusters of huts in thick jungle. These bandit camps, built in deep jungle which would have cost many lives to storm, were blasted from the air. The Communists grew to hate and fear these raiding aircraft, and they drew up their own ' air-raid precautions.' They ordered their men to scatter immediately the drone of a plane was heard and to lie low until the danger had passed. The bandits very soon learned, too, that if they were on the edge of jungle and rubber their best ' fox-hole ' was rubber land, for the R.A.F. had strict orders not to drop bombs on rubber-estates. Quite apart from injuring the industry, the R.A.F. could be asked to pay heavy compensation for damaging valuable trees. So it was from the safe glades of rubber that the bandits cocked snooks at the R.A.F.

The Air Force had other equally valuable jobs to do. They flew reinforcements of troops and police and arms, ammunition, and stores from point to point. They brought supply dropping in jungles to a fine art, which enabled police and troops to keep on the trail of bandits for days without having to return to base for supplies.

The Navy had their rôle. They took over operational control of all in-shore as well as off-shore patrols. They were there to intercept possible Communist reinforcements by sea, or the smuggling of arms and ammunition into the country. The Government and the Navy have always maintained that these patrols deterred the Communists from sending reinforcements by sea, but the Malayan coastline is a long and ragged one, and not every inch of it can be closely guarded. It was inevitable that penny-packet groups of Communists should succeed in landing from junks that sailed down with the north-east monsoon. In fact, this occurred infrequently.

More Emergency Regulations were devised to give the Government further powers over life, liberty, and freedom. The police could now detain suspects for periods up to two years without trial, could control movement of traffic and food along roads, impose curfews, and search houses without warrants. There were heavy penalties for the crime of assisting bandits, and it became compulsory for judges to impose the death sentence on people convicted of carrying arms and ammunition.

The British Government did not have such sweeping powers in Britain during World War II, but the people of Malaya accepted them in the belief that they would go far towards ending the Emergency quickly. They were let down, not by the Regulations, but rather by the complacency of the men who had fashioned them and wielded them, and by their own failure to co-operate.

As time went on it became necessary to improvise a system of separating the bandits from the law-abiding population, of distinguishing one man from the other. The Government accomplished a master-stroke with compulsory National Registration. Every man, woman, and child over twelve years of age had to possess an identity card bearing his photograph and his thumb-print. The Communists rightly regarded this as an extremely dangerous move against them. Essentially they should be men with secret faces and names. They were quick in the field with anti-registration propaganda. Their attack on it was related to basic themes—asserting that the object of Registration was to conscript men for the Army, to levy oppressive taxes, to facilitate forced labour, and to requisition food supplies.

Registration was labelled as " tyrannous enforcement of Fascist methods, devised to consolidate oppression of the people." Crude slogans written in Chinese, Jawi, or Tamil on strips of paper were hung on rubber-trees and on village doors. They threatened death to ' running-dogs ' who registered, and to photographers. Leaflets called on readers to " Use your identity cards as joss-paper " because they were " trouble-causing things."

The Communists launched a brutal campaign of intimidation and murder during the months of National Registration. They killed photographers and they shot people who carried identity cards. They attacked Government registration teams visiting remote kampongs.

When they found that all these vicious steps were not bringing registration to a halt they turned their attention to destroying identity cards. They raided villages, collected every card, and either burned them or tore them up. They halted buses, lined up the passengers, took their identity cards, and burned them in the vehicles, which had been set on fire. They also retained cards for themselves, and substituted their own photographs, but these forgeries were apparent in any security check. The police carried out continuous security checks on villages and groups in bad areas. Sometimes these checks demanded the use of both troops and police. They found men or women without identity cards. Such people were suspect on the grounds that citizens who had nothing to fear would possess a card, so they were taken away for interrogation. Many of them were detained for months merely on suspicion of being sympathizers. It was harsh treatment and inevitably there were innocent people who suffered, but they were few in number.

The successful completion of National Registration in the country was a heavy defeat for the Communists.

7

The Party Structure

WHAT is the structure of the Malayan Communist Party, its fighting arm (the Malayan Races Liberation Army), and its supply unit (the Min Yuen)?

In supreme authority is the Central Executive Committee, which is believed to number between ten and thirteen men, most of whom are chairmen of State Committees. In the first two years of the campaign Central was able to meet every six months, but since then the trials and tribulations of life in the jungle, the difficulties of communications, and pressure by the security forces have reduced them to much more infrequent meetings. Captured documents indicate that Central gets together so rarely that when it does it issues campaign directives to cover the next six or more months.

The brains of Central are three men who form the Politburo, the all-highest. They are Chen Ping, the Secretary-General, a tried Communist fighter named Yeung Kwo, and a remarkably efficient propagandist named Lau Lee. They have on their heads the highest rewards offered by any Government in the history of crime. Chen Ping's is 250,000 dollars (nearly £30,000), and there is 120,000 dollars (about £15,000) for each of the other two.[1]

Spencer Chapman in his book described Chen Ping as "Britain's most trusted guerrilla," during the Japanese occupation. He can as well be described to-day as the Malayan Communist Party's most trusted Communist.

The next important man in the Party and the one most likely to succeed Chen Ping as Secretary-General should anything happen to him is Yeung Kwo, a sickly looking individual. Born in 1917,

[1] These rewards were withdrawn in 1953.

he too comes from the northern part of Malaya, which incidentally, has bred several of the Party's leading men. He joined the party when he was fifteen.

In 1946 Yeung Kwo was appointed a member of the Central Executive Committee. He hated Loi Tak, and was one of the very few who suspected the Secretary-General of treachery. It was Yeung Kwo's allegations which eventually led to Loi Tak's flight.

Lau Lee, the third member of the Politburo, was born in China in 1916 and was brought to Malaya by his parents when he was young. He joined the Party in 1935. He adopted the profession of school-teacher and taught in a Chinese school in Johore.

During the Japanese occupation he was a member of the Perak State Committee with Chen Ping, but, with his background as a schoolmaster and his knowledge of writing, he was placed in charge of propaganda. Like Chen Ping and Yeung Kwo, he was appointed a member of the Central Executive Committee in January 1946. He was given the special job of supervising and directing Central propaganda and of running the Party Education Committee. They are jobs he still retains in the jungle-bound Central. He is the brain that produces the booklets, pamphlets, and cyclostyled sheets which the Federation Government's own propaganda experts admit are effective. His is the brain which works out propaganda lines to further the basic objectives of the Party, which makes ideological appeals, drums out anti-British themes, and beckons to Indians and Malays and students to join the Party revolt.

Here is a telling extract from an early Federation Government report dealing with the Party's propaganda machine and system:

> The bandit propagandists, working under very considerable difficulties, have shown intelligence and skill in attempting to give the local people a firm basis in Communist theory of the Marx-Lenin School. Well-informed, they have made intelligent use of the world situation and of the situation in adjacent countries of South-east Asia for local propaganda purposes. They have been quick to seize on local occurrences which could be made to appear to support their virulent anti-British campaign of racial hatred.

Lau Lee's propaganda teams in every State of the country are either ex-teachers, ex-students, or ex-newspapermen.

From the Central Executive Committee there is a chain of command downward to the smallest bandit gang, but co-ordination throughout the country is an impossibility. One reason against this, and probably a more important factor than the lack of communications, is the subordination of the military element to the political.

Even a Central Military Committee which 'controls' the M.R.L.A. is subservient to the Central Executive Committee, and the Party's control downward is maintained by strict discipline, by the operation of political cells in 'Regiments,' companies, platoons, and sections, and by spying on members. Political discipline in the fighting ranks is maintained by a political instructor. He is found in every group of the M.R.L.A., right down to even a six-man section. In most instances these 'commissars' rank equal to, or higher than, the military commanders of their groups.

Branching from Central are three regional bureaux consisting of groups of States in North, Central, and South Federation. Then, descending in pyramidal order, come the State Committees, District Committees, Branch Committees, and finally the cells. This Party organization consists strictly of Party members, who function in the Malayan Races Liberation Army at all levels. A State Committee member can be a regimental commander, or that most important man, a regimental political officer, the virtual ruler of the group. He has the power to cancel a military operation if he considers it in the Party interests to do so. Many wives of Party men also hold important positions at all levels.

From district committee level downward, the members of the Party structure are divided between the M.R.L.A. and the Min Yuen. It is necessary to know a little of the Min Yuen's history and organization to appreciate what importance the Federation Government places on its extermination as quickly as possible.

The name Min Yuen literally translated means "Masses' Movement," the popular name for it in Red China, but one that is wishful thinking in Malaya. When the Malayan Peoples' Anti-Japanese Army worked side by side with Britain's Force 136 against the common enemy of Japan, it was fed, clothed, and given information by a motley crowd of men, women, and children who formed the Malayan Peoples' Anti-Japanese Union.

The Japanese, like the British now, never knew who were

members of the M.P.A.J.U. That Union has become the Min Yuen of to-day.

The Min Yuen is the strongest arm of the Malayan Races' Liberation Army. This organization is far more potent than any Western Fifth Column has proved. The Min Yuen is a vast concourse of spies and suppliers of money, food, and other desirable guerrilla requirements. It is the Supply Corps for the fighters in the jungle, a corps that is not distinguishable or identifiable by shoulder flashes or painted insignia on its transport. A member of the Min Yuen may be the rich man, the man-in-the-street, the villager, the squatter, the trishaw-peddler, the lorry-driver, the barber—anybody. Thousands of people form the Min Yuen. Nobody, not even Central, knows its exact strength. A conservative, very conservative, estimate is 500,000. Not every man, woman, and child in this organization is in it voluntarily. A surrendered bandit, who had been an important member of the Min Yuen, said to me quietly one day, " The people hate the Min Yuen. They work for it out of fear, not willingly out of sympathy for the cause."

The Min Yuen has become the priority target of the Security Forces, for it has been obvious that without this organization the Communist Army cannot continue to exist in the jungle. The security forces rate their kills of Min Yuen and ' district ' and ' branch ' committee members far higher than those of the fighters in the jungle. Commanders say, " Crack the Min Yuen and the bandits must come out to fight for food—and life."

Working as it does either in or close to towns and villages, the Min Yuen is a more accessible target than the Liberation Army; but it has withstood cracking for six years now. The reason is simple. Its existence depends on secrecy, and the public in the towns and villages have not yet worked up sufficient faith in the Government's fight to come forward to give away the names of those whom they know are working for the Communists.

In the last two years the Min Yuen has undergone an important change in character. At the beginning of the Emergency, the armed members of the Party were all in the Malayan Races Liberation Army. The Min Yuen, as the secret service and supply organization, had no armed protection at all.

As the Federation police slowly and laboriously built up its information about the Party and its Min Yuen, and as the security forces gained successes against the latter organization, the M.R.L.A. detailed some of its platoons to be ' on call ' for any local district committee whose Min Yuen was getting into trouble. This apparently did not work out satisfactorily because there never seemed to be a platoon available at the right time.

In most States, then, the M.R.L.A. was forced to detail a certain number of platoons to District Committees, who drafted them out as armed protection units of the Min Yuen. These armed groups come under the direct control of the local Committee instead of under the Army.

Two categories of men form the armed units of the Min Yuen. The first grade are on permanent duty. They usually include members of the Party District Committees. They are practically indistinguishable from the fighting men of the M.R.L.A., for they wear essentially the same uniform and five-starred caps. The second grade are the part-timers, the men who tap rubber or grow vegetables or are salesmen in village shops in between being members of a protection corps.

The functions of the armed protection units have changed radically as the M.R.L.A. has been pushed farther into the jungle. The Party began to realize that the armed units of the Min Yuen could do better than merely produce food and material and intelligence; they could hamper and harass the security forces not only directly by ambushes but also indirectly by sabotage and sideshows of every description which would divert the police and army from the main object of hitting the M.R.L.A. So now the Min Yuen acts as a screen to the M.R.L.A. as well as a supply unit.

The Min Yuen has been the main collector of money for the Party. Large sums were obtained by extortion from big land- and estate-owners and transport companies. Smaller sums came from domination over labour, particularly on Asian-owned estates. At one time the Min Yuen extended this domination over labour. It began by making an expert census of conditions on estates in isolated areas. Next it selected an Asian-owned estate which was paying its labourers a basic wage lower than that in a neighbouring estate—ignoring whatever privileges the men might have received to offset the cash discrepancy. It persuaded the labourers to strike for a higher wage, promising to back them by force or threat of force direct to the owner or manager.

On a few occasions this worked, and for every higher wage-scale won the Min Yuen benefited in two ways—by receiving the approbation of the labourers and by taking a rake-off (a condition laid down was that each labourer subscribed a percentage of his earnings to the Party).

The Min Yuen falls back on two very rich ' treasuries ' for the greater part of its 'contributions' of money. These are the island of Penang, in the north, and the district of Johore Bahru, in the south. Penang has a large and prosperous town with a predominantly Chinese population. Its hills provide excellent hiding-places, and several fishing-villages, inaccessible to the police except by sea, allow Communists easy communication with the mainland. Johore Bahru is the back door to the bigger and richer city of Singapore, which also has a predominantly Chinese population. The teeming streets and the rabbit-warrens of houses in Singapore are natural hiding-places. Where Penang is a rich treasury to replenish the coffers of the Party, Singapore can conceal and feed the southern bandits.

The Min Yuen in some areas went further and attempted to persuade the labourers on European-owned estates to leave ' capitalist ' employment and start food production as peasants. Any success in this direction would, of course, embarrass the estate management and ensure a larger corps of food-suppliers for the Party.

It also tried to inveigle labourers into sabotaging installations on their own estates. This fortunately had little success.

The Min Yuen provides couriers for the M.R.L.A. inside the jungle, and runs its own outside it. Both are extremely slow services. A woman Communist wrote in her diary, which was captured, that it took seven months and twelve months for two letters to come to her from her high-ranking Party husband, who functioned in a neighbouring State. " I am losing touch with him," she jotted down disconsolately. These two Communists are not the only ones who have lost touch with each other. Harassing tactics by the security forces have continually broken communications between State Committees and District Commitees. In Negri Sembilan, for instance, the State Committee once lost touch for over a year with all but one of its district committees.

The Min Yuen in Penang and Johore Bahru district still remain largely intact. In Penang the organization, backed by its ruthless protection corps, instituted a reign of terror which lasted three years. It assassinated people who actively opposed it or refused to pay subscriptions, or were suspected of giving information to the police. Members of this Communist Protection Corps committed murder in daylight in busy streets with the certainty that no eyewitnesses would assist the police. Dark fear reigned in Penang, and it was only lifted by the patient work of the police Intelligence branch, which eventually obtained certain Communist documents. These led raiding-parties to camps and communication posts in the hills overlooking the town. They found a printing outfit which had consistently produced propaganda for distribution in Penang, and in Kedah, on the mainland. Many important members of the Min Yuen and Protection Corps were arrested. By the end of 1951 the Penang police had gained the initiative over the Communists, but it had taken them three years of slow and arduous work to do so.

In the early days of the campaign every mite of information was accepted by the police as if it were gold. Captured documents and prisoners were the main sources. Unfortunately, there was not the staff to deal properly with the great quantities of documents picked up in Communist camps or found in packs dropped by fleeing bandits. As the police and the Army were still groping in their efforts to build up a picture of the enemy, the interrogation of prisoners was not then as thorough and detailed as it might have been.

As the interrogation staff grew in numbers as well as in experience, however, much fuller detail was extracted from prisoners, many of whom, as a matter of interest, even volunteered to add more important facts and names of comrades in the jungle after they had been fed. The prisoners had no hesitation or compunction about telling the security forces of the sites of their camps, even though this meant that friends would be killed. It was a *volte-face* which no British officer would accept with equanimity. Captured or surrendered bandits are the worst form of traitors.

In those spacious Communist days of 1948 and 1949 the Communist Army lived in large and well-built camps standing in thick jungle and away from beaten tracks. Some of the largest camps could take 600 men, many had accommodation for 300. Each had a parade-ground, administrative offices, separate quarters for officers, and kitchens and latrines. They were solidly built wood and bamboo snuggeries, and a great deal of care and thought had been given to their construction and layout.

Although many of them occupied a considerable area of ground, all had admirable cover from the air. Every possible ground approach was guarded. Some strategically placed sentry-posts stood as much as a quarter of a mile out, and the guards used thick string which led back to an alarm in the centre of the camp, to give the signal of enemy approaching. In most posts the sentry's orders were to fire two quick shots as an alarm and then scuttle for safety, as did the rest of the gang. Every camp had its retreat road.

Recruits were trained in these camps, square-bashing on the parade ground, complete with its flagstaff from which hung a Red flag. Around the square was a command hut, and a ' school ' with tables and benches. The camps were always near a stream or a river, and the latrines were hygienically situated below the spot where water was drawn for cooking and drinking.

Reveille was at 5.30. A roll-call and two hours of drill followed before breakfast at nine o'clock. An hour later began the first discussion of the day on ' politics.' It lasted for two hours. ' Complete freedom ' from noon to half-past was followed by three hours on camp chores. Supper came at five-thirty. From seven to nine o'clock, there was the evening political session, which included the phenomenon peculiar to all Communist countries—self-criticism. A comrade was expected not only to criticize himself but also his superior officers: in fact, he was encouraged to do so for their good. It was considered one way of ' inspiring ' a man. The two hours of self-criticism was a privileged period for the ordinary comrade. No commander could punish a comrade who criticized him.

Men of this Liberation Army have rigid rules and regulations to observe. Foremost are the four offences which carry the death penalty:

1. Disobedience or acting against the command of any leader or assistant in the war front.
2. Openly or secretly endangering the Army or trying to organize small groups of people to endanger the unification of the army.
3. Revolting, revealing secrets to the enemy, or helping and serving the enemy.
4. Killing or plundering people for no reason.

I make no comment on whether these crimes fitted the punishment, but if the last rule had been rigidly observed a large number of terrorists qualified automatically for the death sentence.

There are also the " Ten Points to be observed in Camp ":

1. Speak gently.
2. Observe custom.
3. Return borrowed articles.
4. Pay for damage done.
5. Be honest in buying and selling.
6. Treat prisoners of war well.
7. Keep living quarters clean.
8. Keep personal belongings in good order.
9. Go every day to the lavatory, which must be far away from the camp.
10. Avoid the fair sex when bathing.

Comment on the sixth point is superfluous, for the majority of " prisoners of war " received short shrift, and the principal enemy, white men, were never taken prisoner but killed.

The Party has rules for an " Army on the March " and regulations for sentries who are warned not " to play " with their guns while on duty. " You are not allowed to retreat unless you are ordered to," is, for instance, a general order that can only have been observed rarely. There are a couple of simple but sensible orders for going downhill—" Be silent," and " Be careful of branches and trees." However, told on the one hand to " live and work for the benefit of all," the Communists are also warned that " Free movement is not allowed," and that they should keep the " rigid army discipline " in mind.

In the first two years, when the Communists had the upper hand and life in the jungle could be taken leisurely, they observed all the trappings of a Communist State. New comrades were welcomed ceremonially. (Later they were forced in at point of gun or bayonet). A " Circular of Approval " was handed to every accepted member of the Party. A new adherent was a ' Reserve ' who had to go through a ' waiting period.' If he passed this he received the membership letter which told him in Chinese:

> During this period you worked hard, improved your knowledge and achieved progress. The State Executive Committee are satisfied

with your work and find that you have passed the qualifications for becoming a member of our Party.

To-day you receive an extremely glorious title: a Communist Member, a Bolshevik Warrior—and as such your responsibility will be heavier.

The responsibility of striving for the liberty of the proletariat in Malaya is now upon your shoulders. That is why from now on you must overcome all your defective points, improve yourself, and keep on building your knowledge of Communist politics and culture.

Look upon the Party as your vocation in life. Strive and fight for the Party, fulfilling your duty to the last.

The next few remarks, however, brought the jolt which reminded the new comrade that he was being carefully watched. I quote from the certificate given to one man:

According to our report, we find that you have the following defects which you should take heed of:

1. A bad temper.
2. Inexperience of our working system.
3. Insufficient enthusiasm for learning.

You must show the determination and perseverance of a Bolshevik to overcome these defects quickly.

A salute to Bolshevism!

Membership of the Peoples' Liberation Army does not itself qualify a person as a member of the Malayan Communist Party. Recruits are told this in no uncertain manner. A booklet given to them to digest has this revelation:

Having joined this glorious army, does it mean you are members of the Communist Party? No. The Communist Party champions the fight for liberation of the suppressed and exploited people of the entire world, and its members are the cream of the proletariat. They will endure any hardship and are even ready to sacrifice their lives for the prosperity of the human race. To be members of the Party you must first go through endless training and tests of endurance and discard all bourgeois ideas.

Communist training manuals reveal that sixty per cent of a man's day is devoted to political lectures in conformity with a directive from the Central Executive Committee. Every formation, including the small section of six or seven men, has a political officer whose control, as I said earlier, is paramount, even in military affairs. During his lectures all ranks have to stand to attention.

Discipline is the chain which binds the comrade to the Party, the recruit to the army. Every platoon commander has books instructing him on the training of comrades, on the reasons for discipline, and how it should be executed. One book I saw directed the platoon commander to " make every one understand " the four death-penalty rules and the " Ten Points to be Observed." He was exhorted to arrange periods of discussion and self-criticism, in which he should participate not as a leader but as a comrade among comrades. Theoretically his deficiencies could be laid bare by aggrieved comrades, and he had no remedy—except, of course, when they were discussing " examples of punishment " for the breaking of discipline, when he could if he wanted suggest some as punishment for a man who had broken a cardinal rule of showing no respect to his leader.

Just as forcibly he was exhorted on the need for " winning over " men who had been punished. One way was " to make them understand their mistakes." " Misunderstanding of discipline must be corrected at once."

The political discussions might be compared to a teacher taking a young and inexperienced group of children in a subject above their intellect. The political commissar delivers his lecture and then asks comrades for their views. One by one they stand and repeat what he has said, and they each receive a condescending pat on the head with the words: " That is quite right." Actually, there is generally no exchange of views at all.

The subjects for discussion are Communism in its every aspect. Naturally enough, what democracy means is not on the curriculum, and it is a serious breach of discipline for a comrade to stand up and ask questions about it. No criticism of Communism and the actions of the Malayan Races Liberation Army is permitted. There are only two punishments for these foolhardy acts—suspension from the Party for a period and death. A man who wrote in his own private diary that the slashing of rubber-trees was wrong was killed. Another, who rashly asserted that the Chinese forces fighting in North Korea were not volunteers, was reduced to the ranks, deprived of his arms, and dismissed from Party membership.

Waverers, men who become uncertain about the rightness of their deeds, are carefully watched. For minor offences the form of punishment is discussed by the entire group, including the offender himself, who is asked to suggest his own penance.

Self-criticism periods, according to reports, are animated and forthright. I have read several Communist documents containing full reports of these sessions. (In those early days when they had plenty of time Communists had a mania for writing down every detail). One section commander wrote that he had been described as " being unable to give an example for others to follow " and that he was always " liable to commit mistakes." Another commander learned that he had a " dislike for being criticized," an understandable failure for any non-Communist but a heinous offence for a commissar.

On a page headed " Mutual Criticism " I found criticisms of every man in a group: " a lack of fighting and struggling spirit," " a dislike for learning," " lazy," " careless in daily life," " talking when on sentry duty," " cannot stand hardship," " sleeping in a camp for a night without making a report," " smoking and dozing when on ambush," " helping to crop a comrade's hair." Why this last should be a subject for criticism I was not able to find out.

Field punishments are severe. An offender may be tied to a tree and exposed to the sun for hours without water to drink. He can be beaten with a bamboo pole for as much as thirty-six strokes —and a bamboo pole can be a most painful weapon. Men have been executed by being buried alive. Discipline is in accord with the background. It is jungle discipline.

In the first years of the campaign comrades were permitted casual leave to their homes to visit their families. After a year, however, this facility was withdrawn; too many men, apparently, were not returning. The withdrawal of leave produced dissatisfaction in the ranks. Intercepted letters complained of lack of leave.

Only after two years, when their Min Yuen gained access to large stocks of jungle green or khaki cloth from shops and stores, did the bandits achieve the dignity of some kind of uniformity in their dress. Shirts are cut in the British Army style, and trousers are tucked into rubber shoes and wrapped around with puttees. Every fighter wears a cap with the five-pointed red or yellow star as a badge on the peak.

The fighter once received a ' salary ' of thirty dollars (over three pounds) a month, a part of which he spent on buying towels, cigarettes, and sweets. This scale called for an income of nearly 1000 dollars (about £112) a month for most of the platoons of the ' Army.'

The Malayan Races Liberation Army does not adhere to any accepted military dimensions. Each State has one or more ' Regiments.' The strength of each regiment once ranged between 400 and 700 men. The deployment of M.R.L.A. troops is as follows: in Johore there are the 3rd, 4th, and 9th Regiments, in Pahang the 6th, 7th, and the 10th (Malay) Regiments.

In Perak the 5th Regiment is one of the strongest in the country. In Negri Sembilan there is the 2nd Regiment, in Selangor the 1st, and in Kedah the 8th. Far-away Kelantan had the " Pulai Gang," and now the " 7th Company of the 5th Regiment."

Perhaps the only facility for training that the Communists did not, and still do not, have was target practice. They had to preserve their bullets, which they unearthed from hidden dumps. Strange as it may seem, in six years of fighting the Communists have never really been desperately short of arms and ammunition.

The Federation Government asserts it has not heard of any instance of " outside supplies," but the general belief is that the Communists must be receiving weapons and ammunition from somewhere.

It has been established that there are few specialist troops among the guerrillas, but with their native ease at adapting themselves to anything they have men who have become good armourers and gunsmiths, working with tools either stolen or contrived out of ingenuity and resource. There has been plenty of evidence of rifle bullets having been filed down to fit sten breeches.

8

Plans for a " Republic "

ON January 25, 1949, the headquarters of the Malayan Communist Party announced its plan for a Peoples' Democratic Republic. This came in the form of an open letter to " the brethren of all races." A copy fell into the hands of the Government. Its full terms were never disclosed to the public, but here are the essential sections.

The manifesto described the Emergency as a " Colonial War " launched by " British Imperialism " against the Malayan people. It was purely in retaliation that The Malayan Peoples' Anti-British National Liberation War had " universally flared up."

The Malayan people could obtain " warmth and salvation and have a brilliant and democratic future " only by evicting the British Imperialists, completely eliminating their military, political, and economic systems, terminating the methods of Colonial administration, and establishing the Peoples' Nation.

In the Malayan Peoples' Democratic Republic, which would unite Singapore and the Federation, citizenship would be synonymous with nationality. The national constitution was to be determined democratically by Malayan citizens. There would be " complete freedom for association, assembly, speech, publication, person, residence, movement, correspondence, religious creed, political creed, strikes, demonstrations, etc." The administrative body would be the Central Peoples' Council, which would be formed in accordance with " the principles of racial equality " with " safeguards for backward sections of the community."

The manifesto gave the pious assurance that the National Constitution of the Malayan Peoples' Democratic Republic " will neither be a Soviet Republic of proletariat despotism, nor will it be a republic of bourgeoisie dictatorship, but it will be a New Democratic Republic, which will be a combined autocracy of various revolutionary classes."

A possible scoring point with the Chinese squatters was the Party's assertion that upon the establishment of the Republic farmers would own their own land, although in the same breath they were told they would be given " ownership of sufficient land for their support." The Party proposed replacing " extortionate taxes " and miscellaneous Imperialist levies with " reasonable and light simple taxes." Malayan industry would be protected from foreign exploitation.

The difficulties of peasants, hawkers, and small-scale businessmen would be particularly borne in mind. For instance, they would be exempted from paying taxes " in the early stages " of the establishment of the Republic.

The Party described in detail how the Republic would " care " for the people's livelihood, their social welfare and their education (" Colonial culture and education must be eradicated as hostile to national emancipation, and replaced by a new democratic cultural education ").

A National Defence Army under the control of the people would be established, and in the sphere of foreign policy the Government of the Republic would establish friendly relations with all territories prepared to treat it " with equity."

The Party explained how this estimable State could be achieved. There were two alternatives.

The first was to travel along the " running-dog path of Malay and Chinese leaders "—a path that " encouraged capitulation to British Imperialists, betrayed the peoples' interests, protected the income of monopolist capitalists, and forced people to starve."

The second was the noble path of revolution which " resists death and seeks life."

After an appeal to workers, peasants, and people of all races to unite in the struggle against the British Imperialists, the Party warned that the revolutionary war would be " long, difficult, and relentless," but it could not possibly fail because its object was to effect the liberation of the people and the establishment of the Peoples' Democracy with " prosperity of economy and the blessing of livelihood."

The Malayan struggle, it asserted, was part of the World Peace Democracy Movement, in which the Malayan people were taking their place with " progressive countries " throughout the world. The struggle was timely in view of the failing power of the " American-led Imperialist Camp."

Led by the Soviet Union, and encouraged by " the successes of the Revolutionary War of the Chinese people whose population is one-fifth of that of the whole world," the " liberating forces of Communism must inevitably prevail."

The Party propaganda machine quite naturally plugged this manifesto for all it was worth—but not always in its original dialectical form. Four months later its writers had broken it down and simplified it in words and phrases intelligible to the " workers and the peasants."

The terrorists' tactics had, however, sounded the death knell to any Communist efforts to win over the simple-minded masses. The Party had obviously forgotten the lesson the Japanese conquerors had learned too late in their occupation of Malaya. At that time the Malayan people, disillusioned by the failure of the British Army and Government to defend the country, had shrugged their shoulders, and they prepared to give life under the Japanese Government a try. If it was as benign, tolerant, and open-handed as the British, and encouraged free enterprise and liberties, they were prepared to remain Japanese subjects, and, indeed, when the time came, to assist in the defence of the land against its reoccupation by Allied forces.

The heavy hand of the Japanese, the brutalities of their military police, their failure to welcome brown- and yellow-skinned people as real brothers, and the introduction of a system where the Japanese were right whatever they did, brought swift disillusionment. There was a swing back for the return of the British system of government " despite its faults."

It was the same with the Malayan Communist Party. There was little doubt that the thinking Chinese in Malaya, loyal to the core to their own motherland, China, were curious about the Communist Government of Mao Tse-tung. They were prepared to wait and see how Communism differed from the corrupt Nationalist Government.

They were ready to assist Mao Tse-tung with their riches if he proved worthy of it, according to their estimation. But in Malaya, in their own homes, the vicious manner in which the local Communist squads killed, committed atrocities, and extorted money by bandit methods made them recoil. They ' co-operated ' with the Communists under duress, and they likened the glorious Communist promises of an ideal land to just so much pretentious vaunting.

At this point mention must be made of that all-important Chinese political organization, the Malayan Chinese Association. It was formed to try and convince the Government, the Malays, and the rest of the country that all right-thinking Chinese were anti-Communist, that Chinese were, and always had been, the principal targets of the Communists.

It pointed out that only because of fear had the Chinese hesitated to strike back and refused suggestions that they should form local self-defence corps. Through fear they would not give the police or Army information about the enemy.

Undoubtedly one important reason for Chinese reluctance to take any kind of offensive action was the absence of Government protection and security. The squatters, for instance, were beyond the range of effective administration, let alone policing.

Consequently bandit law superseded Government law in most villages and every squatter area.

Unfortunately, the failure of the majority of Chinese to resist the Communists, even morally, created doubts and suspicions about the genuineness of their loyalty to Malaya. This dangerous and growing state of mind was appreciated by the Chinese leaders who began to organize their community to protect its own interests in the country. They formed the Malayan Chinese Association. Among its professed objects were the preservation of good intercommunal relations and support for Government in its efforts to maintain law and order. In ten months the Association gained 100,000 members, especially among the non-English-speaking Chinese.

The Association has not, however, been an unqualified success. There has been too much dissension within itself.

In various parts of the country its quality of leadership has varied a great deal. In some areas its officials are good men; in others they are bad. Only the sincerity and honesty of its president, Dato Sir Cheng-lock Tan, a venerable statesman, has prevented the Association from collapsing.

The Communists from the first disliked the Malayan Chinese Association. They realized that if it succeeded as an organization it would present them with a united Chinese front.

So they brought the Association under heavy verbal and physical attack from its inception. Less than six weeks later they flung a hand-grenade into a meeting of the Association at Ipoh, in Perak, and wounded Mr (as he was then) Tan Cheng-lock and four other important Chinese. This fortunately failed to frighten these leaders.

Other M.C.A. officials were murdered. Communist propaganda called the Association " a British bandit-supported organ of puppets and running-dogs," and they dubbed Tan Cheng-lock " the British bandit running-dog Chief."

The Association did good work in other spheres. It took on as its first task the cause of the harassed squatters and also, despite the Chinese dislike of the Federation Agreement, it began to urge Chinese to become Federal citizens.

The Association foresaw that full Communist control in China would eventually result in Mao Tse-tung's Government turning its attention to the Chinese living in Malaya. Before this happened, it was essential, they considered, that the Malayan Chinese should strengthen their ties with Malaya, their country of adoption, and also their own unity as an integral section of the Malayan population.

These intentions of the Association must be considered as the most important development in Chinese affairs during 1949.

On February 1, 1949, the Communist Party announced that its Anti-British Army had been converted into the Malayan Races Liberation Army. This was an attempt to disguise the revolution as nationalist in spirit and to imply that it incorporated all races. To give extra weight to this argument it also formed the Tenth Regiment of Malays in Pahang.

Most of the original members of this ' regiment ' were left-wing Indonesians, but by the end of 1949 this body, harried more by Malay kampong guards than by regular security forces, had almost completely disintegrated. Its remnants took refuge with Chinese units. As they gained more experience, however, they re-formed into the Tenth Malay Regiment, and exist to this day.

There seemed a hope at the beginning of 1949 that the Communists had begun to crack. They were reluctant to attack guarded targets. They never moved except in large forces and never swooped unless they could command surprise. Their main forces were often inclined to retreat to bases deeper in the jungle, where they could evade the offensive operations of the Army and the police and continue training.

Loyalists were heartened by the unusually sober analysis found in a Central Executive Committee document captured in a Communist camp.

Entitled " Our Opinion of the Battle," it stated that the Executive was disheartened at the way the ' revolution ' was going. Their bases were being destroyed, they lacked " popular support " and confidence in victory. Their campaign, they said, had been badly planned and improperly directed.

A bandit diary picked up in June confirmed the situation revealed in documents seized earlier—that the Malayan terrorist bands had been forced on to the defensive, and that they were " war-weary," weakened by internal dissension.

The diary told of hardships in the jungle, the lack of training and the loss of guns, " the deterioration of morale and the lack of popular support." Indeed, by the first week of August 1949 bandit incidents reached their lowest-ever figure of twelve.

There were the first definite signs that the Emergency might terminate by the end of the year. Encouraged by these signs, the Federation Government finally acceded to popular request that surrender terms should be offered to the bandits. Chinese opinion had always been that, as the majority of the men of the M.R.L.A. had been ' forced ' to join, they would desert once they were assured they would not be hanged if they surrendered.

On September 6, 1949, the Government announced surrender terms to the men in the jungle by dropping from the air a million leaflets. These declared there was no intention of relaxing the law against those known to be guilty of murder and other serious crimes, but that the law had been amended so that other men who surrendered voluntarily would not be charged with any offence involving the death penalty. Each case would be dealt with on its merits.

By the end of the year 116 bandits had surrendered after reading the leaflet; but the flow never attained the avalanche that armchair exponents had so fondly prophesied. The higher command of the M.R.L.A. looked after that by imposing stricter discipline over their wavering rank and file, by cutting their forces down to small sections of ten or twenty men, thereby making it easier for a leader to maintain watch and control.

Harsh treatment by company commanders and section leaders of men whom they suspected of the Communist crime of 'deviationism,' made others think twice about attempting to escape. The Party propaganda machine whipped into action. It described the Government offer as "resulting from the weakness of the security forces and the successes of the bandits."

The Government went on to make "surrender" its most attractive bait. As the months went by more cleverly thought-out leaflets were showered into the jungle or left by Army and police patrols along known bandit tracks for terrorists to pick up and read. Bandits who surrendered later said that the Communist High Command had made the reading of surrender leaflets an offence punishable with death.

Surrender and, as will be related later, the resettlement of squatters have been the two most powerful weapons available to the Government.

In the meantime the armed forces had grown in strength, if not in ability. Technique in jungle warfare improved slightly. The police had more than 200 jungle squads which acted as 'fire-brigades' in dashing to the scenes of incidents. These also went into action with the Army.

A police Frontier Force patrolled the Malayan-Thai border, a line that moved raggedly through deep jungle and high hill. The jungle in Thailand had become a resting and retraining ground for Malayan bandits. The South Thailand police, then lazy and engaged in their own personal battles with the Thailand Army, had turned blind eyes to the menace in their land, although their Government in Bangkok had declared they would have no truck with Communism.

Lachie Macdonald, of the London Daily Mail, and I found

proof of this one day during a visit to Kota Bahru, in Kelantan, when we went across the border to the nearest Thai village of Golok. It was typical of most Malay villages, except that the signs on the shops were in the Thai language and the people were bilingual.

Nobody stopped us or questioned our presence. We saw no Thai police on beat, but we glimpsed Chinese in jungle green uniforms on the verandas of houses during our casual walk through the village.

We spoke to shopkeepers and to peasants. We talked to the station-master of the little railway station at which trains from Malaya turned round for the southern return journey. They all admitted that Chinese bandits lived among them.

"Why aren't they arrested?" we asked. The eloquent shrugs of shoulders were the only answers.

The Thai police-officer in charge declined to be drawn into conversation about the armed Chinese who roamed the streets day and night. He never even asked us for our passports. The Thai customs-officer admitted that an unusually large quantity of tinned foods, rice, flour, and biscuits were being brought across the border along open tracks. Small children and old women forded the Golok river—a shallow stream which is the frontier boundary—carrying a couple of tins of condensed milk, or a tin of biscuits, or packets of cigarettes, or a tin of corned beef.

If stopped, all they had to say was that they had bought them in the Malayan village of Rantau Panjang, across the river, for themselves. Under a mutual agreement between the two Governments, Thais and Malays living within three miles of the boundary can move across the river without the formality of a passport. They carry instead a border pass. They are permitted to buy non-dutiable food in either territory.

In this way the resting bandits north of Kelantan obtained food and help from both sides. They and their cohorts along the rest of the frontier knew they were safe enough, for neither the Malayan Police nor Army could cross the line in pursuit.

This impossible situation was modified late in 1949 when the Thai Government agreed to allow Federation police to go across the frontier in pursuit of terrorists. They were allowed inside three miles of Thai territory, but Malayan police had to be accompanied by a Thai police-officer. To facilitate this arrangement small detachments of Thai police were stationed at villages along the entire border, particularly in Kedah. This agreement worked satisfactorily and produced a greater measure of co-operation by the Thai police, but the border has never been effectively sealed. This has not been from want of effort by the Malayan police.

9

Airstrip among Aborigines

ANTHROPOLOGISTS say that some of the world's most primitive people live in the great Malayan forest and that they know little about them.

Many of these aborigines live nomadic lives in unexplored regions into which they have been driven by 'civilization.' During the Japanese war hardly any aboriginal groups living in accessible areas were unaffected by the attempts of the Japanese conquerors of the country to spread their grim gospel of the 'Greater East Asia Co-prosperity Sphere.' The people fled back into the fastnesses of the jungle, driven by fear, leaving the gardens on which they had depended for much of their food. Many died from hunger. The aborigines came to dread the sight of armed men in uniform and they quaked at the sound of a Japanese aeroplane.

The Japanese surrender brought some of them out of the jungle again, but their efforts to resume a peaceful life were frustrated when into the shoes of the once-feared Japanese soldiers stepped more merciless armed men, the Communists. Once again helter-skelter into the jungle there leapt the Temiar and Jakun and Negritos, hoping to leave their new enemy on the fringes of the jungle as they had done the Japanese. There was, however, little hope of this, for the Communist killers also found that their own haven lay only in the forest; and they turned to the timid jungle-people for food. The Communists forced them to grow tapioca and sweet potato and buy tobacco on their behalf, to spy for them, and even to kill for them.

The aboriginal races presented the Government with problems that had to be faced and dealt with quickly. They were the people most vulnerable to Communist influence, and under Communist domination they could play havoc with any Government measures in the jungle. They could easily be frightened into becoming a most valuable ally of the Communists.

One such tribe was the Semelai, living in South Pahang around Tasek Bera, and along the Triang and Serting rivers.

Anthropologists believe that, like certain other aboriginal tribes in Malaya, the Semelai are descended from hill-people of Indo-China who migrated southward about a thousand years ago. Up to the time of the Japanese war between five and six hundred of these dark brown, stiff-curly-haired, long-faced people had lived in splendid isolation, for the area of Tasek Bera, a great lake surrounded by thick jungle, was unexplored territory.

There did not seem any need in those leisurely, easy-going pre-war days for any British Government officer to make the heart-breaking journey to Tasek Bera just to see the Semelai. Scientists, anthropologists, and ethnologists were interested in them, but very few visited them. The tale became different during the hazardous days of the Japanese occupation, however, for the Tasek Bera suddenly emerged as an important link in the Chinese guerrilla route from South Pahang to Johore. It was then that the peace-loving Semelai (as animists, they fear death in any violent form) first came to know of thuggery and slavery. They saw no British guerrillas, for even that jungle-hardened fighter Spencer Chapman said in his book *The Jungle is Neutral* that the journey to Tasek Bera was " extremely hazardous " for the Chinese and " quite impossible for a European."

But it was in pursuit of militant Communists that British troops in 1949 forced through that " impossible " jungle to liberate the Semelai and bring help to them.

Major-General Charles Boucher, G.O.C., Malaya District, introduced me to Tasek Bera in 1948. It looked most uninteresting on the map, just swampy land surrounded by thick jungle with no tracks to it, a large lake surrounded by many small ones.

" That's the place the bandits are going to—in that direction," said General Boucher. He believed it, and so did a lot of other people. The conception then was that the best thing to do with the bandits was to drive them into the jungle, and leave them there to fend for themselves. They would not last long then, as it was considered that the jungle was deadly to the enemy.

Tasek Bera was still a mystery to the Government. How or in what condition the Semelai were, and where their sympathies lay in this new local war, was uncertain.

Early in 1949, however, it became evident that something had to be learned, and done, about Tasek Bera. The bandits were reported to be using it as a resting- and training-ground, to have large, well-organized camps there, and to have subjugated the Semelai.

The Government decided to send an expedition to Tasek Bera because, apart from Communist exploitation of the Semelai, the territory had again become a direct link in the Communist communications between Johore and Pahang. It was considered essential to the general plan that Tasek Bera should be 'occupied,' first by British troops, then by the police, who would have the triple rôle of protecting the Semelai, of denying food to the bandits, and of disrupting Communist communications. A large reconnaissance party was planned, and its journey was timed to fit in with an operation to be launched on the border of North Johore and South Pahang; this was "Operation Borrowdale," named after an area in the Lake District of Britain.

A company of the 1st Seaforth Highlanders was detailed for the march under the commanding officer, Lieutenant-Colonel Jock Douglas, O.B.E., Mr William ("Jock") Neill, D.S.O., Assistant Superintendent of Police, ex-major of the 1st Airborne Division and a veteran of Arnhem, was to find the site for a police post.

This, though, is not the tale of Jock Neill, of Carstairs, Lanarkshire, although he has a lot to do with it. It is the story of how the Semelai were won from the bandits, how a police post was built, and how inexpert British and Malay policemen laid an airstrip, using primitive equipment, ingenuity, and resource, and at the cost of only twelve bags of rice.

Information about the quickest and easiest route to Tasek Bera was scanty. A man who had been guided there about two years before, Dennis H. Collings (then Curator of Raffles Museum, Singapore), was ready to go with the party as he could speak a little of the Semelai language.

It looked as if the reconnaissance party would have to force its way through the jungle blindly, but the police heard of two

Semelai working as tappers on St Hilliare Estate, in Bahau, Negri Sembilan. These men agreed to be guides.

From the map it seemed that the quickest route would be from the north-east corner of Ladang Geddes Estate, striking north-eastward towards Kampong Baapa, the main village of the Semelai. The distance was sixteen miles in a straight line. As it turned out, with the many diversions and obstacles, the journey was twenty-four miles. Thanks to the guides, it took a three-day forced march instead of an estimated eleven days without guides. The big force expected to encounter large numbers of bandits at Tasek Bera.

The Seaforth Highlanders realized they were in for a tough time and that it might mean death for some of them if they came to battle with entrenched Communists. So they set off on a mission that was one of battle and mercy combined. They took a doctor and a dresser. The going was extremely difficult. The troops were carrying heavy loads—rations for five days, ammunition, and weapons. The way was so rough that very soon Colonel Douglas ordered half-hour marches with five-minute halts. Jock Neill, with his compass and the two guides, acted as pathfinder. The three of them cut a path and blazed trees for their return journey.

It was typical of a hundred other journeys into the Malayan jungle made by the security forces in their fight against the bandits. The Malayan jungle has been forced to open up its secrets, and the future military maps of Malaya will show hundreds of tracks criss-crossing the peninsula. The geographical data which these expeditions have picked up will help when the jungle-ways are opened up to commerce.

The expedition sank into swamps, and climbed out again, muddy and odoriferous; they crossed rushing little rivers and emerged covered with leeches; they had to make diversions of hundreds of yards to cross fifty yards of territory. They clambered over giant jungle trees that had been blown down. Everything—swamps, rivers, thick undergrowth, ten-foot-diameter trees—had to be tackled with full packs. It was an endurance test of the devil's own making.

Once they came across an expanse of jungle which had been wind-swept. Great jungle trees had been uprooted and flattened by Nature. There was something awesome in that spectacle. Man with his explosives and his electric saws could not have created such havoc. "Just bloody murder, climbing over that stretch," said one man later.

The capacity of the British Army to produce immortal words in the midst of trials and tribulations is well known. The journey to Kampong Baapa had its moments. There was the Scot who, when a halt was called, wearily took off his pack with the remark, "Whin I get hame, I'll niver hae the bluidy hert tae herness a cuddy again." Those who heard him laughed, but they knew what he meant.

The second evening out camp was being laid, and the Semelai had got their own little cooking-fires going, when Colonel Douglas, anxious for a cup of tea, asked his sergeant-major, "Haven't you got the fire going yet, sergeant-major?" and received the bland reply—in the middle of the jungle—"Canna fin' ony wud, sur."

The difficult terrain made it impossible to send out leading scouts, but as the country nearer Tasek Bera opened up a section went ahead with a bren-gun. It was none too soon. Towards the end of the second day's march they bumped into bandits. "We almost shook hands," said a Jock later. There was no friendliness in this meeting, however. The bren opened up, but the bandits dived into the undergrowth and squirmed their way out.

The expedition moved on, taking more precautions. On the same afternoon, four miles south of their destination, they came across abandoned dry rice-fields and bare tapioca grounds. These were old Semelai ladangs, but decrepit bashas also were still standing, little huts that were not Semelai in design. The troops estimated that this bandit camp could have held about fifty men.

As dawn broke on the third day the column marched ahead in great expectations of seeing their mystery lake soon. And it was not long before the two Semelai began chattering excitedly in their monosyllabic language as they heard a cheerful noise that sounded something like "Ho-hu, ho-hu." This came, as the expedition found later, from Semelai musical windmills, affairs with wooden sails, ten to eleven feet long, with bamboo flutes tied to each end with rotan. These were stuck on tall trees. To the Semelai out in his scrabby field the sound of the windmill is a welcome-home. Some Semelai have almost a mania for making windmills, and sometimes those setting them up in tall trees break their bones or are killed in a fall to the ground. Even a slight puff of wind will blow the sail round strongly.

There were other signs that the expedition was at last at its destination. There were more Semelai huts and cleared land planted with vegetables, but, except for the sound of the windmills, the land was quiet. The troops climbed to the brow of a small hill and looked down on Tasek Bera, a lake eleven miles long with a breadth varying from 100 yards to 600 yards, and covered with weeds waving four feet above water. There were cleared narrow channels criss-crossing the carpet of weeds, with a main wide channel running down the centre. These were the waterways for the shallow dug-outs of the Semelai, and, as the troops learned later, they needed a guide to cross the water maze in any direction.

A strange stillness hung over the scene. The place seemed deserted. The Semelai were hiding, and they refused to come out, even though their two tribesmen chattered loudly to them. The Communists had done their work well in sowing the seeds of distrust of white men.

Neill and Colonel Douglas realized that before they could begin their work the Semelai had to be won over. It appeared that the only way of making contact would be to catch a Semelai. The faces of two men were seen peering from blukar. Two Jocks sauntered away and made a wide detour to come up behind the hiding men. Once again the two soldiers showed that the British Army can make friends with any race under the sun. Although the Semelai were frightened and bewildered, they emerged from the weeds, were given cigarettes and biscuits, and when another white man, Collings, spoke to them in their own language and hailed them as long-lost brothers the rest was easy. The Jocks nicknamed Collings " The White Sakai."

The headman of the tribe, the Batin, appeared with his family, and soon the whole tribe was settling down beside the grinning Scotsmen, who were nevertheless appalled by the advanced malnutrition of their new friends. The Batin explained how the Communists had come and lived among them for months, had subsisted on their crops, forced them to grow more, and had threatened them when they had not worked hard enough.

Where were the bandits now? The Batin waved his hand vaguely. " Gone," he said. " They heard you coming." The Batin was right. In patrols during the next few days the Seaforths found a well-built and well-planned camp for 150 men, which had been evacuated hurriedly. The Seaforths took over, and from that moment the Semelai were freed from Communist influence.

The next job was to make that freedom secure; but there was an engagement with bandits seven days afterwards. One man was captured, and from what he said it semed likely that Kampong Baapa could expect pressure from the enemy. It was decided that the police post should be built as soon as possible. Neill found a site at the top of a small hill rising by the lake.

Meanwhile the Seaforths were learning about the Semelai and their ways. The Semelai gave a feast, with the younger men and bare-waisted women wearing their best sarongs and bamboo jewellery. They produced their favourite drink, brews of bananas and of sugar-cane, kept in big Chinese glazed earthenware jars which had been half-buried in scrub for more than a month. The drinks were mildly alcoholic, the one made of sugar-cane tasting like rum.

The Semelai drink only on great ceremonial occasions such as the annual planting of a garden. Dreams play a large part in their life; on these depend the success or failure of their new garden. Collings, for instance, learned that dreams of the killing of deer, elephants, or other animals meant that the ground would be unfruitful and that another site should be looked for. Dreams of a European meant that the "ghost of the soil" (who has a beard and moustache of iron wire) would not let his land be used, but would point out another site. To dream of another aborigine meant that there would be wild pig for the next day's meal; but dreams about burials, digging up sand, wandering among graves, or climbing up the steep, high bank of a river were good auguries for the garden.

The Semelai believe in kindly elves and frightening jinns, and that if they die a natural death their spirits go to an island filled with fruit-laden trees on which they live with long-dead kinsmen and friends, but that violent death sends their spirits to a lonely hell.

Among the Semelai the Batin, the tribal chief, has absolute power. He controls his people according to unwritten customs handed down through the generations. The only offence he can punish by death is incest, and the sentence is carried out by drowning the condemned man in the Tasek Bera.

After eleven days Neill, Douglas, and the main body of the troops marched back to Segamat. Neill was to return with a building party. They left a rear party to consolidate and protect the Semelai from marauding bandits. There were plenty of supplies for maintaining friendly relations, apart from the cheerfulness and open-heartedness of the Scots troops. Food, tobacco, sarongs, and native axe-heads had been dropped by Dakotas. When the first Dakota circled overhead, the old Batin amazed his visitors when he pointed at it with a gnarled thumb and asked, " Is that a Communist aeroplane? " The Chinese had told them that the Spitfires and Dakotas that roared overhead belonged to the " Communist Army." When he finally understood that the *orang jahat* (bad men) had been telling him lies, he said that his ambition was to see an aeroplane on the ground. He did not have long to wait.

On July 2 Neill set out again from Segamat with a police party composed of Mr J. V. Spooner, Cadet Assistant Superintendent of Police, Sergeant D.C.M. Todd, from Midlothian, Sergeant C. J. Philips, a Londoner, Sergeant A. Love, of Glasgow (radio operator) and fifty-three Malays.

The march from the same north-eastern corner of Ladang Geddes Estate to Kampong Baapa was uneventful. This time it took only one day.

A formidable task faced the police. They had to clear jungle, excavate and prepare sites for the police station and barracks, erect these buildings, and make roads. They were now on their own, the rear party of the Seaforths having left immediately after their arrival. But the jungle trees fell quickly before the whipping bliongs (axes) of the Semelai, who helped in clearing the sites. They cut through large trees quickly and easily.

As station and barracks were pegged out, Neill made some attempt at 'town planning.' He " surveyed " by compass and by pacing until a Dakota dropped a measuring tape. Stumps and roots were removed to level the site. Then up went the walls of the buildings on bamboo floors. Up went the dining-hall and the kitchen for the men. The police station gradually took shape in local hardwood. It was twenty-five feet broad by forty feet long and twenty-five feet high, and had a charge room, a wireless, planning, and map room, a large store, and a small dispensary. Everything was completed in three weeks, and all had been done with two hammers, two saws, three cross-cut saws, and some felling axes and parangs. Nails were dropped by air; instruments for providing levels and horizontals were made or improvised on the spot.

Neill considered an airstrip essential, but an officer of the Royal Engineers who had been with the original party had asserted in writing that this would be impossible in Tasek Bera. Neill decided to look round again. He was impelled by the fact that Kampong Baapa was remote and the route to it was dangerous. A police casualty would have to face a long carry-out and then a tedious journey by road to the nearest hospital. Neill began a detailed reconnaissance of the area. He thought he had found a reasonably level piece of ground, but when he cut a patch it proved to be undulating and full of dips. He tried again elsewhere, and this time cut a patch with seven smaller paths leading off in the shape of herringbone. This gave him a better picture of the various levels.

The preparation of the jungle airstrip began. Apart from felling and clearing tall, thick jungle trees, the police and Semelai had to tackle great ten-foot high ant-hills, solid as cement. These were blown up with explosives; so were the stumps of the trees. Ex-saboteur Neill taught the sergeants how to place the explosives, then run for it after lighting the fuse.

Once again jungle gave way to man. It took some time to explain to the mystified Semelai why a padang (cleared area) was being made, and why they should help. When they heard that this work would end in a big air-bird coming down among them on its two wheels they said "Wow," and set to work with their bliongs again.

As the trees were felled and their stumps removed, clearings were burned. When this was completed there was a piece of ground which looked nothing like a potential airstrip until the blackened trunks of trees were manhandled away, gaping holes were filled with wood and earth, and dead timber was put into undulating sections to build up a level.

There was improvisation all the time. There were no wheelbarrows to cart laterite to make a rough level over the strip, so canvas (previously wrapped round packages dropped from Dakotas) was cut into strips and each piece was fixed to two poles to make a carrier.

Small ' carts ' were made. Their wheels were solid wood running on a wooden axle lubricated by milk tins filled with margarine. When it became necessary to lay a good surface—and digging near by produced ideal red clay—rollers to smooth down the strip were improvised from logs of wood.

After forty-four working days the strip was completed. There it lay, 280 yards long by 40 yards wide. When the news was radioed out, it was not believed at headquarters, but a test landing was arranged.

The great morning arrived. The Semelai flanked the field. The police waited anxiously. Torn strips from parachutes lay on the earth as guide lines for the aircraft. A windsock operated from the top of a primitive windmill. As an extra precaution, smoke also gave wind direction.

At ten o'clock there came the soft noise of an approaching Auster. The pilot circled three times, then came round as if to land. With flaps down and throttle back, he almost touched down —then took off again.

Neill signalled frantically to the pilot to land. The aircraft came round again, the pilot put on full flap, throttled back, and made a precautionary landing thirty yards inside the strip. It was an historic moment for isolated Kampong Baapa.

The pilot clambered out to the cheers of the police. He confessed that as he touched down he had fully expected to go up on his nose.

Kampong Baapa celebrated the occasion with tea.

The Semelai wonderingly touched the fuselage and wires of the Auster and peered at the mysteries in the cockpit. That airstrip opened up the Malayan world to them. They saw more strange but friendly faces. Doctors and dressers flew in with medicine, treated their yaws and their other illnesses, and gave them vitamin pills to counteract malnutrition.[1]

[1] Two years later the police post was abandoned. In 1953, however, a new post was constructed and called Fort Iskandar.

10

Birth of a Plan

ALTHOUGH bandit incidents had dropped in number by the middle of 1949, the Min Yuen organization had grown steadily and had forced into its ranks thousands of Chinese squatters living throughout the country in areas bordering the jungle. Their vegetable-gardens and houses were ideally sited for the collection and distribution of food. Rubber-planters and tin-miners, who drew most of their labour from the squatters, were among the first to realize their great potential value to the Communists. They urged the Government to take drastic, even ruthless, action against the squatters. It was necessary, they said, to cut off the Communist fighting squads from their sources of supply.

Sir Henry Gurney acknowledged the force of this argument and asked the Government of each Malay State to investigate its individual squatter problem and recommend action which, he suggested, should be uniform throughout the country. The Malay Governments settled down very slowly to the problem—why, I shall explain later.

A solution had to be found. Mass detention and repatriation of bandit helpers to Communist China had become impossible. Ships from Malaya had ceased to call at occupied ports in China, and no port on the mainland of China was available to disembark Chinese repatriates from Malaya, quite apart from the fact that the new Chinese Government had to give its formal consent first to accept these people.

The Federation Government suddenly introduced an unpleasant measure called Emergency Regulation 17D. This gave its officials power to detain the residents of any village, area, or district against which there was satisfactory evidence of aiding, abetting, or consorting with the bandits.

It was a distasteful measure because inevitably innocent people suffered. Communities were torn up without warning and moved bodily into concentration camps euphemistically called " detention camps." Compensation was paid for property and livestock left behind, but no compensation was made to people who proved innocent for their loss of freedom, which extended in most cases over months, or for loss of livelihood.

Regulation 17D emerged as one of the harshest measures the Federation Government introduced, although it described it as essential to deprive the terrorists of large bodies of voluntary or involuntary supporters. In fairness, I should add that after 1949 and the introduction of the very acceptable 'resettlement' policy the Government rarely fell back on this disagreeable form of punishment. It turned too many people against them. It made thousands of Chinese bitter. Nevertheless, between January and October 1949 Regulation 17D was enforced sixteen times in various localities and 6343 people were thrust into detention camps.

The Government has never disclosed how many of these were not Communist sympathizers, nor how many were people who had been visiting the areas the day the police descended and swept them up into detention willy-nilly, nor for how long most of them were in detention camps before they proved their innocence and were released.

The early bright hopes that the Communists had had enough had been built on flimsy evidence. The bandits had merely been drawing their second breath. They had withdrawn into the jungle to retrain.

On September 11, a week after the Government's offer of surrender terms, 300 bandits attacked the railway town of Kuala Krau, in Pahang. They burned the station, the houses of the Indian station-master and the railway inspector, and the water-hose.

They lay in wait for the help they expected would come. They derailed an armoured train sent up to investigate the attack. By the time they withdrew the bandits had killed four policemen, two Malay women, and two British railway engineers.

On September 25 another 150 armed bandits attacked a small village in Pahang. On October 4, 200 burned the British manager's bungalow, labourers' quarters, the smokehouse, and other buildings on Kemayan Estate, in Pahang. These were big raids, and in the last four months of 1949 the graph of bandit-incidents rose rapidly. The Communists were showing that neither the reported " internal dissension " nor the presence of such high-class troops as the Guards Brigade and the Gurkhas could stop them.

This then was the situation when the Emergency entered the third year in 1950, but nothing that the Communists had done in recent months hit the country harder than the British Labour Government's recognition early in January of that year of the Chinese People's Government. This was a step which the Federation Government and the Chinese leaders in Malaya had feared but fervently hoped would not be taken in Britain. Sir Henry Gurney attempted to assure the Chinese that " nothing that may happen in China will weaken the determination of the people of this country to eliminate militant Communism here; rather will their efforts be strengthened." The Chief Secretary, Sir Alec Newboult, said the same thing, that the fight against the bandits would not be affected if the British Government recognized the new Chinese Communist Government.

And when the announcement was made in London the Commissioner-General for South-east Asia, Mr Malcolm MacDonald, declared in Singapore that this recognition did not involve any slackening in hostility in Malaya against the Communist terrorists, who were the enemies of the Malayan people.

The recognition, however, had two serious effects in Malaya. On the one hand the bandits were encouraged by the news. One important Communist jubilantly jotted in his diary (which was captured later), " China will send troops to Malaya."

On the other hand there was a significant change in the attitude of a very large number of Chinese. They became less ready to help the Federation Government, and, in the words of a Government report, became " more disposed to insure themselves with the other side, for they feared that if they openly sided with the Government in Malaya their relatives or their property, or both, in China, would suffer at the hands of the Communist Government."

Back went a lot of them to the old game of fence-sitting. It took more than two years to get many of them off that fence again and on the side of law and order.

Perhaps the country can be thankful to the Chinese that they did not all slide down the fence on to the Communist side. Had they done so, there would have been a different and darker story to tell. By now Malaya might have become a member of the Soviet bloc.

Certainly the British Government's act prolonged the Emergency in Malaya by many, many months, because it took this period of time to regain the confidence of the Chinese.

The Communist bandits began stepping up their attacks on people and estates, mines, railways, and homes. The M.R.L.A. had spent most of the latter months of 1949 in concentrated training. Their killer squads and gangs emerged from the jungle exhilarated, not only by confidence in their secret preparation, but also by the news about China.

Bandit-inspired incidents rose to 221 in February 1950, an increase of 80 per cent. over the average monthly figure of 1949. The Communists stormed and burned the village of Simpang Tiga, in the Sitiawan area of Perak, making 1000 people homeless. Estate factories and stores of rubber were destroyed. Estate managers and labourers were murdered. Trains were derailed, buses were held up and set on fire. Policemen were ambushed and killed.

It was a bad month which reached a climax when a well-led force of bandits surrounded an isolated police station at Bukit Kepong, in Johore, and tried to capture it. Thirteen constables, six kampong guards, two women, and two children were killed and three constables were seriously wounded in a heroic stand. Seven bandits were killed and approximately fifteen wounded.

The bandit campaign continued in its viciousness. A gang in Selangor savagely attacked a village and fired indiscriminately into a crowded cinema, killing five and wounding twelve others. There was, however, retribution for the leader, because as he turned to escape a Chinese Home Guardsman lifted his rifle and shot at him. The bullet struck. The bandit was identified as Chan Sam Yin, for whom there was a reward of 20,000 dollars, dead or alive.

In May the bandit incidents totalled 534, nearly double the previous highest monthly figure recorded since the beginning of the Emergency. There was little doubt that the Communists had the upper hand again. They killed so many planters in South Pahang that, as one survivor put it bitterly, those that remained were not enough to furnish the required number of pall-bearers at the next victim's funeral.

A critical stage was being reached in the operations against the

Communist rebels. Whitehall obviously had no real conception of the problem, nor any idea of the growing dangers. They met recrudescence of Communist activity with complacency and half-hearted measures. It was obvious that the strategy must be changed. New methods of fighting the bandits and fresh inspiration were demanded. More troops were also necessary.

Co-ordination between the Army, the police, and the administrative officers was not as close as it should have been. The Army had never felt comfortable in their rôle of supporting the civil power; they were soldiers, many of them said, fighting with one arm tied behind their backs. They were irritated by the slow, methodical tactics of the police. For their own part, the police were becoming irritated with the Army's superior attitude.

Operations were carried out on a basis of compromise between police and military methods. There was always divided authority on any large-scale operation involving troops and police. There was the inevitable clash between the soldier trained to deal with the enemy by all means within his power in the quickest possible time, and the policeman trained to act only after the fullest investigations and after convincing himself that he had got the right person.

It was also impossible to train Asian or British policemen to be both good policemen when they were outside the jungle and good soldiers when they were in it.

Administrative officers worked in their own lanes as they did not wish to interfere with police and Army tactics, quite overlooking the fact that their duties were an integral part of the operation of war.

While all these matters were in the melting-pot the Army announced that they would be strengthened by the arrival of the 26th Gurkha Infantry Brigade from Hong Kong, and that the Royal Air Force was to be introduced by additional aircraft, beginning with a heavy Lincoln bomber squadron from Australia. The use of Lincolns in support of ground troops operating against jungle bands was something of a military novelty, but if they could help to crush jungle terrorism there was a place for them.

The British people were also beginning to get restive over the slow course of the campaign in Malaya. The House of Commons was the scene of heated debates as Members of Parliament attempted to push Mr James Griffiths, the Secretary of State for the Colonies, and Mr John Strachey, the War Minister, into corners with demands for more troops, more material, more action.

The war was doomed to failure unless there was one man placed in charge of operations. It was clear that Sir Henry Gurney could not carry out the important political rôle of High Commissioner and also fight the bandits. It was no surprise, therefore, when Malaya learned that the British Government was finally considering appointing some one to do nothing but wage war. The question was who—and what was his fighting reputation?

In March came the announcement that Lieutenant-General Sir Harold Briggs, of Burma fame, was to be Director of Operations "to plan, to co-ordinate, and direct the anti-bandit operations of the police and fighting forces." Malaya took new heart.

General Briggs was fifty-five years of age. He was a veteran of the Western Desert and of Burma, where he had commanded the famous Fifth Indian Division during the Japanese war. After Japan's surrender he had been appointed General Officer Commanding-in-chief in Burma. He retired in 1948 and went to live in the lovely island of Cyprus. He had just begun to relax in retirement when he received a personal request from his friend Field-Marshal Sir William Slim, then Chief of the Imperial General Staff, to take on the job of Director of Operations in Malaya.

Briggs accepted it for a year. He stayed eighteen months before he returned to Cyprus a sick and spent man, disillusioned, and critical of the failure of the Federation Government to give him all executive powers they had promised him.[1] All this, however, did not emerge until after he had handed over to his successor, General Sir Rob Lockhart, another noted warrior.

Good soldier that he was, General Briggs had battled quietly with the odds heavily against him and let no word of his difficulties leak out. Had all this been known earlier, it is certain that Sir Henry Gurney would have been forced to urge London to give Briggs almost all the power he wanted. Malayan and British newspapers would have ensured that. General Briggs was too good a man. As it was, he left Malaya not with a reputation shattered, but rather without having enhanced it, although what he did in effect laid the foundations for what can only be victory.

[1] General Briggs died in Cyprus in October 1952, eleven months after he had left Malaya.

Briggs was possibly the best choice the War Office could have made at that time. He was an expert in jungle warfare, though possibly not in guerrilla warfare. He was a quiet man whose very quietness attracted confidence in his abilities. He worked directly under Sir Henry Gurney, not as an Army officer, but as a civilian. He wore no uniform.

Briggs asked for a small staff and began travelling and meeting all kinds of people, supplementing by personal observation the information he had picked up about the problems of Malaya in both the War Office and the Colonial Office. He allowed himself a public announcement that there was no quick or easy way of ending the Emergency.

It did not take long for the people in the front line, particularly the harassed planters and miners, to recognize that a leader had arrived who would try to get things done. Briggs had the manner and the understanding to get the best out of everybody, from District Officers down to frightened squatters.

Within a fortnight of his arrival he had issued his first directive. It was the master-plan for the defeat of the Communists. It was as simple and direct as the man himself. In a few words it meant, " Protect the populated areas, cut the enemy lines of communication, and force him out to battle."

His operation became known, and will endure in the history of the Emergency, as the " Briggs Plan."

It set out these four aims:

(*a*) To dominate the populated areas and to build up a feeling of complete security, which would in time result in a steady and increasing flow of information coming from all sources.

(*b*) To break up the Communist organizations within the populated areas.

(*c*) To isolate the bandits from their food and supply organizations in the populated areas.

(*d*) To destroy the bandits by forcing them to attack the security forces on their own grounds.

He laid down that the police should give top priority to fulfilling their normal functions in the towns and the villages. The Army should maintain a permanent framework of troops deployed in close conjunction with the police to cover the towns and villages which the police could not adequately deal with themselves.

The Army was to be the striking force with the priority task of dominating the jungle " up to about five hours' journey " from a town or village. Units were to establish headquarters in a town or village, thus increasing the sense of security. Sub-units were to deploy and live in the fringes of the jungle up to a distance of about three hours' march from the roads and jungle paths.

The Government, he ordered, should increase—by duplicating or even trebling—the number of District Officers in the field, to enable it to administer effectively and to provide the normal social services.

To initiate action, Briggs established a War Council consisting of himself and the heads of the Administration, police, Army, and Air Force. This Council mapped the Emergency policy.

He created War Executive Committees in each State and Settlement to wage the war in their own territory. This chain of war went right down to the smallest district, which had its own tiny war executive committee. By this means Briggs brought the men in the various levels of the Government, the Army, and the police into the conference room to exchange information and plan operations. It forced every member to take a personal interest in the action in the field. It made every man examine the reasons for failures and encouraged him to exploit the measures that brought successes.

Through these little war cabinets, Briggs took the strings that were tugging in all directions and wove them into a rope of coordination. He brought what might be described as " joint thinking " into planning the end of the Emergency. Ideas were pooled. The good ones went all the way up to the Federal War Council to be examined, approved, and disseminated all over the country.

In his first directive, too, Briggs ordered the establishment of joint police-army operations rooms in every district. He drew up a massive master-map of the Federation of Malaya. On it in a variety of colours were shown where the Chinese and Malays were living; where the scattered communities were thickly massed and how close to jungles they were; where lumber-camps, rubber-estates, and tin-mines existed; and where the aborigines lived and travelled.

" The Briggs Map," a most remarkable picture, was built slowly from information garnered from every conceivable source. The idea was extended by enthusiastic police and Army officers. In one police office much later I noted that the map of the district also showed good dropping zones for aircraft.

Out of that map developed the sites for the plan for the resettlement of thousands of Chinese squatters whom Briggs agreed were the prime source of assistance to the Communist fighters in the jungle. All the squatters were Chinese, hard-working men, who had come from China to seek a livelihood. They were peaceful people, who asked for nothing more than to be allowed to live on their own with no interference in their affairs by either District Officers, or police, or by Communists.

There had not been too many of them before the European war to present a problem to the Government. With the outbreak of the European war, however, and the consequent decline in the importation of food from Britain and Australia, to name only two countries on which Malaya had been dependent, the Government encouraged the production of food everywhere.

Chinese tappers were given every facility for opening up small plots of land, either in or surrounding estates, to produce vegetables, and, as the demand exceeded the supply, there was a large movement of Chinese from towns out into areas where agriculture was possible. When the Japanese war broke out thousands of other Chinese ceased to be completely dependent on the rubber and tin-mining industries, and turned to food production, if not as a basic economy, then as a part-time economy. There was no rubber or tin produced, so they had to find some other means of subsistence.

Families in towns and villages, through fear of the Japanese, also moved out towards the jungle fringes. There they hoped to be left alone. They began " squatting." They set up huts and tilled the soil from early morning to late evening, growing food desperately to make them independent of the distant shops. They were also shrewdly aware that considerable profit might materialize from the produce as months of the War passed and the Japanese failed to import food.

Into the picture then stepped the Chinese guerrillas, who found in the squatters allies ready and willing to supply them with the vegetables and the rice they were growing as their own little contribution to the underground resistance to the Japanese. It was strictly business, because the guerrillas paid for their supplies. The guerrillas, planning their lines of communications of their own accord, established their own " squatter areas " near to their camps.

By the end of the Japanese occupation, therefore, there were great stretches of vegetable gardens, radiating from the principal towns and villages throughout the country. They existed in jungle clearings, in pockets adjacent to roads, rivers, and railways, on old mining lands, and on the outskirts of hundreds of towns and villages.

With the liberation, the squatters did not all return to the towns and villages. There was still much money to be made from vegetables. Food was scarce and prices were high. Their fortunes rose steeply until, by the end of 1947, many of them could be rated rich even by our standards. Indeed, one small group of market gardeners toiling on the slopes of Cameron Highlands, in North-west Pahang, were considered to be among the richest people of their class. Their gross profits for one year ran well above a million dollars (about £125,000). Each man could have bought several expensive, high-powered American cars had he wished to.

When the Emergency was proclaimed it became obvious to the planters, miners, and the police that the squatters would once again fill the Communists' larder, either voluntarily or involuntarily. As the months developed, this happened.

Out of easy reach of the Administration, the squatters became most vulnerable to the terrorist domination. Reports showed that most of them were not willing allies of the Communists, certainly not as willing as they had been during the Japanese occupation when they were inspired to co-operate out of sheer hatred for the conquerors. At the worst, the majority of squatters did not appear to hate the post-war Malayan Government. They only wanted to be left alone by both the Government and by the new enemy, the Communists.

But the isolation which had proved such a boon against the Japanese proved the reverse in this new war, because, willy-nilly, the squatters came under the subjection of the Communists, and thus to the attention of the Government. They were the first prey of the armed gangs who wanted to establish Communist-controlled regions from which an assault on the centres of government could be launched.

The squatters could be useful to the Communists not only for the food they could supply. They had money, or could find it.

They could produce voluntary or involuntary recruits to replace casualties in the Communist ranks. They could also play a valuable rôle as spies on the movements of security forces. So, throughout the country, the independent units of the Communist army found, without much planning or trouble, an effective fifth column. Nobody could distinguish a Communist squatter from an untainted man. There was therefore no need for disguise. And so the squatters became an important section of the Min Yuen.

It was not until December 1948 that the Federation Government decided to examine the extent of this menace and how it should be eradicated. In commendably rapid time a special committee produced its findings. Admitting there was a serious problem, it stressed that this had to be dealt with by the individual States and Settlements because of the different land laws followed by each of them. It recommended that squatters should either be settled in the areas they already occupied, or if this were not possible, brought into alternative suitable areas, and that if any man refused to be settled or resettled he should be liable to compulsory repatriation.

Sir Henry Gurney instructed each Government to investigate the extent of squatterdom within its own boundaries and to consider how and where they could be resettled. This in effect presented the Malay States with an important principle to overcome. Almost all the valuable land each possessed had been set aside as " Malay reservation," and resettlement meant sacrificing many of these areas to foreigners, a policy which went against the grain of most Malay Rulers and their advisers.

The greatest tact and persuasion had to be employed by Sir Henry Gurney to impress upon the Malay States the fact that times had changed, that, whilst preferential treatment for Malays would still be maintained by the Government, it was essential for the future well-being of the country that they should change their policy and accept aliens as citizens. Indirectly, it was hinted that " another Palestine " might develop in Malaya.

Most of the States were still not satisfied that good land should be handed over to Chinese, but, fortunately, there were a few enlightened examples among them. In Negri Sembilan resettlement had begun even before a policy had been enunciated by the Federation Government. Johore let it be known that it was prepared to give Chinese permanent titles to land.

With almost maddening deliberation, the policy of resettlement was accepted by each State, but even so the problem was still far from being solved. The movement of squatters raised complex problems of administrative control. Field investigations by British officers, in the face of grave danger, and aerial photographs showed the tremendous areas that had to be dealt with. Preliminary rough estimates indicated that at least 500,000 men, women, and children would have to be moved to security and new lives.

Briggs had been quick to put his finger on the squatters as being the crux of the immediate problem. He agreed with planters and experienced Government officers that moving the squatters would disrupt the bandits' source of supply and probably force them eventually to fight for their food and life.

He saw the urgent need for bringing the squatters on to the side of the Government by giving them protection from the intimidation, extortion, and murder that they so mortally feared. He knew it was essential to follow this up with a more permanent token of the Government's desire to treat them as citizens, and this could only be achieved by giving them a stake in the land.

Resettlement required careful planning, which also had to be on a national basis, because the squatters played a most important part in the economy of the country. They grew most of the vegetables consumed in the areas in which they lived. They also provided much of the labour for rubber-estates and tin-mines.

11

Uprooting Half a Million People

RESETTLEMENT became one of the greatest social experiments carried out by any Government. Nearly half a million people had to be moved from established homes to new settlements to begin a new life. It has been said since that resettlement was not just an Emergency problem. It was an administrative problem which the Government would have had to tackle in any case eventually, because the squatters were spread far and wide in the country. No one had any idea where they all were exactly or what they were doing. It would have been essential, therefore, in the ordinary course of good government to have brought them within administrative control with all the benefits of social, educational, and medical services. The effect of the Emergency, though, was to force the Government to carry out resettlement in a matter of months, instead of tackling it leisurely over years.

Resettlement was an immense and complex task. Questions of economy, communications, and security governed the choice of sites for what became known first as " resettlement areas " and much later, for potent psychological reasons, as " New Villages." The economic questions were rubber and agriculture. The squatters who worked on estates and vegetable gardens could not be too far separated from them.

Sites of new villages had to be bound by the existing system of roads, which were poor in the country. There are a little over 6000 miles of roads in the Federation, of which over 4000 miles are metalled and by Asian standards are first class. Johore, one of the largest States, has just under 1000 miles of metalled road. Pahang, the largest State, has only 600. The survey of where the squatters existed took the longest time. Generally it was a vague affair, as a clear count later showed. This was quickly followed by a survey of suitable areas of land on which the people could be settled. Survey parties, protected by ground forces, trudged hundreds of miles looking for good land which could easily be cleared of its trees and undergrowth and was near to roads and water but far from thick jungle. The Royal Air Force co-operated with air photographs of likely areas.

Every piece of suitable land had to be acquired by the Government before resettlement could begin. Then legislation imposed controls on all building materials to ensure that wood, nails, and wire did not go to luxury homes for rich people.

In the early haste to get squatters away from the Communists, little " town-planning " was done in some States. Huts were erected willy-nilly. Inevitably slums developed and forced the local authorities to carry out what became known as " re-resettlement."

The other States, however, took resettlement seriously and ordered proper town-planning. Roads and drains were laid out, houses built in orderly rows, wells were dropped, and latrines erected with an eye to health and sanitation. In all these the bases of model villages were laid.

The next great problem was staffing these areas with administrators and police.

The plan was to put a Chinese-speaking British Civil Service officer in charge of each new settlement. With him would be a young man of the country—preferably a Chinese, otherwise a Chinese-speaking Eurasian or man of any other race—who would be an assistant until he was trained to run the settlement, and then the British officer moved on to another area, and he would take over.

There was good psychology behind the desire to have Chinese-speaking men to help ignorant, illiterate, as well as frightened Chinese families to begin a fresh life under this mysterious thing called " government," of which even in pre-Japanese-war days they had taken little cognizance.

It was imperative that their confidence should be won. A man who could speak their language, who already had a glimmering of understanding of the way in which the Chinese mind worked, whose office was open to everybody, and who could say a jolly good-morning to the housewife or pat little children on the head, would succeed far better in this task than would an experienced administrator who did not know the Chinese, or who disliked them as a race and could not have cared less if they were all put into detention camps. Smiles had to be won from the bewildered, uncertain men and women, who obviously feared the meaning of government just as their ancestors in China had feared the unscrupulous war-lords.

There were very few Chinese-speaking Britons in the Government. As resettlement was top priority, they were taken from their jobs and given more important new ones. Young Civil Service officers who had been sent to Macao to learn Chinese were brought back before their course had been completed.

The search for men extended to Britain, where Christian missions were approached. Communist China had stopped the work of the missionaries, a large number of whom had already returned to Britain. Would they offer their services in resettlement work? A few accepted the opportunity of a new form of service to mankind, and they have been among the most successful resettlement officers in Malaya.

Resettlement officers were carefully selected men. Their ability to make friends, their powers of persuasion, were just as important as their competency in organization and administration. They also had to have imagination, the type of imagination, for instance, of two young Englishmen who were administrative officers in Temerloh District in Pahang, and in the neighbouring district of Triang. Their interest and zeal led to an " inter-zone " badminton competition among teams representing the Government, the police, the Army, and the new settlers. They were quite practical about it. " The settlers will get to know us better, and we will get to know them better on the badminton-courts," one said to me. " It is worth trying. It will give us and the settlers an additional interest in life."

The British officers in resettlement areas were lone Britons among strange people who might be squatters by day and either bandits or Communist supporters by night. They were the first of the new type of pioneers in the Malaya of the second half of the twentieth century. They had to introduce to alien people beset by danger not only an appreciation of government for and by the people, as in Britain, but also an acceptance of their future responsibilities as citizens in the Federation. They had little legal authority, and therefore had to employ diplomacy and their own powers of persuasion to bring this about, as well as to bring contentment to the squatters.

I have walked through some settlements where the British resettlement officer received the same friendship and hospitality as the early Malayan pioneers such as Hugh Clifford and Frank Swettenham received when they walked through Malay kampongs. Just as they spread warmth, sincerity, good understanding, and fellow-feeling among the Malays, so their successors of to-day were doing with the Chinese squatters.

I have also walked through settlements where ominous quiet prevailed, where there were sulky looks and a certain amount of hostility and stony resistance. The British officers here were men whose daily task among these hostile populations could end in death. They knew it, and it was a sign of their courage and greatness that they continued trying to win the friendship and understanding of these would-be disciples of militant Communism. Several were killed for their sense of duty to the people of Malaya.

As resettlement gained momentum throughout the country there were more and more demands for staff. The Malayan Chinese Association was asked to help to find young men who were ready to face the dangers which attended the job of assistant resettlement officers. Of those who came forward, the majority were inspired by a genuine desire to help. There was a minority, however, which saw in resettlement work an opportunity to get rich quick by corrupt methods. Those who were found out were sent to gaol.

To ensure that the energies of every available Government officer and department were concentrated on resettlement, the Forestry, Game, Mines, and Surveys Departments, whose activities had anyway been cramped by banditry, were to all intents and purposes shut down; a few clerks ran them on a care-and-maintenance basis. Their British officers were moved into the field to advise and survey, and to undertake the building of settlements.

As an illustration of staff requirements, in Johore fifty senior officers and a hundred junior officers had to be found for a hundred thousand people who were moved into about fifty settlements.

There were the problems of logistics. There was the wood and the roofing to be found for huts, reception lines, police posts, and offices in every resettlement area. For twenty thousand huts in Johore twenty million pieces of attap were required. Attap is the leaf that comes from the nipah-palm, which grows in tidal mud and round the estuaries of fresh-water rivers. Its leaves are dried, folded over a rod of hard wood or bamboo, and then stitched, thus forming a thatching material which, with not much overlap, is light and effective. As roofing material, attap can last two years. But twenty million attaps could not be obtained in the space of a few months. Indeed, the supply of attap ran out and the Government scoured the markets for alternative roofing material such as asbestos and aluminium.

Timber was also difficult to get in sufficient quantities, so the Government obtained wood from its forest reserves and sold it cheaply to settlers. It restricted the output of timber-yards to normal trade, and diverted the timber to the villages so that there would be enough wood for the fences, the huts, the police barracks, and the stations and the watch-towers to be built to bring protection to the people.

At this stage the people had to be moved. There was not enough transport available. In Johore alone the Government considered itself fortunate when it was able to buy ninety trucks from the Army for resettlement work in the whole State.

The only thing that was not a problem was finance. Malaya was in the throes of a rubber boom, and the imposition of extra export duties on the industry produced millions of dollars. The Federation Government was not concerned at this time with the money it had to spend.

Another factor was time. Briggs wanted to complete resettlement in certain States in a matter of months. It took a year to complete the work roughly in Johore alone, and then only after Briggs had cracked the whip and fixed a target date.

In most instances resettlement had to be conducted as an operation of war. From the very first hint of this new weapon against them, the Communists had directed propaganda and terror tactics against squatter communities. They did everything possible to wreck resettlement. Their propaganda frenziedly told the squatters that resettlement was a " plot to overthrow the masses' movement." Their political groups tried to form cells and even protection corps among squatters before they were moved, so that their work could be continued inside the settlements. In some areas they formed secret ' dormitories ' on the fringes of the jungle, and tried to persuade young men always to sleep in them at night, so that if the community were moved suddenly (and in many districts dominated by Communists surprise tactics by the Government were essential) they would be left out.

They tried go-slow tactics. They urged squatters to tell the Government officers who came round to them that they could not move until they had rounded up their pigs " which had gone into the jungle," or that their crops were about to ripen and should be harvested before they settled down in new locations.

The Government countered all these efforts by compensating the squatters for loss of pigs and harvests, and then either harvested the crops in due time or destroyed them if they were too far from roads.

The actual removal of squatters had to be planned to the final detail. It was a task which called for compassion, understanding, and speed. Secrecy was essential to avoid possible flight. Before first light of day, therefore, troops surrounded a squatter area. Police screened the people, and in this way caught many Communist sympathizers and helpers.

Then teams of Government land officers, veterinary experts, social welfare workers, doctors, and nurses moved in. Every man, woman, and child who was willing was medically examined and sent to hospital if suffering from any disease or illness.

Each family was allocated a truck. On it they loaded their old homes, which were easily dismantled, their stocks of food, and everything else they wanted to take. They were given receipts for livestock, such as poultry and pigs, which they had to leave behind, and later received payment for them at market prices. The squatters were convoyed to the site of their new homes under military protection.

In the actual transfer of these people to their new abodes, the British soldier played a great part. He provided the finest propaganda in showing that resettlement, although a harsh measure, was to be carried out as sympathetically as possible.

The British soldier in his jungle uniform not only kept a tight look-out for bandits who might attack moving squatters, but he also helped the old and the infirm to carry their pathetically small bundles to the trucks and then from the trucks at the other end to the reception huts.

The soldier took fowls, baskets of clothes, or babies off old women, mothers, and grandfathers, trudged behind them along the footpath, and then hoisted them all into the trucks. At the destination he helped them down again. He put up a wonderful show. The British soldier is among the greatest supporters of the underdog, and he tackled the work of resettlement with tact and sympathy.

All through the country the friendly attitude of British troops was praised, and many an old Chinese man or woman grinned toothlessly and brought a hand up to the forehead and down to the chest repeatedly in the ancient Chinese form of thanks. In Perak a group of resettled people were so grateful for the way they had been treated by the husky Coldstream Guards that they asked for and received permission to name their village Kampong Coldstream.

Resettlement was one of the more unusual tasks allotted to the troops in Malaya, but they never allowed speed, efficiency, and dispatch in picking up people and dismantled homes and placing them down again miles away to interfere with their traditional friendliness, tact, kindliness, and helpfulness.

Resettlement took two forms. Either new villages were created by bringing together all homes scattered in splendid isolation over extensive areas of padi-land, blukar, or the jungle fringes, or the limits of existing villages and towns were extended to embrace hundreds of new families brought in from near-by locations. For instance, Mentakab, in Pahang, once a town of between 3000 and 4000 people, has doubled its population. Broga, in Selangor, once a village of about 700 people, now has more than 1400 living within its barbed-wire protective fence.

Uniformity in resettlement schemes was somehow achieved throughout the Federation. Inside each new fenced-in village every squatter was given one-sixth of an acre of land—equal to two full-size tennis-courts—on which to build his shack, keep his poultry, and plant his fruit-trees.

All vegetable gardens within a two-mile radius of the perimeter of the village continued to be cultivated by their occupiers, but squatters brought in from beyond that distance were given new plots not less than two acres in size within two miles of the settlement.

Squatter families were compensated for being uprooted from their homes. Those within the two-mile radius received a subsistence allowance for a fortnight plus a cash grant of nearly forty pounds to help them purchase material to rebuild their home inside the village at sites selected (within certain limits) by themselves. Families brought in from beyond the two-mile limit received a weekly allowance to cover subsistence for five months, by which time it was expected their new plots would be in production.

Shops were opened in each village, and so were schools. Their function was not only to educate children, but to create Federal citizens and a Malay-speaking and Malayan-thinking generation in each area.

Great boars were specially imported from England to encourage better pig-breeding among the squatters. A British boar is nearly three times the size of a Malayan animal.

The task of resettlement was carried out smoothly in the majority of areas, and no persuasion or force was necessary. The only hesitant ones were those whose lives were governed by horoscopes—and even they moved house on the propitious day.

The Government was not the only surprised body when squatters began moving into settlements of their own accord. The Communists were taken aback. They tried long-distance appeals with pamphlets saying, " Beware of spies in your camp." Also, " How can you help us with food supplies? "

A directive issued by the Communist high command, captured in Selangor, dealt with the Communist attitude to resettlement. " If the masses are unwilling to oppose resettlement," it stated, " they are to be intimidated, and any of the masses trying to take refuge in the jungle as a result of our agitation should be tactfully discouraged and induced to return to their houses owing to the shortage of food in the jungle."

There was no doubt that resettlement began to hit compact bandit groups severely. Tan Guat, the military commander of a Communist company in Johore, admitted on surrender that his company's plans for food storage had been considerably disrupted by resettlement. He said that operations of any size were made " extremely difficult because of the problem of feeding a large gang. Before resettlement," he added, " bandits could visit relatives and close friends at any time of the day or night to get information."

The bandits again embarked on a jitter campaign against resettlement villages. They fired through the perimeter wires at night, cut through the wire, and burned houses and killed people. Strangely enough, not one resettlement area was evacuated by its inhabitants because of this murderous form of intimidation.

Ampang, six miles out of Kuala Lumpur, was sniped at every night by the incensed bandits, who shot from the safety of some hills overlooking the settlement. The village committee went to the resettlement officer and complained to him that the shooting was keeping them awake at night. Could something be done? R.A.F. bombers went into action for several days. After that there was peace.

The difficulties the Government faced in resettlement work were tremendous. One great problem arose from the conflicting claims of security and the care of the people. In thinking of security, the Government was inclined to harshness in achieving " results."

One tremendous obstacle lay in the fact that the Chinese as a race are not—and some say never will be—public-spirited. The entity that calls for a man's loyalty and energy is not the country but the family. His neighbour and his community mean nothing as a rule. If a man comes to some harm it is most unusual to find anyone except a relation coming to the rescue. The Chinese also hate to get involved in anything they may be answerable for. It will take a long time to instil in them a community spirit.

In two years the geographical face of the Federation was changed. Resettlement had created four hundred new towns and villages where none had existed before; it had stretched the boundaries of existing towns and villages beyond anything that had been contemplated by their planners for the next ten years. In fell swoops it had cleared great expanses of land of human habitation. In one area in North Negri Sembilan nearly sixty-four square miles of cultivated land was cleared for the sake of the security of a few thousand Chinese and Malays.

The rotting timbers of drunken uprights, the weather-torn attap roofs of evacuated huts, the tall grass growing over once-neat beds of vegetables, the jungle creeping in to dominate once again—these are the mute remains of homes and livelihoods of Chinese and Malay families who had to sacrifice their independence in areas beyond the bounds of administration for the " cause of Freedom."

12

A 'Deviationist' Executed

THERE is an affliction which strikes Communist parties throughout the world. They call it " deviationism," which is a " traitorous " misdemeanour in any Party man. In 1950, as the Briggs Plan swung into motion, the Malayan Communist Party suffered two grievous examples of deviationism by members of their Politburo. The Central Executive Committee had the satisfaction, however, of being able to execute one of the two, a man named Siew Lau. The second man, Lam Swee, succeeded in escaping from the jungle. He surrendered to the Government, and has since been considered a valuable cog in the Government propaganda machine.

The story of Siew Lau is particularly interesting and enlightening. The only aspect of the Lam Swee story that compares with it was the violent reaction of the Party to his post-surrender charges against it. Government experts on Malayan Communism described Siew Lau as a " would-be Malayan Tito." He held a most important position in the Communist hierarchy. He was State Secretary and terrorist leader in Malacca. As State Secretary, he was automatically a member of the Central Executive Committee. A Malayan Chinese, he was born in 1923 and educated in Kajang, in Selangor. He spoke English and Malay well. He became a schoolmaster, a rather well-educated and intelligent one, a contrast to the general run of Chinese school-teachers then in Malaya.

He joined the Malayan Communist Party some time before the Japanese war, and he was among the original recruits it sent to the Special Training School in Singapore to be trained as a guerrilla. He eventually became a leader in the M.P.A.J.A. in Johore. After the declaration of the Emergency Siew Lau was appointed political commissar in North Johore. Eventually he was given control of Malacca. It was probably because of his influence that terrorism in Malacca never achieved the heights it did in neighbouring States. Siew Lau was never a militant Communist.

Some of his writings which came into the possession of the Government marked him as a "true Communist." That is, his knowledge of the theory of Communism and the teachings of Marxian Leninism was comprehensive; he was an idealist. He had studied the theory of Communism intensively and from afar watched it being put into practice in various countries. He considered he knew exactly what should be done in Malaya when the 'revolution' opened, and he reacted violently after studying the policy directives of the Central Committee.

Early in 1949, when he was undisputed leader in Malacca, he wrote three theses severely criticizing these directives. They were entitled, "Rectify our mistake, and fight on with determination," "Keynote of the Malayan Revolution," and "Discourse on the principles of equal distribution of rubber-estates." His "Keynote" particularly brought him into disrepute with his brother Committee comrades.

In it, after a critical examination of the Malayan situation, he drew several conclusions:

(*a*) That the Party had been compelled to adopt a "defensive" and "passive" policy due to the great weight of the British Government attack, to its inability to establish a firm supply base, the poor standard of its army, the inadequate and inferior quality of its arms and ammunition, and the loss of what he called "operational grounds" (the trade unions which had formed the foundation of the People's Movement).

(*b*) That these weaknesses, in their turn, were having a demoralizing effect on the Party members. Some, conscious of the fact that the majority of the operational grounds were Chinese, and that the Chinese must bear the full brunt of the British attack, even "doubted their chance of survival."

(*c*) That under these conditions any prolongation of the armed struggle was suicidal, because the "defensive" and "passive" policy was not only doomed to failure but would also seriously impair the future fighting strength of the Party, both militarily and politically.

(*d*) That a prerequisite condition of success in the armed struggle was the creation of a strong racial front and a large army founded on the mutual economic interests of the three main races, the Chinese, Malays, and Indians.

Siew Lau thought that armed revolution was " indispensable " and that it provided the only effective means of dislodging so powerful an enemy as the British Imperialists. He agreed also that the primary objective of the armed struggle must be the outlying villages, where the influence of the British was weakest.

In Malaya, he argued, over seventy per cent. of the population consisted of labourer-farmers and farmers whose one outstanding demand was for land. The answer to this demand, therefore, was land reform which gave to farmers and labourer-farmers the right to own the lands they tilled and to share in equal parts the lands developed by, and confiscated from, the British Imperialists and their henchmen.

He emphasized that heavy industries in Malaya were pitifully few and the number of industrial workers proportionately low, that rubber-workers constituted the greatest force of workers and the great majority of them were Chinese and Malays, and that the proletariat, therefore, was weak and could achieve nothing without the co-operation of other classes and races.

The pressing task was the mobilization of the Malays for the overthrow of the British Imperialists. Without Malay support and participation in the revolution, hope of success was " an idle dream." Without their support, the tasks of establishing bases in backward hamlets and ultimately of driving the British from the towns and villages could not be achieved.

Siew Lau held the view that, because of the dependent nature of Malayan economy, Malaya could not become a Socialist State till long after the revolution, though the general trend of development must consistently be towards Socialism. He visualized three stages of development:

(*a*) The production by individuals of small articles of merchandise, and of rubber, coconuts, and pineapples from small estates and plantations.

(*b*) The expansion of private enterprises, light industries, and medium-sized rubber-estates.

(*c*) The nationalization of commercial enterprises, industries, plantations, mines, and transportation, with nationalized enterprises and co-operative societies competing with, and finally exterminating, individual capitalists. The rubber-estate land which would be divided in the initial stages would ultimately be reformed into large estates.

The Central Committee lost no time in attacking Siew Lau. It published a long directive condemning his " open opposition," and sent it by couriers to bandit commands all over Malaya. In the course of this " instruction," it said:

> Siew Lau and his supporters are unwilling to accept the basic principles of democratic centralized policy of the Party—the minority should submit itself to the majority—the whole Party should submit itself to the Central Executives. His booklets are a tissue of lies, many of them the result of ignorance.

The Committee was furious that anyone should dare to challenge its statements, and it described him as a " deviationist." That marked the end of Siew Lau.

It declared that his policy of land reform differed in material respects from that enunciated by the Politburo in its " Plan for a People's Democratic Republic " announced in January 1949, and that his views and attitude offended the fundamental principles of democratic " centralism."

It contended that his notions on the nature of Malayan rural economy were misconceived. Although the land which produced rubber might be classified as agricultural, " when regarded from the proper social and economic standpoint it fell fairly and squarely, with tin, into the industrial class, and was, in fact, an enterprise for the production of raw material."

It was a fatal error, therefore, to place rubber-workers in the category of peasants, and to conclude from this that the rubber-workers were entitled to equal shares of the rubber land to be confiscated from the British Imperialists. On the contrary, the Party plan was to nationalize, or socialize, the big rubber-estates owned by British Imperialism in the interest of the peasants.

Referring to Siew Lau's criticism of the Party's failure to obtain the support of the masses due to its inability to offer tangible benefits, the Executive adhered to the policy of the " greatest happiness of the greatest number," which, in its implementation, it said, demanded the sacrifice of the interests of the minority to the interests of the overwhelming majority.

Central's charges did not deter Siew Lau. He continued thinking and writing. In August 1949 the Central Committee issued fresh instructions for dealing with him. These instructions were recovered by a patrol of the 4th Battalion the Malay Regiment from the body of a bandit courier killed after a short engagement.

Siew Lau was to be demoted, and, in the event of the slightest suspicion of defection, he was to be destroyed without hesitation. " It is not necessary to wait to follow the rules and agree with Siew Lau," said the instruction. " It is essential to isolate and destroy his influence." He was to be " checked up," and if there was no evidence that he was " an enemy spy," and if he was " willing to accept criticism," then he was to be punished by being made a reserve member. However, if he was not willing to accept criticism then " he must be destroyed." The instruction blandly and cold-bloodedly added that " if watching his movements and actions are tedious, then it will be better to go ahead and destroy him without further bother."

In November 1949 Siew Lau was expelled from the Party. He was allowed to live with his wife, but under guard. There were reports that they worked as rubber-tappers on a remote Chinese estate in Malacca with another leading Communist in Malacca, a man named Chee Ping, who had been demoted from platoon commander.

Although he was carefully watched, Siew Lau still went on writing pamphlets and booklets. Indeed, he sent letters to his friends asking them to join him in his fight against the Party leaders. Some of them did.

He exposed the actions which he thought were wrong. He disagreed with the stealing of identity cards from the public and with the policy of slashing rubber-trees. He criticized the Executive openly for the way they employed the bandit forces. He called them " Ngau Kung," which means " Buffalo Communists." It was an alarming situation for the Central, for there was a possibility of Siew Lau's views spreading.

Then the Party leaders began to fear that he would seek the opportunity to surrender. In April 1950 they ordered his execution. In May he and his wife and some of his closest supporters were shot by Communist killer squads.

After his execution, the Central Committee issued their reasons for killing him. They brought additional charges against him: unjust criticism of the democratic life of the Party in order to satisfy his personal ambitions; splitting the Party organization and policy; refusal, despite expulsion from the Party, to admit the error of his ways; and displaying tendencies which if allowed to remain unchecked would inevitably lead to his defection to the British Government.

To make these charges clear, the Central Committee quoted the following examples of activities subsequent to his expulsion from the Party in November 1950: an attempt to enlist the assistance of another comrade in order to reach the "outer perimeter" by obtaining an identity card; persisting in writing a book entitled *Discourse on the Principles of Equal Distribution of Rubber-estates*; and inciting other comrades to treachery by distorting the principle of democratic centralism, and by accusing the M.C.P. of lack of grasp of the fundamental principles of Marxian Leninism and the misapplication of these principles to conditions in Malaya.

A member of the Federation Government who studied the Siew Lau case thoroughly gave me this note:

> It was not unique. It was cold-blooded murder by Communists in the name of Communism. But Siew Lau was exceptional by Malayan Communist standards. He was an idealist. His quarrel with the Central Committee, unlike that of Lam Swee, had its origin in a genuine divergence of opinion on matters of high policy and not in any reasons of personal spite.
>
> Blatantly frank and open in his criticism, indiscreet in his letters, he never by word or action permitted his distaste for Central to outweigh his hatred of the British Imperialist. Nor did he plot treachery or physical harm to its members. He was confident in the justice of his cause and the correctness of his reasoned attitude and determined, to the point of obstinacy, and despite the inevitable consequences, to stand by his principles in defiance of superior authority.
>
> By contrast, the members of Central appear characteristically sensitive of criticism, conscious of the inherent weaknesses of the present situation, and ruthless in their determination to smother

any deviation from the set party line. Even had Siew Lau succeeded in his intention of reaching the "outer perimeter" it is exceedingly doubtful whether he would have contacted the authorities, or whether, if compelled by events to do so, he would have assisted them in any way to defeat the Communist threat.

Lam Swee was a different kettle of fish. He had been a member of the Party for more than ten years. He surrendered out of sheer pique because he had been demoted. Nevertheless, his was an important surrender—indeed, the most important up to that time, for he had been a member of the Central Executive Committee.

Born in 1917 in Ipoh, in Perak, of Cantonese parents, Lam Swee became a rubber-tapper. He came to Singapore in 1939 and joined the Communist Party. He was a clever young man, but he was not a real Communist. He said after his surrender:

> I did not make a deep study of Marxian Leninism. I read some documents on Communism and understood that the realization of a communistic society must necessarily pass through the stage of socialism before arriving at the communistic society, which was the most desirable social order among men. Therefore I entertained grave dissatisfaction regarding the existing social order, and at the same time longed for the realization of a new, logical, free, and equitable social order, in which each would be given full opportunity for the manifestation of the best he possessed, and in which each would be enabled to obtain what he needed. Everybody would have rice to eat, and everybody would find employment. There would not be man preying upon man or man killing man.

In Singapore Lam Swee, through the manipulations of the Communist Party, became the secretary of a stone-masons' union on a near-by island. He left this a few months later, returned to the village of Rengam, in Johore, where his mother was living, and became a barber. During the Japanese occupation he became an important cog in the Communist wheel in North Johore.

After the war, when trade unionism was spreading throughout the country, the Communist Party appointed him secretary of the Singapore Federation of Trade Unions, and later gave him the important job of General Secretary of its Pan-Malayan Federation of Trade Unions. By this time he had set up a barber's shop in Singapore with borrowed money.

On June 16, 1948, he followed other Singapore Communists

into the hills of South Johore. He was appointed local leader. He eventually rose to the position of political commissar attached to Central headquarters in Johore, and soon afterwards became commander of the 4th Regiment in Johore.

After his surrender Lam Swee sat and took months to write a booklet which he entitled *My Accusation*. This was his retort to a denunciation of him by the Central Political Bureau entitled *Lam Swee's Surrender to the Enemy and Betrayal of the Party*. The accusation that he was a traitor to the Party filled Lam Swee "with intense disgust."

In his booklet he disclosed that there was dissension among the comrades of his Regiment over the "callous" attitude towards the troops of the Central Committee. He said he had presided at an "indignation meeting" of his platoon commanders, one of whom said he "felt good only when members of the Central Committee were arrested and shot." Lam Swee added, "The question of shooting Central members was not discussed in the meeting, only the means to solve the existing difficulties."

Just about this time, Lam Swee said, he began to have little confidence in the "success of the revolutionary undertaking," but he had no desire to surrender. However, as the months passed, "the hateful Malayan Communist Party Central took every measure to create ideas and plans to get rid of those who went against them, so that I was finally forced to take a risk. If I had not escaped in time to surrender, sooner or later I should have been murdered by these conspiring elements."

What he meant, of course, was that he had been demoted, relieved of his badge of rank and his pistol, and that Central even refused to allow him to retain a hand-grenade for "self-defence."

At this time Lam Swee had a 10,000-dollar reward on his head. He and the troops of the 4th Regiment had moved from South Johore and were operating in South Pahang.

Lam Swee walked out of the jungle and into the police station at Bentong, Pahang, to give himself up. The date was June 27, 1950, but the Federation Government did not announce his surrender until November. In the interim period he had, as a traitor, told them everything they wanted to know about the terrorists in Central Pahang and Johore. He proved more than willing to answer questions.

He has since proved an excellent anti-Communist propagandist. In July 1951 he went on a six-weeks' propaganda tour in his old hunting grounds of Johore, and lectured to crowds in estates and villages numbering from 500 to 2000.

To-day Lam Swee enjoys a very considerable degree of personal freedom. He spends all his time writing.

13

Journey through Malaya

IN the beginning of January 1951 a Chinese colleague, Goh Teik Boon, and I were sent to find out how the battle was going and to write about every aspect of the war, which was soon to enter its fourth year. Our job lasted two months. We travelled hundreds of miles, every bit of it by road, including the " red roads," meeting men of all strata, including surrendered bandits.

The Federation Government gave every assistance. Indeed, it went further. It opened confidential files to me. It also instructed all officers from Mentri-mentri Besar (Prime Ministers) and British Advisers down to district and resettlement officers to talk to us freely, untrammelled by any fear of consequences for not " saying the right thing." That letter was the open-sesame to the hearts and tongues of British, Malays, and Chinese who worked for the people and, by doing so, faced death every day.

For me it was a revelation to find a new throbbing spirit dominating the country. I met young British civil servants who had become old before their time, grey hairs thick on their heads and lines of weariness in their faces, but their eyes burned brightly with the sincere belief that the initiative was with them now, that the Briggs Plan was the right one going the right way, and that Briggs, the man, was the right leader. Many, in fact, were optimistic enough to say they saw the end in sight.

They were critical, too. Despite the arrival of a few hundred men from Britain there was still a shortage of manpower. There was still too much paper-work for the police and the district officers. There were still dunderheads at Government and police headquarters in Kuala Lumpur, who knew little or nothing about the men in the field. Those chairbound officers were the stumbling-block to real efficiency. They ran their secretariats and their little departments in the same maddeningly slow way that they had done in peace-time. Letters had to be in duplicate and triplicate. Copies had to go here, there, and everywhere. Minutes and files were imperative before a decision could be made or a reply given to an obviously urgent Emergency matter. Those men in Kuala Lumpur created as much paper work as they could so that the well-worn path of Government red-tapery could be trod. It was disheartening, because even Briggs could not break this system.

The cry of the police was for more armour. Too many lives were being lost in ambushes, which formed more than 40 per cent. of the total of bandit incidents. The police travelled on duty and to scenes of incidents in vehicles unprotected by armour. They moved in open trucks. They trundled along dangerous roads in wooden-sided lorries. They were open targets.

Mr Gray, the Commissioner of Police, was vehement in his refusal to put his men behind armour-plating, contending that this would destroy whatever " offensive spirit " they possessed. He was bitterly attacked, but he remained adamant until public opinion in Malaya and in Britain forced the Government to counter his policy. By that time, however, the police had lost many valuable officers and men. By the end of 1950 two hundred and twenty-two had been killed, sixty-four more than in the previous eighteen months. Three hundred and twenty-one had been wounded—double the number for the previous period. It was a sorry story.

British and Asian police officers began to regard themselves as sacrifices offered in the anti-Communist war. Their wives lived under a more agonizing mental strain than the wives of planters and miners. They were terrified when they saw their husbands rushing off on a mission in their naked vehicles. They were thankful when they saw them return, but the agony continued every day.

More than one police officer who described narrow escapes in ambush said to me, " We could do absolutely nothing. We just had to get out of our vehicles, leaving behind the men who had been killed and wounded in the first burst of fire, and fight back from whatever cover we could find—if we reached it. The only reason *I* am alive is because the bandits withdrew."

The police devised a system for foxing bandits who might be

waiting on tortuous stretches of roads. A mile or so from these danger-points the men jumped off their trucks, and then walked up along both sides of the road while vehicles went ahead to a rendezvous at a safer point farther along. In this way only the drivers and a couple of men were targets for the bandits, who, on the other hand, might be surprised in their positions.

The police did not regain confidence until they found themselves on a par with the Army, who had already been equipped with armour. They had to wait more than two years before this happened.

It took only three weeks of travelling and talking to feel the new atmosphere. When I began to write my articles on the situation I opened optimistically but cautiously, by saying, "I have found a breath of victory in the Federation. There is a new spirit and a new hope." The signs were there too.

Maps in the joint-operations rooms throughout the country gave a graphic picture of how the situation had changed in six months. Black pins showed how large enemy groups, which had once been clustered in thick masses in almost every State in the west of the peninsula were now widely dispersed and broken into small gangs. Almost all these gangs were now ringed with the red pins of security units.

In their secret rooms the police had a formidable tally of the M.R.L.A. and the Min Yuen. Every police district headquarters had compiled a dossier on many of the Communists operating within its boundaries. This was a most remarkable achievement and a tribute to the painstaking methods of efficient policemen. From surrendered bandits, from agents, from captured documents and photographs, they had built up these files. An elaborate index-system enabled them to identify a killed bandit in a few hours.

Where bodies of dead bandits could be manhandled easily out of the jungle to the nearest police station for identification, this was done; but each Army-police patrol went out on operations equipped with a simple box-camera to photograph the face of dead bandits. These photographs were checked with those in the secret rooms or shown to surrendered bandits. A name would then be scored off and a file marked "Dead."

The vast machine which General Briggs had set in motion was now at work. It was helped on by an extended Intelligence system, resettlement of squatters and agriculturalists, the regrouping of estate labour, and some control over the movement of food.

The hard core of bandits headed by the Central Committee was being forced away from its source of existence and power, its thousands of willing or unwilling supporters. The wedge that was splitting the two halves was the gradual movement of more than 400,000 people from isolated areas to new protected settlements.

The impression I gained was that the Federation Government and its security forces was in nearly complete harness at last for the slow drive to establishment of law and order. There was quiet optimism from the planners in Kuala Lumpur right down to the commanders in district battle-grounds, in some of which the enemy was beginning to show signs of despair.

The confidence was there, but it was tempered with common-sense caution born of more than two years of hope and frustration, and of the realization, too, that before *finis* was written to this Red Emergency the embittered Communists could be expected to hit back by any means in their power.

General Briggs himself hoped that, by the middle of the year at least, the three priority areas of Johore, Negri Sembilan (together with Malacca), and South Pahang would be cleaned up. The military and the Government machine would then turn to flushing every other bandit area.

Although the first object was to kill bandits, it was realized that the morale of the bandits must be broken. This would inevitably lead to the disintegration of the part-time followers. It would leave the " hard core " isolated in the jungle, where they could either stay or come out and fight for their food and their lives.

Figures showed part of the success-story. The onset of the Briggs Plan in 1949 had stirred up bandit activity. The black graph of incidents had joggled up and down in the hundreds month after month—380 in April, 509 in May, 457 in June, 354 in July, 426 in August, 558 in September, until it reached a peak of 571 in October.

The situation then was grave. In Johore six battalions of troops and more than 2500 police could make no impression on a few hundred bandits of the 3rd, 4th, and 9th Regiments.

Early in November General Briggs had changed the military tactics. He put an end to unwieldy, wasteful operations carried out in battalion and company strengths. The groups into which the bandits had broken down their regiments and platoons were sought out by flexible, small patrols. Guerrillas were to be fought by guerrillas. The police were to be left to dominate the towns, the villages, and resettled areas.

The Security Forces were hammering at the cracks in the jungle armour. In many areas the enemy was hungrier and was finding it difficult to get food. As against this, there were still many stubborn areas, where the bandits had plenty of food supplies and where they were building hidden dumps for the future.

My travels supported the picture of a changed situation. I joined an expedition that was about to proceed into South Pahang with Sir Henry Gurney and General Briggs. Under a light escort we motored in convoy the forty-five miles from Kuala Lumpur southward to Seremban. Then we turned north and took the notorious Jelebu pass. Our escort was three jeep-loads of policemen. The Jelebu pass had been an evil road along which the enemy had inflicted serious losses to security forces in well-planned ambushes. Then cunning was matched with cunning, and the bandits holding the pass found themselves ambushed instead. The Army took control of the summit from which the bandits had had an untrammelled view of all traffic. There is majestic scenery along the Jelebu pass, and it was a relief to be able to look at it appreciatively without having to wonder what was going to happen round the next bend and the next and the next . . .

We arrived at the little rubber-growing town of Bahau. It is also a main station on the railway line which has been pushed northward again through Pahang and Kelantan to the north-eastern port of Tumpat. It was rebuilt on the track of the pre-war line. The railway was indeed a boon to the people in the country through which it ran. It was their only means of communication. Up and down it took people and freight. However, isolated as it was, the line had been a popular target for Communist saboteurs. They had continuously torn up the track between the district of Jelebu and Bahau and then south to Gemas. They had shot up the slow-moving passenger trains trundling the people with their rubber, vegetables, and rice. The railway had suffered an average of an attack a week. Sometimes it was so badly mauled that travel was disrupted for days. The people who used the train had learned to be patient about trips to town. They knew they had a very good chance of being stuck by the wayside for many hours while the sabotaged track was repaired. There was little doubt that Communist supporters living along the line were responsible for much of the sabotage. Once sixty yards of railway track were removed in two hours, the time lapse between up- and down-trains on this particular section. The work showed the technical skill of permanent-way labourers, and railway experts were emphatic that at least fifty men equipped with the necessary tools must have been engaged in this quick bit of destruction.

A considerable number of troops and police were concentrated between Jelebu and Gemas to patrol the line and chase bandits after incidents. Railway labourers no longer lived in their brick-built lines along the track. They had been withdrawn to the comparative safety of the nearest village. Too many railway tools had been stolen by bandits, and there was also concern that, out of fear, the labourers if they were left in isolation would be forced to help the bandits. So the labourers were taken to work every morning under a police escort, which stayed with them the whole day to protect them from attack.

The security forces used armoured trains, which had absolute right of way between Jelebu and Gemas. These trains proved most useful in the war in the parts where there were no roads at all. On one epic occasion the commander of a Gurkha battalion which was following up a large force of bandits used the line to push fresh reinforcements into the chase every day until the enemy disappeared into dense jungle and went into hiding.

Resettlement appeared to have had an effect on sabotage of the line because attacks on it had become less frequent. A twelve-hour curfew from 6.30 P.M. shut down life in every village and kampong within half a mile of each side of the track.

We climbed aboard one of the four armoured trains which roved up and down the twenty miles of isolated track. It was not a comfortable journey. The heavy train jolted over every foot of the line. We rolled past the empty blocks of railway labourers' houses standing desolate in their weed-covered clearings on the edge of the track. Their emptiness was all part of the great, expensive plan to give security to every one living in isolation and vulnerable to militant Communism.

Gurney and Briggs got off at various halts. The first was at a place called Kemayan, where there was a new settlement of six hundred people, set on a ridge below which was an airstrip.

We met men who were seeing a High Commissioner for the first time in the history of this part of the country.

Kemayan was run by its own elected committee. Wai Chee, forty-six-year-old headman of fifty tappers, many of whom had lived in the area for sixty years, had gone off on election day to the near-by town of Kuala Pilah, to marry. He returned to find himself elected first chairman of the village committee. His wife became the ' first lady ' of the settlement.

We journeyed on and stopped again, climbed into motor transport and travelled two and a half miles over a road laid down by the Royal Engineers to a new settlement of agriculturalists at a place called Paya Lang, once the rice bowl of the bandits in South Pahang. It was a neatly-laid-out village of three hundred zinc-roofed homes, occupied by 1200 Chinese. Every agricultural squatter in the district had apparently come willingly into the relative security of the wired-in settlement. They humped everything they owned on their backs or on bicycles and lugged them to the site of their new home.

The Chinese headman was one of the cheeriest individuals I met in the whole of my two months' tour. He was outright anti-Communist, and his grizzled face broke into delighted smiles as he showed Gurney and Briggs around his domain and proudly told them that Paya Lang was so self-sufficient already that it had begun to sell rice to neighbouring villages.

Our next stop was Triang, a little village on the banks of the Triang river. It was also the local military headquarters. Attached to it was a new settlement of smallholders, men with money of their own, becoming richer with every day that the price of rubber went up.

The District Officer said that when resettlement had been mentioned to them they agreed to it on the condition that they paid for their own homes. The Triang ' suburb ' became one of the neatest of its type in the whole country. The smallholders laid it out as a garden village. One resident said to me, " We want to grow trees along our roads and build a temple for our community."

Triang was still in the process of erection. We walked past smiling Chinese nailing windows, hingeing doors, or laying sheets of corrugated zinc on to the roofs. Piglets crossed our path. A little Chinese girl played with a pet—a brown- and black-striped baby wild boar, caught in the jungle some distance away.

A little farther north was the one-street village of Mengkarak, which had been attacked by 150 bandits a year before. Here Gurney met the village committee and gave it the first stern warning of the trip: " The Government does not want to punish this village, but if it does it is because you have not helped us."

This warning was really not deserved, because, according to the District and Army officers, the village had been co-operative. Gurney's words, however, had the effect of making the village committee think still more; the threat also went up and down the line by word of mouth.

So, without any incident, we eventually arrived at Mentakab, a town which had doubled its population of 3500 in the past months, as all people living within five miles of it had been brought within its extended perimeter. The same thing had happened to Temerloh, an important town six miles east. The stretch of river along which both towns sit was closed to river traffic to prevent possible food supplies going out by water.

When chain-link fencing had been erected around both towns there were no Chinese living outside any wired-in towns or villages in the extensive isolated territory between Mentakab and Bahau, over forty miles south. Thirty-five thousand people had once lived scattered lives in that stretch of land, which was beginning to give itself back to jungle.

I stayed in Pahang to learn how the Briggs Plan had changed this seriously afflicted State, whose greatest limiting factor for operations was lack of roads in its 14,000 square miles of jungle and padi-land. The tale was the same as I was to hear later in every other State I visited. The completion of major resettlement schemes and the regrouping of estate labour were making the bandits desperate for food.

Jungle bands operating in the Bentong-Karak-Manchis road—where in Japanese days the M.P.A.J.A. had one of their greatest strongholds—had been warned by their leaders that supply sources were poor and that they could expect worse times. A few bandits who had surrendered had been "terribly emaciated," said police officers.

Pahang's enemy was a well-organized, well-led jungle corps known as the 6th Regiment. In two and a half years of war the security forces had found 950 of their camps, each of which had accommodation for from 10 to 600 men. Like bandits elsewhere, those in Pahang carried what the British Intelligence described as "emergency rations" on which they fell back whenever supplies were short in their meanderings from one feeding-place to another. These included a tin of British rolled oats, and it was in Temerloh that I heard the story of how one bandit had lost his freedom through his tin of oats.

Mr D. W. Stewart, a young British Administrative Officer in Temerloh, was walking with a group of policemen through an estate after serving resettlement notices to Chinese squatters when the younger junior Chinese Affairs Officer with him gave a quick, low warning. About seventy yards ahead a uniformed Chinese was talking to Chinese estate labourers in front of their lines. He wore a three-star red cap, and was armed.

The Chinese Affairs officer and the bandit fired at each other at the same time. Both missed, and the bandit disappeared round a smoke-house with the others after him.

They turned the corner to find tall grass in front of them but no bandit and no movement. Thinking he might be hiding in the grass, Stewart threw a hand-grenade forward. He then saw a movement and fired in its direction twice. A voice cried out in pain, but the man disappeared again.

Stewart and his men went forward. They picked up a hat which the bandit had left behind. They next saw him slipping down a slope into a ravine some distance away. They shouted to him twice in Malay and Chinese to stop, but he retorted with a hand-grenade, which landed ten yards from his pursuers. It was their turn to run. They did so for three seconds, then flung themselves flat on the ground. The explosion did not injure any of them.

The police put a cordon round the area, and Stewart and his Chinese officer began a close search along the banks of an eighteen-inch-wide stream in the ravine.

Stewart then noticed the red colour on a tin of British rolled oats, standing out brilliantly against the green ferns and undergrowth in the stream. He thought it strange for it to be there, so he stooped to pick it up. It would not come away from its "bed."

"I pulled again," Stewart said later, "and then saw a pair of eyes looking up at me. It was the bandit, lying on his back in the stream with ferns and undergrowth cunningly placed around his head. His feet were well in the water. The tin of oats had been strapped to his belt. I jumped back, and we covered him with our guns as he scrambled up."

The bandit was only eighteen years of age. He had two wounds, and he still carried two grenades. He was a Min Yuen food collector, and had been interrupted in the estate during his work.

It was in Pahang, too, that I heard the most fascinating stories of how kampong Malays had revolted against the domination of some Malay bandits who had styled themselves the 10th (Malay) Regiment, M.R.L.A. Cloak-and-dagger tactics broke this 200-strong force and led to thousands of Malays in Pahang buckling on their parangs to face the threats of Chinese terrorists.

The original 10th Regiment operated in preponderantly Malay territory in North Pahang, north of the Karak-Mentakab-Temerloh road, through the riverine kampongs, up to the Pahang-Trengganu boundary. This vast area, criss-crossed with little streams struggling through forest and sparkling through kampongs, was inhabited by simple-living Malay padi-growers, who observed the laws of Mohammed religiously and acknowledged the sovereignty of their Sultan if they felt like it.

Pahang Malays have always been a strong-minded set. Their history records wars with other Malay States and among their own chiefs. In 1892 a Pahang chief, Bahman, of the district of Semantan, which now borders the Karak-Mentakab road, rebelled against his Sultan and the British. A force was led against this fierce and turbulent fighter, and he was vanquished. Strangely enough, it was in this same district of Semantan that in 1950 sprang the seeds of the revolt against the domination of Communist-minded Malays, most of whom were of Indonesian stock.

The 10th Regiment was led by a Malay named Wan Ali, who seemed to bear a charmed life. Soldiers of the Malay Regiment and police jungle squads had failed to get him. Among the Malays he had built up a reputation for "invulnerability," because he was reported to wear charms. He had a bodyguard of six Malays, and he roamed where he liked and was contemptuous of the people around him. " Might is right " was his motto, and, because his area of operations happened to be territory far from Government administration, the inhabitants dreaded him.

Wan Ali's wife, Samsir Pakeh, helped him considerably by running the Malay supply organization. She had Malay women assisting her. The only difference between them and the other women they talked to was that they carried hand-grenades which they had been taught how to use.

Another prominent bandit was a young, stockily built man named Wahi Annuar. He was attached to a gang which was harried so much that he decided to leave it. He slipped away and then wandered eleven days in the jungle without food before giving himself up to the police.

Like many other Communist leaders, however, he had surrendered out of sheer pique. As he said afterwards, he had been promised the command of a " Malay Regiment," but he had found that it was, in fact, about two hundred men and women, many very old, and all " ruthlessly " dominated by the Chinese, and he was not its commander.

A third important bandit was squint-eyed Manap Jepun (" Manap the Japanese "), a name that came to him because his mother had been Japanese. He was born in the Temerloh area of Pahang in 1919, and he was sent to a Government English School in the State capital of Kuala Lipis. On the outbreak of the European war, like quite a number of other Malays in the country, he joined the Federated Malay States Volunteer Force, a fighting unit. During the Japanese occupation he traded on his Japanese descent, turned traitor, and became notorious in Pahang, if not throughout the country. Like many other Malay youths, he developed into an ardent nationalist, and when the Malay Nationalist Party was formed soon after the liberation of Malaya he became secretary of the Temerloh branch. The Malay Nationalist Party was extremist in its views and its actions, and it was eventually banned by the Government; but Manap Jepun allied himself with the Malayan Communist Party, and he followed it into the jungle on the outbreak of the Emergency.

When the Party arranged to form the 10th (Malay) Regiment

Manap sat on the Regimental Board of Command. One of its first platoons was handed to him for command, and one of his first acts was to murder an Indian veterinary officer travelling in a motor-car on duty.

At this time Manap was thirty-three years of age, a sharp-faced, slightly stooping man. He was a savage and ruthless terrorist. Kampong folk fled their homes when they heard he was in the area. He murdered and plundered in his fanatical efforts to force the Malays of Pahang to support the Communists. All the same, he was casual in some of his duties, a trait which did not endear him to his Chinese masters, who were great disciplinarians. In 1949 they demoted him for neglect of duty, but he did not sink utterly into oblivion. His star was to rise again much later.

The existence of the 10th Regiment was alarming to the Government, for if it succeeded in its work there was every possibility of other pockets of Malay resistance being formed in the name of nationalism, if not of Communism.

To the Malays in the kampongs the bandits were *Musang berbulu ayam* (literally " foxes in chicken skins.") Nevertheless, they were frightened of these " musangs." The Regiment held sway so completely that little information about them was given to the Government, and aggression against them could only be negligible.

It became imperative that something should be done. It seemed that this could only be done by falling back on the use of intrigue —and in the history of pre-British Malaya the courts of Pahang Sultans and chiefs had been dominated by intrigue.

A young Malay named Yeop Mahideen was selected for the onerous, exciting, and dangerous task of bolstering up the morale of riverine Malays, of building up their resistance, and, if possible, breaking up the 10th Regiment. Yeop Mahideen was the ideal man for the job. He had been among a small number of Malays who had escaped from Malaya when it was overrun by the Japanese. In India he had joined Force 136, and he had been parachuted into the jungles of Pahang to build up a resistance among the Malays. In this he had done outstanding work. An essential part of his new job was to rally anti-Communist Malays in each frightened kampong, instil them with faith in the project, and then secretly arm them. Yeop Mahideen decided to work on his own. He made Temerloh, the heart of Malay Communism, his headquarters. He knew that the job of winning over antipathetic Malays, even though they were anti-Communist, was going to be a tough one. Their antipathy had developed out of the lack of Government administration, the failure of the Sultan and his officers to go among them, the lack of counter-propaganda to rebut the claims and promises of the Malay Communists, and the comparative freedom of the Malay bandits from onslaught by the security forces.

The peasants had swallowed the promises of the bandit leaders that when the Pahang Government was defeated they should receive everything that had been denied them. The small Chinese community among them was indifferent. They described their own attitude by quoting a Chinese proverb—" I follow the river. If it bends I travel crookedly; if it is straight I travel straight."

However difficult the problems facing him, Yeop Mahideen realized that initial successes might result in a sweeping victory. He set to work to achieve them. The first area that he worked in was Sanggang, a little district north of Temerloh. It was in danger of being cowed by unruly elements in the neighbouring area of Bangau, which was completely dominated by the 10th Regiment. Two Malay kampongs standing opposite each other on the river secretly agreed to form kampong guards of twenty men each. They were quietly armed with shot-guns and told how to defend themselves. No sooner was the existence of kampong guards known than the Malay bandits harassed them almost nightly, but fortunately the two kampongs held out. One kampong in fact advanced to meet a number of bandits heading towards them and drove them away, a victory which raised the spirits of the 3000 people in Sanggang. It was not long before guards were formed in other kampongs in the district.

The next difficult area to win over was Bukit Segumpal, south of Temerloh, a remote mukim (parish) where bandits held sway. They had forced the penghulu (headman) out of his kampong, but, instead of fleeing, he had gathered around him about forty loyal friends, and they had created their own kampong.

" When I arrived all I had to do was to provide them with arms; they were ready to fight," said Yeop Mahideen later.

One night, reinforced by the police, these kampong guards raided a Malay bandit camp near by. The bandits fled, leaving behind nine rifles and a tommy-gun. It was a real victory. Very soon bandit influence in the mukim waned as more people plucked up courage to stand up to them.

Also in the Temerloh District was Mukim Songsang, completely under bandit domination. Here too the penghulu had been driven out and forced to stay in Temerloh town.

The leader of the bandit group was Budin bin Choh, who had a price of 2000 dollars (£235) on his head. In an atmosphere of deep conspiracy two Malays planned to kill him. They had no weapons. They made Budin's acquaintance. They offered him a mat in their hut whenever he wanted one. They fed him, they laughed with him. They became in two months great friends. One night they waylaid him and killed him with shot-guns that had been smuggled in to them, piece by piece.

The next day armed kampong guards suddenly appeared in Songsang. They too had been armed secretly, and they repelled three bandit attacks. Morale rose and the penghulu returned to his home.

Later Wan Ali, a notorious leader, was shot dead in Pulau Tawar. It happened like this.

One day ten kampong guards who knew him volunteered to get him. They were brought before the Sultan of Pahang, and they took an oath to kill Wan Ali. Like the killers of Budin, they contacted Wan Ali and pretended to agree to his plans, because they had already received the Sultan's titah (royal approval) to proclaim themselves anti-Government in order to achieve their end. They noted Wan Ali's movements. They learned his habits. He boasted of his invulnerability, but this, they thought, could be looked after when the time came by specially prepared bullets over which prayers had been pronounced.

Early one fine morning they got Wan Ali as he was coming out of his hut in the kampong. He was dressed in his uniform, ready for whatever the day might bring him. He toppled down the steps in death. His bodyguard of six put up a weak retaliation and then fled. The two Malays carried Wan Ali's body to Jerantut in triumph, and there received 10,000 dollars reward and the congratulations and thanks of the Sultan.

Jerantut district, which Wan Ali had terrorized, breathed again. It was the beginning of the end for the first 10th Regiment, and

SEVEN CHINESE TERRORISTS WHO SURRENDERED TOGETHER IN PERAK

Third from the right is the leader of the party, himself the vice-commander of the Communist company. His wife is third from the left.

Photo "Straits Times"

A SAKAI GIRL WITH THE SHOTGUN SHE KNOWS HOW TO HANDLE

A Malay Policeman

A fine example who has been fighting the terrorists for many years.

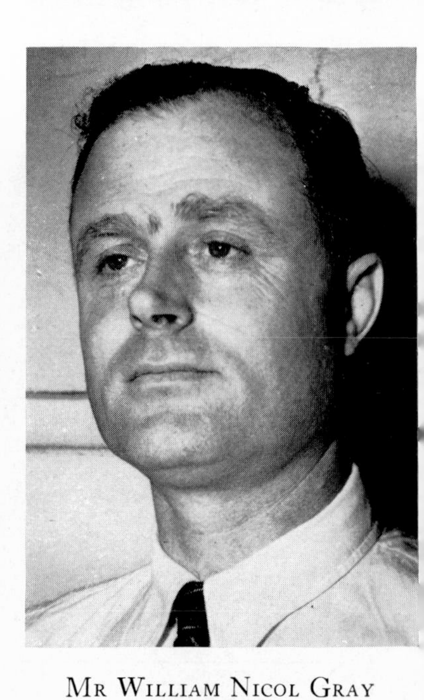

Mr William Nicol Gray C.M.G., D.S.O.

Commissioner of Police, Federation of Malaya from 1948 to 1952.

Photo "Straits Times"

Mr Michael Codner

One of the heroes of the famous 'Wooden Horse' escape from a German prison camp during the war, he was killed by Communist terrorists in Malaya.

[*See p.* 206]

Photo "Straits Times"

Awak anak Rawang

With the George Cross he won in Malaya.

Photo Sarawak Information Department

soon afterwards his successor, Wahi Annuar, surrendered in the same district.

Wan Ali's death, and later the surrender of Wahi Annuar, broke the 10th Regiment. In three months about a hundred men surrendered, and the rest of the organization deteriorated so rapidly in morale that it was distrusted by the Chinese masters. It was inevitable that the Central Executive Committee should strip it of its last vestige of authority, but its downfall was not taken lightly by them.

They planned to reorganize as soon as possible. They diverted some of their best Chinese guerrillas to the survivors, giving the unit a firm base. They sent it to work in the Kuantan area. Manap Jepun was restored to favour and given command of one platoon. There was no denying his smartness. He built up a good intelligence system, which always came to his aid when security forces planned attacks on his camps. On many occasions he flitted from his camp just before the attack.

He recruited men by force and he stole guns. His operations were well-planned. He employed " Q " tactics. Once a group of special constables appeared in a village. The sergeant in charge said he had been sent to inspect the village's armoury. He paraded the village constables without guns. His own men walked into the armoury and walked out with the shot-guns. Their sergeant followed them very soon afterwards. He proved to be Manap Jepun.

His Sino-Malay force operated in the Kuantan district, along the east coast, and menaced south Trengganu. Manap Jepun won almost legendary fame on the Pahang-Trengganu border. Nearly every incident was attributed to him. Two years later, in May 1952, troops of the 1/10th Gurkha rifles met twelve bandits in the jungle twenty miles from Kuantan. They shot at a man wearing a red-flowered sarong who had turned to escape. Bullets shattered his jaw and thigh and killed him. A loaded sten-gun dropped with his body.

When the body was brought to the Kuantan Hospital mortuary a hospital assistant noticed the squint eyes and a mole on the right side of the nose.

" It's Manap Jepun," he cried, and it was.

14

School for ex-Terrorists

AS my journeys continued I found bright spots and dark shadows in every State and Settlement. Squatter resettlement had begun to smoke out the bandits, who were making spirited efforts to build up stocks of food.

In Pahang men of the 1/10 Gurkha Rifles uncovered a tank normally used for latex, similar to the petrol-carriers on trucks, buried on the fringe of a rubber-estate. Only a small section of its turret was visible. Removed from its chassis, the tank had been filled with two and a half tons of rice and other food. After its burial rubber-tappers had stamped down the earth around it with their feet.

In Johore the forces found food-dumps which could have kept small bandit groups going for six months.

There were also contrasts in the atmosphere of neighbouring towns. While Bentong, in South Pahang, was free from menace, Raub, only twenty-five miles to the north-east, still lived in fear.

Raub is a picturesque gold-mining town. Malaya's only gold-mine lies two miles from it. In the jungles around it were bandits who relied on supplies from the 5000 squatters living on land owned by the gold-mining company.

Gold smuggling was rampant. Much of it went into the bandits' treasury. There were more goldsmiths in Raub than in any other town of its size in the Federation.

The roads out of Raub were no-man's-lands. In the town business closed early, and although there was no curfew, the streets were empty after nine o'clock. Some residents were on the bandits' black-list. One prominent Chinese, it was reported, had not gone out of his house for nine months.

The gold-mine itself had long been a Communist target, so it maintained its own private army, which included Gurkhas recruited from Burma, and Malay, Sikh, and Indian auxiliary policemen. At strategic points in its 9000 acres of hilly land, all good ambush country for bandits, stood defence towers, armoured with steel. Every house in the mine occupied by a British or Australian miner had its own bullet-proof room.

The mine had its own fleet of armoured cars, used not only for journeys round the property but also along the two twisting miles of road to Raub. Motor-cycles became unpopular for the town trip after the escape of one miner who was passing a group of 'grass-cutters' when one of the men took a swipe at him with his scythe.

The Raub police were having a busy time suppressing terrorism. Their enemy were three companies of the 6th Regiment. Among their souvenirs was an "efficiency" pennant captured by five privates of the 2/7 Gurkha Rifles after a moonlight ambush on a large force of bandits. The Chinese characters on the pennant proclaimed that it was a Communist award to the headquarters section of the 25th Independent Company, 6th Regiment, on August 25, 1950, for exemplary conduct during a "bravery and efficiency period." The Communists were beginning to hold these morale-boosting periods frequently, and gave prizes to groups which had shown bravery in the face of the enemy by pulling their wounded or dead colleagues away.

I found that territories had their own peculiar problems. Ipoh, the capital of Perak, had two. The first was that it had suffered more grenade-throwing attacks by sneak terrorists than any other town in the country. There seemed to be no method of counteracting these attacks except with information about the grenade-throwing group. But no information had been forthcoming. The police took an unusual security measure. They banned bicycle-riding in the town after 7 P.M., because most grenade-throwers had escaped on bicycles. The ban, coupled with increased patrols on the streets by auxiliary police and Home Guards, stopped this sneak terrorism. The gang apparently declined to operate by day.

The second problem lay in the numerous limestone hills ringing the town. They are fascinating places, these wooded limestone outcrops, but they have hundreds of caves which make perfect lairs for bandits. There are obvious physical difficulties in clearing these hills of Communists.

Selangor had not yet felt the impact of the Briggs Plan, and it was depressed. Planters and police declared that until more troops were available in the State there could be no substantial improvement. Kuala Lumpur, the Federal capital, a sprawling town, was the headquarters of a vast supply organization for the bandits. The Min Yuen was several hundreds strong. Many large Chinese businesses were paying protection money. Kuala Lumpur was feeling the strain of the Emergency. There was a sense of insecurity, an undercurrent of fear, even though the town was packed with police and ringed with troops, because it was essential to guard this Government capital and the person of the High Commissioner against frontal assaults by fanatical Communists.

In the north the rich island of Penang was held in thrall by a group of fifteen men who formed a killer squad. This was a strange but stark fact. Nearly 200,000 people on the island, among them men earning incomes of nearly 12,000 dollars a month, declined to give any information whatever about the terrorists.

The precise reason for Penang's attitude was difficult for the police to determine, unless the Hokkiens and Teochews, who form the main part of the Chinese community which was the most affected by terrorism, were observing the age-old trait of not allowing anything to interfere in their normal daily occupation of making money. The Penang Chinese were markedly unwarlike.

Communist activity in Penang island was run by the Penang Town Committee, which formed a part of the Northern Malayan Bureau of the Central Executive Committee. It had two offshoots, the Penang Anti-British Alliance Society, which was the equivalent of the Min Yuen on the mainland, and a strange organization called the Bereaved Families Relief Society, about which little was known.

The Anti-British Alliance Society was most active. It ran a Women's Branch and a Students' Branch, which, under the guise of the Penang Students' Association, carried out much of the non-violent Communist work in Penang. This association was causing concern as its tentacles extended into every possible sphere of youth activity in Penang. It was recruiting Chinese youths from both Chinese and English schools. The Party was using all the school organizations, including the Boy Scouts, for its own purposes.

The average age of the members of the Students' Association was seventeen years. The boys were organized into cells of four, each of which had specific tasks, such as collecting subscriptions or distributing the Penang Communist pamphlet *True News*. Some of the more indoctrinated boys acted as couriers in Penang and worked on the mainland occasionally. The cells met wherever they could.

Whenever it was possible to do so the Penang police had quietly warned parents of the Communist activities of their children. Some parents went to extraordinary lengths to prevent their sons and daughters " going Communist."

One girl was indoctrinated in a Chinese school. When her father, who lived in a Federation town a long distance away, was told of it he brought her home and kept a close eye on her for five months. She was then permitted to go to an English school in Penang, but she again picked up her old contacts. The police arrested her and informed her father, who, emotionally upset, said to them, " Kill her."

In Perak is the pretty little town of Taiping, nestling under a group of hills up which climbers and hikers used to go at week-ends before the Emergency. The Taiping hills became notorious bandit lairs, and from their hideouts the terrorists to-day can look down upon a finely laid out school, established principally to reform Communist-minded men and women. Taiping is a Chinese word meaning " Great Peace and Tranquillity." The school is popularly known as " The School of Great Peace and Tranquillity." It stands on the delectable site of the pre-war race-course, which had been the pride of the district.

The establishment of the school was inspired by experiments at Macronissos, in Greece, where ex-Communist guerrillas were prepared for entry into the Greek Army, and at Wilton Park, in England, during the War, when Nazi prisoners-of-war were shown by practical demonstration and lectures what advantages a free democracy had to offer over a military autocracy. There are, of course, important differences between Taiping and the Macronissos and Wilton Park schemes.

Taiping has to conform to the peculiarities of the Chinese character. It cannot carry a patriotic appeal, as did the experiment in Greece, nor can it appeal to the intellect, which was the policy at Wilton Park.

The majority of its pupils, known as Hok Uens (students), were illiterates. They had no loyalty to Malaya, and they had to be treated like grown-up children. Most of them went into Communism by force of circumstances rather than through any deep political convictions.

The Taiping school does not set out to convert Communists into democrats. Its theory is simple. By educational and vocational training, followed by resettlement, it hopes to be an antidote to anarchy. Taiping, to quote one of its supervisors, " conditions Communists so that they can take their place in society without danger to that society, and educates, or re-educates, them mentally, morally, and physically into the type of free citizens who will be a credit to their land of adoption."

As the Emergency continued it became necessary to detain more and more people, and the problem of what to do with them presented a real challenge to the Federation Government. It was decided to continue to detain the tougher cases, to repatriate aliens either voluntarily or compulsorily, and to release the others either unconditionally or on bond. The Taiping camp represents part of the third method.

Prospective inmates of Taiping go through a fine-selection process before they are accepted. The initial choice is shared by the police, by Detention Committees of Review, and by various Chinese-speaking British Government officers. Admission is limited to Chinese men between the ages of eighteen and forty (the average age is twenty-six), who are not known members of the Communist Party, and who are not accused of crimes of violence. They include food-suppliers, subscription collectors, spies, recruiters, propagandists, couriers, and supporters generally. Every man has three official interviews with the Superintendent. On arrival he is told in Chinese what the camp is and what is expected of him. " We do not discuss politics at all," the Supervisor told me. Politics is also avoided by the staff when they mingle with the detainees.

The second interview some weeks later traces the progress made by the Hok Uen. If it is satisfactory his occupation after release is discussed.

At the final interview just before release he is told about his future responsibilities and warned of the two dangers encountered after release which can lead to his rearrest. The first danger is from the bandits, who, on learning of his release, might try to inveigle him into helping them again. The second is from the police, who naturally remain suspicious of him until he has proved himself a good citizen.

In one year only one man was rearrested by the police after release. Immediate investigation by the Supervisor of the school disclosed, however, that he had been arrested for being a member of the New Democratic Youth League—for which he had already served detention. He was released the same afternoon.

How long does a detainee have to stay in Taiping before he is considered fit for release? The period varies from two to six months or even longer. His behaviour and reactions are carefully watched and reported, and it is on these reports that a decision is made. His resettlement is considered to be the most important phase in his rehabilitation, and it is here that the Malayan Chinese Association gives considerable assistance by finding him work and by keeping in close touch with him later.

The school, quite naturally, has been the target of attack by the Malayan Communist Party. There have been two lines of Communist propaganda against it, the usual one that any detainee who enters it will be severely beaten and tortured by the Government, and the second that on leaving it he will become a Government agent. This is a much more difficult line to counteract.

It is a fact that the very first batch which came to Taiping had to be forced into trucks at the start of their journey to the school. They objected strongly to being transferred to Taiping, and their objection was assessed by the Selection Board as being natural fear rather than recalcitrance or insubordination. On the day of their departure they became mutinous. They were still difficult to control when they arrived at the camp. The Supervisor who received them recalls that " at the end of the following day, after they had been interviewed and shown their facilities for education and recreation, their sullenness had gone. They were polite to the staff and among themselves, and they had obviously decided that there was nothing to be feared."

This change of attitude is one of the most noticeable features in the day-to-day existence in the school. The Hok Uens arrive from their detention camps badly demoralized by the close confinement and the aimless existence they have led. The well-laid-out school with all its amenities provides a sharp contrast, and the hope of release takes some of the sullenness out of the men. The freedom they experience brings them out, and they enter into all the activities with enthusiasm.

I was told that instances of continued Communist activity after admission to Taiping are rare. In detention camps, on the other hand, there is a high proportion of well-indoctrinated Communists, who organize groups to intimidate other detainees. In Taiping the few indoctrinated Communists speedily become known to the Supervisor and his staff. The other students do not fear them and invariably report the slightest hint of Communist activity.

The armed guards around the perimeter of the school are posted more for defence against possible raids from the terrorists in the hills above than to prevent escapes from within. The single barbed-wire fence is certainly no effective bar against escape, and no secret is made of this fact to any Hok Uen on his arrival. He is also told that any attempt to get away will mean recapture, return to a detention camp, and loss of the chance of freedom and self-respect. There have been no attempted escapes at all.

Nowhere in the whole of Malaya have I seen more agreeable conditions for detention than in Taiping. Brightness and cleanliness predominate. In between the long, attap-roofed dormitories, which can accommodate 600, are flower-gardens and vegetable allotments developed by the Hok Uens. There are pitches for basket-ball and badminton, and teams occasionally go into the town on parole to play against local sides.

The grandstand from which punters once watched their winnings or losses pile up now house offices and classrooms, and workshops for carpentry, tinsmithing, motor mechanics, bicycle repairs, tailoring, and cobbling. Poultry, duck, and rabbit farms thrive. The Hok Uens are paid seventy-five cents a day for work which is remunerative to the school generally. This money goes into a central fund for extra comforts for all. The men have their own Chinese orchestra, and the radio set is popular. At the beginning of the Chinese Communist attack in Korea they listened assiduously to Radio Peking. No ban was placed on this, for it was considered that any attempt to prevent listening-in to Peking would not be in line with the democratic way of education within the camp. The Hok Uens, however, were casually referred to the versions of the war as published by Malayan Chinese newspapers sent daily to the camp's growing library, and it was noticed that as time passed the radio was rarely tuned in to Peking.

The Hok Uens awake at 6 A.M., answer roll-call a quarter of an hour later, have breakfast at seven, followed by physical training. ' School ' begins at 9 A.M., with a break at 10.45 A.M. for the midday meal. There are more classes between 11.45 A.M. and 1 P.M., and then there is a resting period until 3.45 P.M., after which games are played.

Following the Chinese way of living, the last meal of the day is served at 5.45 P.M. ' Prep ' occupies four hours from 6 P.M. The Chinese, Malay, and English languages and arithmetic and book-keeping are the basic subjects in the school. At the time of my visit fifty Hok Uens were also learning Jawi, the Malay script, in addition to the Malay language.

Vocational training during school hours is varied. The school has even turned out its own women's hairdresser. The Hok Uen who wished to learn this profession was allowed to work in a saloon in the town on parole. Fifteen men were working on various jobs outside the school at the time. Some were learning to handle bull-dozers. Three times a fortnight there are cinema shows. American Westerns are the most popular.

The camp's staff consists mostly of Chinese, but includes Malays and Indians, who are employed either as teachers, instructors, or clerks; but, whatever their category, they all fit into the life of the school. Their relationship with the Hok Uens is " Friendliness without easy familiarity, discipline without bombast, and no courting of popularity on either side."

The Supervisor is always prepared to give practical examples of how re-education in Taiping has produced useful citizens, and how the school functions as a valuable weapon against Communism. As an example, a well-educated Hakka Chinese, aged twenty-nine, was a schoolmaster before his arrest as a Communist. In Taiping he took classes in Chinese studies. On his release he returned to his village, where he received such a friendly and warm welcome that his former headmaster offered to re-employ him.

He has revisited Taiping frequently, lectured to the inmates, and also clubbed together with several other released detainees to sub-scribe 100 dollars to the school for the furtherance of its objects.

There was also a twenty-year-old, almost-uneducated Cantonese forest labourer, who was at first lazy and sullen, then became a good student, showed an aptitude for motor mechanics, and ' graduated ' to a garage in Taiping as an apprentice fitter.

" To date," said the supervisor to me, " the results have been good and up to the expectations of those who conceived the idea in the face of much criticism from certain factions in the country." Opposition once existed to the scheme, and this was due to the mistaken notion that here was an idealist's paradise rather than a very practicable and workable solution to a difficult problem.

Taiping appears to be succeeding in its aim of making ' good Chinese,' with the hope that the instruction in the Malay language, coupled with the lectures and films on Malaya, will encourage these men to develop ultimately into ' good *Malayan* Chinese.' This is even more important.

15

High Commissioner Murdered

THE Briggs Plan gathered momentum, but its great scope, which made more and more demands on the police, the Army, and the people most closely concerned, proved its weakest point.

Its first year was primarily intended to turn much of the Army into semi-guerrilla units to contact the terrorists on the fringes of the jungle. Its second most important task during that year was to ensure that no armed Communist forces interfered with the resettlement of squatters and the regrouping of estate labour. It was essential, too, that the Communists should continue to be harassed, so that they could neither rest nor reorganize.

Briggs said, " The terrorists must be baffled everywhere in their attempts to dominate the populated areas." He insisted that they must not be allowed to maintain their supply sources or organize new channels for them.

Although the original terrorist supply and extortion organizations had been disrupted by the resettlement of the squatters, they still had widespread reserves, and they adopted new tactics to get more. They scattered among the remaining squatters and especially among estate and mine labourers, whom they intimidated into feeding them and aiding them in incidents such as rubber-tree slashing.

It became obvious that steps had to be taken in the estates and mines to break up these supply lines. As a Government spokesman pointed out, up to this time the machinery, but not the labourers, in both these industries had been specially protected by guards. Briggs therefore ordered the regrouping of labourers and placed the responsibility and cost on the shoulders of the employers, much to their indignation.

Regrouping meant concentrating the homes of labourers near to already stabilized defence areas on estates and mines in order to avoid erecting more defence posts and employing more special constables. In many instances it meant abandoning during the Emergency brick and concrete homes and erecting temporary wooden shacks for labourers. It meant extending barbed-wire fences and installing perimeter lighting. For companies it meant the extra expenditure of thousands of dollars.

Each estate and mine presented a separate and distinct problem, and regrouping committees, which included representatives of the planting associations, were formed to solve them.

As the programme developed the terrorists established a system of food dumps planned to maintain them for an indefinite period until they were able to renew and reopen contact with their former helpers in the resettlement areas and in the estates and mines. It was known all over the country that labourers and villagers were obeying the orders of Min Yuen agents to take from their homes one cigarette-tin of food each daily and to give one day's pay per month as protection money to the Communists. They had also been ordered to pass food over the fences around their newly situated homes.

Something had to be done immediately to dam this flow of supplies.

General Briggs marked the beginning of the fourth year of the Emergency in June 1951 by announcing sweeping regulations to control food and supplies. This was Operation Starvation, and it was Part Two of his plan. It was to be a sustained offensive to prevent food, medicines, and fighting material leaking out to the M.R.L.A.

Briggs wanted to win over the people of the country to aid the Government and the security forces in this new phase of his campaign. He wanted Home Guards to be formed quickly to assist in the task under supervision. He demanded the active co-operation of estate- and mine-managers.

He drew up a list of foods that were to be denied the Communists through restricted sale in shops and control in movement. He listed padi, rice, tapioca, cooking-oil, sugar, salt, concentrated food, tinned foods, cooking fats, dried fish, paper, printing materials, drugs, medicines, vermicelli, and rice products.

Villages, small towns, resettlement areas, and labourers' homes were to become guarded food larders. Any area from which bandits got or could get their food supplies might be declared "food-restricted areas."

Residents in these areas were bound by law to keep a thirty-five-yard wide belt round their perimeter fence clear of undergrowth and obstacles to make it difficult for terrorists to creep up unobserved by day and night. They were forbidden to take out of their homes any amount of food, however small. All meals were to be eaten in the home. The ban extended to clothing and money. Only essential amounts of each might be carried out of a controlled area.

Shopkeepers had to keep full records of customers and their purchases. The State Government had the power to restrict the number of shops in an area by closing some down.

Except for fresh fish, shell-fish, fresh vegetables, fresh fruit, live poultry, and eggs, no food could be moved by road anywhere at night. All transport carrying these foods had to cover their consignments with tarpaulins, which had to be securely roped down. Their drivers could not halt anywhere along the roads except within town or village limits. They could not turn off their direct routes or unload except at their proper destinations.

Theoretically nothing had been left out of these all-embracing measures to cut supplies to the bandits. Briggs told the people, "You will now be able to say to the Communist extortionists when they approach you that you are no longer able to bring them food, money, or other supplies." Indeed, this was a device advocated by the Chinese themselves. "Force us by law to stop helping the terrorists, and we will do so. Do something to us which will enable us to tell the Communists that we really cannot help them any more, otherwise we shall be punished by you," they said.

Briggs made his final appeal: "This is a people's war; I am calling on you, all of you, to help fight this war. By preventing the bandits from obtaining the food and other articles they want, you will be helping to defeat them."

Operation Starvation did not, however, hit the Communists badly in the beginning. None of the villages and estates and mines had Home Guards worthy of the name. Governments seemed to have no plan for organizing and training volunteers. Certainly they had not the weapons to arm them, and they did not want to issue too many weapons for fear they would fall into terrorist hands.

The police were expected to switch as quickly as possible from being a fighting unit to a peace-preservation corps. This was beyond its capabilities, because, with its great expansion and the urgent need to get fighting men into the field, peace-preservation had not been a part of the hurried training of police constables in the past three years.

Concentrated as they were in villages and resettlement areas they had become almost immobile, and as time went on their offensive spirit had slackened. In addition the Special Constabulary, an untrained force to whom the Government had paid scant attention, showed venal tendencies and turned blind eyes on the Communists, and open palms to the terrorist parties foraging for food round resettlement areas.

The terrorists divided their gangs into small units and concentrated on rebuilding their supply lines. The incident rate rose rapidly again, and optimistic hopes were dashed.

Sir Henry Gurney and Briggs were worried men. There seemed little prospect then of persuading the people to co-operate because they had not yet the security they demanded. And then Sir Henry was assassinated.

On the morning of Saturday, October 7, 1951, Sir Henry and Lady Gurney left King's House, their residence in Kuala Lumpur, for the cool of Fraser's Hill, sixty miles north. They often did so at the week-end.

Fraser's Hill is approached by a twenty-mile-long road that winds through most attractive jungle scenery. It is also perfect ambush country. For some inexplicable reason the bandits had never staged a serious ambush on this road. It is probable that neither Sir Henry nor his escort—six policemen in a vehicle ahead and a radio van and a police scout car behind—were expecting trouble. Gurney disliked large escorts, and agreed only to the minimum necessary. He had always refused to travel in an armoured car.

Inside his Rolls-Royce Sir Henry sat behind the driver on the right-hand side. Lady Gurney was on his left. Next to the driver was Sir Henry's private secretary, Mr D. J. Staples.

The convoy came under ambush at an S-bend in the road. Bandits in the undergrowth on a hillside on the right crippled the first vehicle. All the constables were wounded, but they jumped out, took cover, and returned the fusillade. At once Sir Henry's car came under concentrated fire. Its wheels were punctured, and it came to a standstill on the left-hand side of the road about forty yards from the first vehicle. The driver had been hit, but he managed to apply the hand-brake.

Lady Gurney dropped flat on the floor of the car. Mr Staples and the driver crouched under the dashboard. Sir Henry, however, opened the door beside him, got out, and closed the door behind him. He began to walk towards the high bank on the side of the road, but he was shot dead before he reached it. Possibly he thought that by leaving the car he would draw the fire away from his wife, and this was what happened. Neither Lady Gurney nor Staples knew what had happened to Sir Henry until the firing stopped.

Then the driver left the car and threw himself under the cover of the embankment towards which Sir Henry had gone. Lady Gurney and Staples remained in the car.

Intermittent fire continued for about ten minutes. Then a bugle was heard, the bandits withdrew, and firing stopped.

Staples called to Sir Henry, but there was no reply. Lady Gurney said she was unhurt, but she wanted to find Sir Henry. With Staples she crawled from the car. They saw Sir Henry lying near a culvert. When they reached him he was dead.

Lady Gurney, a brave woman, remained there with Sir Henry's body for forty-five minutes until reinforcements came.

When the car was examined later it had thirty-five bullet-holes. Twenty-six had entered from the rear. Investigators of this outrage estimated that the bandits had been in position for at least thirty-six hours.

The S-bend was 200 yards long. Ambush positions for at least thirty-eight men were dotted along all its length. They had been well prepared. Palm-leaves and fresh attap screened the gun positions from the road twenty feet below. The undergrowth had been beaten down at several places. Each ambush position was marked with a 'flag.' One of them was made from a pair of red pants hanging on a bamboo pole. These pants drooped at the main firing-point, a twenty-foot boulder surrounded by bamboo thickets. The boulder commanded a perfect view of the road for more than a hundred yards. It was linked by natural tracks to three other smaller positions near by. Another track led into the jungle. It would have been possible from one of the smaller positions to see Sir Henry's car coming and to signal to the men in the main position so that they could open fire when it appeared.

Police experts declared the bandits had been armed with two bren-guns, a sten-gun, and rifles. They found a note-book which showed that the bandits had posted three firing sections and three 'charging squads.' These squads were generally used to capture the weapons of victims killed or injured. Another document found noted the movements of motor-cars and other vehicles up and down the road from 10.05 A.M. to 3 P.M. the previous day.

It was from police headquarters twenty-four hours after Sir Henry's death that I obtained a copy of this log, which had been discarded by the bandits as they withdrew after the assassination. It was a carefully planned operation.

FRIDAY

10.05 A.M. One motor-car and one jeep with a red-cross sign. Two persons in front and five persons at the back. Soldiers in uniform.

10.47 A.M. Two big-sized military trucks, with four British soldiers, fully loaded with goods, covered by tarpaulin.

11.45 A.M. Eight trucks and three armoured cars (British soldiers). Two fully loaded big-sized trucks.

12.05 P.M. The first jeep with three persons, English. After five minutes another large-sized military truck fully loaded with Gurkhas. About forty persons.

12.30 P.M. A car with a red flag with an armoured truck behind.

1.00 P.M. From Tras [a village a few miles to the east along the road], two military trucks with soldiers (British) and one private car. [This entry, when checked by the police, revealed itself to refer to the escort and car bringing the Chief of Staff, Far East Land Forces, General Poett, back from Fraser's Hill to Kuala Lumpur.]

1.30 P.M. From Kuala Kubu Bahru, two motor-cars.

2.10 P.M. From Tras, three trucks with English soldiers. One of the three is an armoured car travelling very slowly and very alertly. [This was checked as a security patrol.]

2.30 P.M. From Kuala Kubu Bahru, eight large-sized trucks carrying foodstuffs and about two sections of persons.

3.00 P.M. From Kuala Kubu Bahru, three large-sized empty military trucks.

Sir Henry Gurney speaking to Malay Kampong Guards

Shortly before his assassination by Communist terrorists.

A FIJIAN SOLDIER

He is wearing the sort of hat that they call a jungle hat in Fiji. It is made from plaited vines and leaves.

Photo "Straits Times"

MAJOR E. T. CAKOBOU

Second-in-command of the 1st Fiji Infantry Regiment, he was an administrative officer in Suva.

Photo "Straits Times"

A NYASALAND SOLDIER

Taking it easy in his jungle camp.

Photo "Straits Times"

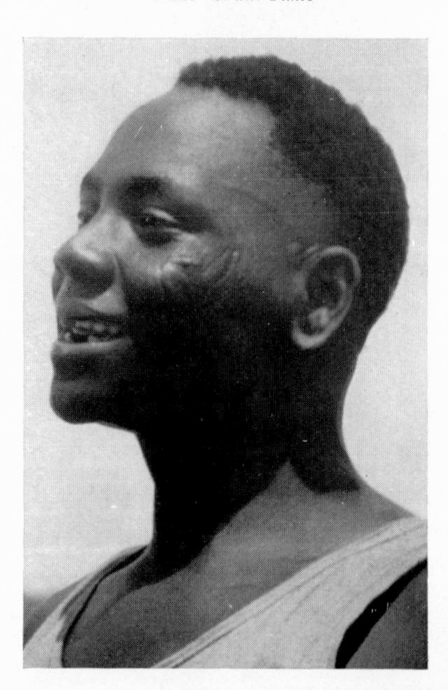

AN EAST AFRICAN WARRIOR FROM THE MKAMBA TRIBE

He shows the tribal identification mark on his face—an arrowhead cut into both cheeks.

This ended the observations for Friday. A curious point was that it should have ended so early in the afternoon. One police theory was that the bandits had left then for a camp situated some distance away.

The most curious fact, though, was that on Saturday morning the bandit observers made only one entry in their log. It was:

10.35 A.M. From Tras, five trucks, two of them armoured, with Malay and English soldiers.

The question in most minds was why the bandits did not continue noting the traffic after 10.35 A.M.

It was after assessing this log that the Federation Government came to the conclusion that the ambush was not laid to intercept Sir Henry Gurney. Neither the Government nor the Army have ever admitted that the bandits were lying in wait for Sir Henry or that there had been a breach in security which may have informed the Communists of his trip, and so allowed them to plan the ambush specifically for him. He did not decide to go to the Hill until the previous Thursday, but his house there had to be prepared. It is not unlikely that telephone-calls were made from King's House, in Kuala Lumpur, to The Lodge, the Hill house, warning the caretaker and servants of His Excellency's arrival on the Saturday. It is not unlikely either that food had to be purchased at the Hill for the visit. On Friday a little truck loaded with the Gurneys' baggage climbed the Hill from Kuala Lumpur. This could have been seen on the Hill.

It has been argued that if the bandits had not really been waiting for Sir Henry they would have attacked military vehicles which had used the road on Friday. Even on Saturday morning ten minutes before the Gurneys arrived the bandits could have attacked a ' soft ' convoy which moved down the road with the Naval ensign fluttering from the bonnet of the centre car. Inside that were the Flag Officer, Malayan Area, Rear-Admiral H. W. Faulkner, and his wife; but the waiting bandits did not make any attack until they saw the Rolls-Royce with the Crown and the Federation pennant flying on its bonnet.

That was how the second High Commissioner of the new Federation of Malaya died. In the three years that he had been chief executive Sir Henry had won from the Malayan people high praise for his courage and his statesmanship. He had regarded his job as a mission and a crusade. He believed in the brotherhood of all men.

Sincere, able, and highly principled, he had worked for the peace and welfare of the people of Malaya. He travelled fearlessly through the worst bandit areas to see for himself the work of the security forces and of his Government officers. He was a brave man, and he insisted that the Federation flag should flutter from the bonnet of his car whenever he used it. He wanted to show the people that it was the 'Tuan Governor' who was flying the flag, and that he, the 'Tuan Governor,' was not afraid of the Communist scum. He agreed to escorts and other necessary precautions—but that flag had to be on the bonnet of his car. He sincerely believed that his expeditions into the ulu, to the resettlement areas, to the small towns and villages, and up-river to isolated kampongs were an essential part of his job during the Emergency, and he is still remembered in those out-of-the-way places.

Not long before his death he had spoken prophetic words:

> We know it to be true that this war is not to be won only with guns or the ballot-box or any other material instrument which does not touch the hearts of men. Nothing less is at stake than truth itself. The true British contribution to the future strength and structure of Malaya, born as it must and will be of a tradition of long centuries of political freedom, has perhaps yet to be seen.

The murder of Sir Henry loosed against the Communists a bitterness unsurpassed in the three years of fighting. It is unfortunate that the Government did not take advantage of the opportunity to use this widespread emotion to the uttermost.

The largest force ever gathered to unearth a tiny group of bandits failed in their task. It was not their fault. The jungle was too thick, the odds were too much on the side of the fugitives.

As the Royal West Kents moved off into the jungle after the ambush Gurkha troops, men of the 12th Royal Lancers, of the 93rd Battery of the 23rd Field Regiment, Royal Artillery, and the police also went into action. They each had a specific task. The Royal Air Force, flying every day from Singapore, and the guns of the Royal Artillery, operating from the main road, put down a curtain of fire. The bombs and the shells fell in a pattern designed to make, as an observer described it, " a sort of moving box with the lid open at the place where the Gurkhas wanted the gang to go."

It was a supreme effort by the forces to avenge the death of a man who was not only the High Commissioner, but one who had been admired by all; and it failed. The little gang was able to move and hide in the protective jungle. They found the loop-holes in the box, and they escaped.

Then their tracks were picked up again. The main Gurkha force took up the chase, maintaining it at the fastest pace possible, and that was from 800 yards to a mile a day. Two days later the Gurkhas were three hours behind the gang. The bandits began splitting into small groups. They moved round in circles in a desperate effort to confound the trackers.

At this moment ill-luck dogged the pursuers. Violent rain and a thunderstorm slowed up the Gurkha trackers and washed away the bandit tracks.

So it went on until a month later the operation was called off. Five members of the gang had been killed. The rest had retreated deep into the jungles of Pahang.

A month after Gurney's murder the Government descended on the little town of Tras, which stood just a few miles from the scene of Sir Henry's death. Tras was a ' sealed lips ' town, the most tightly sealed in Pahang, if not in the Federation.

It had a bad Emergency record. In three years fifteen battles had been fought in or around it, twenty people had been killed and fourteen wounded. There had been twenty-five attempted murders. Twenty-four supply dumps and fifty-two bandit camps had been found round the town. It had been the main source of supply of food to the bandits in Western Pahang. Captured Communist documents had named it as a centre of immense importance to the terrorists in Western Pahang. It had its own Protection Corps Organization, but this had not been revealed to the Government.

The final indictment against Tras came when a man was killed as he tried to break in through the cordon which had been thrown round the town on the day Sir Henry was killed. From his body, police recovered a bundle of letters to Tras sympathizers and relatives from the men who had killed Sir Henry. They wanted food, medicine, and money.

Early on the morning of Wednesday, November 7, troops, police, and Government teams moved into Tras to obliterate the place.

The Government detained the 2000 inhabitants under the dreaded Emergency Regulation 17D, which permitted the collective punishment of the entire population of an area. Tras was closed as a centre of life. The Government never disclosed why action had not been taken against Tras earlier. Why had Tras been allowed to assist the Communist cause for so long?

The killing of Sir Henry Gurney brought the entire question of the direction of Malaya's war, leadership, operational responsibility, mobilization of manpower, action against the fence-sitters, and other aspects under scrutiny. There was a fresh determination to end the war. There was a cry for new policies, new drive, new blood, a more dynamic approach.

The Government began by calling for sincere public co-operation as one way of avenging Sir Henry's death:

> "If every citizen who is worthy of the name will translate into action the abhorrence which he must feel for the crime, we have the ability quickly to rid this country of the terror which lurks under cover in holes and corners, and claims its victims, striking now at the highest in the land, but even more often at the lowest. I ask you —do not leave this feeling of abhorrence as a pure sense of regret and frustration."

This was the way the Attorney-General, Mr M. J. Hogan, a personal friend of the Gurneys, put it, broadcasting in his temporary rôle of Officer Administering the Government.

The public of Malaya pondered, paid tribute to the memory of Sir Henry Gurney, mentally hitched up its trousers and sarongs with an oath of determination, and did nothing at all. The reason was simple. The Communist victory at the U-corner on the Fraser's Hill road had had a shattering effect on public morale, which had fallen low indeed.

Back in England the British Government—now Conservative—was forced yet again to face the unremitting problems of Malaya. General Sir Harold Briggs was retiring in November, so they appointed General Sir Rob Lockhart to succeed him as Director of Operations. General Sir Rob, who was fifty-eight, had retired from

India in 1948. The Federation Government announced that he would be given new powers which would make him virtual supreme commander in all spheres relating to the Emergency. This seemed to indicate that the British and Malayan Governments had at last, after forty-one months of Communist terrorism, realized the need for a real supreme commander; but when Sir Rob arrived in mid-November in order to take up his duties, and was interviewed by the Press, he said that he was not very clear himself about the wider powers which were to be given to him.

The widespread public dissatisfaction was aggravated a few days later by General Briggs, who in a farewell Press interview declared he had not been completely satisfied with his powers as Director of Operations. It was his dissatisfaction, he said, that had resulted in the promised changes for his successor.

On November 29 the Secretary of State for the Colonies, burly Mr Oliver Lyttelton, arrived in Malaya to see for himself and to discover how to bring the war to a speedy end. In addition to this he wished to sift the views of leading citizens about a successor to Sir Henry Gurney. He was told in no uncertain terms that what was wanted was strong leadership and ruthless determination. The conduct of the war and the administration of the country, with its progress towards self-government, had to be geared, he was told, so that they moved in concert. An early victory against Communism depended upon identifying the Chinese community with the struggle. They must be taught to think nationally. The planters warned him that if the situation had not improved materially in six months they would abandon their jobs.

After Mr Lyttelton's return to London various names were mentioned as being possible ' Supremos ' for Malaya. The betting seemed to be on Field-Marshal Lord Montgomery of Alamein, Deputy Allied Commander in Europe. He was the man whom the planters wanted. The problem of selecting a High Commissioner with the right blend of strength and imagination, with political flair and solid ability, above all a man of determination, occupied the British Cabinet for more weeks than Malaya considered advisable. The end of 1951 came and went, and there was still no word.

The year 1952 opened with the people in a worried frame of mind. It was plain that this must be a year of decision, otherwise the campaign would run on indefinitely, and time was on the side of the Communists. The year 1951 had been tragic and had shown weaknesses in the administration and in the field.

As Malaya waited for a decision, Lockhart said publicly that there was no certainty that the year would see the end of the Emergency. He outlined plans to improve the training of special constables, to organize and train the Home Guard, to improve the security of resettlement areas. Malaya once again took heart.

Commonwealth participation in the fight had increased. The 1st Fijian Infantry Regiment and the 1st (Nyasa) and 3rd (Kenya) Battalions of the King's African Rifles arrived as a welcome reinforcement to Malay, Gurkha, and British troops. There was a small contingent from Rhodesia in the Special Air Services Regiment. Australians and New Zealanders were playing their part in the air with the Royal Air Force.

The Fijian battalion had been specially raised to help Malaya in its war. The men were all volunteers, some of the finest specimens of their race. Major Ratu Cakobau, their second-in-command, who had won the Military Cross at Bougainville, had met some of the Malayan bandit leaders in the Victory Parade in London when he was with the Fiji contingent. After they had settled down the Fijians showed their worth. They sang as they killed. Every time they killed a bandit they were like delighted children.

It was the first time that East African troops had served outside their country in peace-time. The men belonged to one of the most historic units ever raised in the Colonies. The Nyasaland battalion was formed in 1888 when Lord Lugard needed local men to help in the British efforts at putting down the slave-trade. These troops later fought against the 'Mad Mullah' in 1902, and in Germany and Portuguese East Africa during World War I. In World War II many of the men served in Italian Somaliland, Ethiopia, Madagascar, Ceylon, and Burma.

The Africans called the bandits *shifta*, an insulting East African term for a bad man of any description. These cheerful but purposeful askaris proved themselves the right type of men for guerrilla warfare. Their powers of observation were amazing in the thick Malayan jungle. It seemed as if they were still in their African brush, lazily scanning the scenery and suddenly saying in Swahili, "There's a buck." The Africans were sent to the Bentong district, in South Pahang. Malay and Chinese Home Guards who went out on patrol with them were amazed at their keenness and their eagle eyesight.

In the midst of new hopes for the year came a sensation. Gray, the Commissioner of Police, resigned and left the country in secret. His departure was so secret that even the Police Secretary in Kuala Lumpur thought he had gone away on tour. It was an entirely unexpected and extraordinary way for the most important individual in the country next to the Director of Operations to leave. The Government never disclosed the reason for Gray's resignation except to say that he had asked to be allowed to resign as long ago as November 1950.

Gray had been a controversial figure from the day he had arrived. Somebody who knew him well said of him, " His great strength was his ruthlessness," and as the months passed even the men in the force, whatever many of them might have thought of him, realized that the situation demanded a strong man. He was a young man and a courageous man. He took a weak force in hand and he put strength into it. When he left the force had expanded from 158 gazetted officers, 188 inspectors, and 10,774 rank and file, a total of 11,120, to 481 gazetted officers, 617 inspectors, 400 British lieutenants and 23,656 rank and file, a total of 25,154.

The special constabulary, which was organized but ineffective when he arrived, was now 39,000 strong, and was an administered force, whatever its other great deficiencies. He had also thrown a police network out to remote villages and Malay kampongs by building eighty-one permanent stations and many temporary posts. He had consolidated an intricate radio network, and completely reorganized the administrative and equipment branches.

With Gray's sudden departure the Federation of Malaya found itself in the unenviable position of having no High Commissioner and no Police Commissioner, in the middle of a very critical time.

Within twenty-four hours of the publication of the news about Gray, the British Cabinet announced the name of the new High Commissioner. He was General Sir Gerald Walter Robert Templer, K.C.B., G.C.M.G., K.B.E., D.S.O., Commander-in-Chief of Eastern Command in Britain since 1950. For two years before that he had served as Vice-Chief of the Imperial General Staff, and before that as Director of Military Intelligence at the War Office. General Templer was to be charged with " full and direct responsibility for the Emergency," and he was to be assisted on the administrative side by a deputy High Commissioner. This division of duties was applauded in Malaya, which had seen Gurney immersed in the intricacies of Malayan administration and attempting also to shoulder the burden of the anti-Communist campaign.

The Conservative Government had apparently agreed with the contention of responsible opinion in Malaya, as expressed to Mr Lyttelton, that in order to make headway against the Communists a combined political and military operation was necessary. The prime political problem was the Chinese. Ways would have to be found to give them a greater political stake in Malaya. This would be an intricate problem for both the High Commissioner and his deputy, because they must first win, or compel, the co-operation of the Sultans and their subjects in this delicate matter.

General Templer as he packed in London remarked that he was "eager to have a go at what will be a tough job." It was an understatement. The High Commissionership of the Federation was the toughest job any British administrator had been given in modern history.

16

General Templer Arrives

IT was with unconcealed curiosity that Malaya read every small item of news about General Sir Gerald Templer, and awaited his arrival. His choice for the post was a surprise; his name had never even been among the 'also-rans.' Templer was to show that Malaya had lacked badly in perception.

He arrived in Kuala Lumpur a pale, highly strung, frail-looking man. He soon lost his paleness in the frequent trips he made under the Malayan sun all over the country. His frailty was deceptive, and he tired younger men by his physical and mental activity.

He turned first to the military problem, and this seemed to indicate that he did not intend to smudge his brilliant reputation by defeat at the hands of "a few idiomatic" Communists. (It may be noted that Templer brought to King's House, Kuala Lumpur, a freshness of idiom which appalled the older and more staid Malayan civil servants as much as it delighted their juniors.)

What is Templer's background and repute? Educated at Wellington and Sandhurst, he first saw active service at the age of eighteen in the Royal Irish Fusiliers. He is a good Ulsterman. In 1936 he performed the unusual feat of winning the D.S.O. and bar in peacetime, when fighting guerrillas in Palestine. His first World War II post was G.S.O. 1 (Intelligence) at Lord Gort's headquarters at Arras. Back in England after Dunkirk he raised and commanded a battalion of the Royal Sussex Regiment, was promoted from colonel to brigadier, then to major-general, and as such commanded various formations in the South of England. At forty-four he became the youngest lieutenant-general in the British Army and he was placed in command of the 2nd Corps District. Templer, however, of his own accord stepped down to major-general and to a divisional command so that he might go on active service in the Mediterranean. At Anzio a mine blew up under his vehicle and damaged his spine. Severe resulting injuries forced him to give up active command for the remainder of the War.

Templer was too good a man to be laid on the shelf and he joined Field-Marshal Montgomery's General Headquarters early in 1945 as Director of Military Government in Germany. Here these unfamiliar duties gave him about a year's experience of civilian problems. All reports indicate that he did well, but he was probably glad to return to Britain as Director of Military Intelligence at the War Office. After two years he was promoted Vice-Chief of the Imperial General Staff. Two years later he was promoted a full General and appointed G.O.C.-in-C. Eastern Command in Britain.

Now here he was in Malaya as civil High Commissioner and, in effect, military Commander-in-Chief. The British Cabinet had broken modern British Colonial precedent by placing a soldier in charge of delicate and complex political problems as well as making him Commander-in-Chief, but Malaya had become a country demanding a break with tradition. It was happy to have a professional soldier tackling the Emergency as long as he got things done, and as long as he was ready to use to the full his authority as High Commissioner and Commander-in-Chief.

For far too long had there been too much of a muddle between the Government, the police force, and the three fighting Services.

It had become clear that there could be no divided control in a country which was waging a small war against the background of a multi-racial political problem which in itself was unprecedented in British Colonial history.

The only doubts expressed about Templer were whether this able soldier possessed also the elements of high statesmanship and administrative capacity to co-ordinate the Governments of nine Malay States and two Settlements, and bring the two principal races, the Malays and the Chinese, to a smooth approach to self-government. If reputation could be relied upon Templer seemed to be a man with enough drive to get things done quickly and to cut his way through the thick tangle of difficulties which was Malaya.

As Templer's Deputy High Commissioner the British Cabinet selected Donald MacGillivray, Colonial Secretary in Jamaica. Although still a young man, MacGillivray already had a reputation for administrative ability. His appointment was immediately criticized in the Federation. The criticism was not against the man himself but against the choice of a man who had no knowledge of the country and its peoples. The traditionalists felt that an experienced Malayan civil servant should have been appointed. It was an unfortunate introduction to a new country for MacGillivray, but he very soon won the critics by his ableness.

Templer and MacGillivray arrived in Kuala Lumpur together two days after the death of King George VI. Templer brought with him a directive from the Secretary of State for the Colonies which stated clearly the British Government's policy towards the Federation of Malaya. It also appointed him Supreme Commander of all land, sea, and air forces in the Federation. The directive stated:

> The policy of the British Government is that Malaya should in due course become a fully self-governing nation. The Government confidently hopes that that nation will be within the British Commonwealth.
>
> In helping the peoples of Malaya to achieve this object—a fully self-governing nation—you [Sir Gerald] will at all times be guided by the declaration of policy expressed in the preamble to the Federation of Malaya Agreement.
>
> To achieve a united Malayan nation there must be a common form of citizenship for all who regard the Federation or any part of it as their real home and the object of their loyalty. It will be your duty to guide the peoples of Malaya towards the attainment of this objective and to promote such political progress in the country as will, without prejudices to the campaign against the terrorists, further our democratic aims for Malaya.
>
> The ideal of a united Malayan nation does not involve sacrifice by any community of its traditions and culture and customs, but before it can be fully realized the Malays must be encouraged and helped to play a full part in the economic life of the country, so that the present uneven economic balance may be redressed. It will be your duty to foster this process to the best of your ability. The Government believes that the British have a mission to fulfil in the achievement of these objects, and that even after self-government has been attained the British in Malaya will have a worthy and continuing part to play in the life of the country.
>
> Communist terrorists are retarding the political advancement and economic development of the country and the welfare of its peoples. Your primary task in Malaya must therefore be the restoration of law

> and order so that this barrier to progress may be removed. Without victory and the state of law and order which it alone can bring there can be no freedom from fear, which is the first human liberty.
>
> You may assure the Malayan peoples of all communities that they can count on the powerful and continuing help of the British Government, not only in the immediate task of defeating the terrorists, but in the longer-term objective of forging a united Malayan nation.
>
> The Government will not lay aside their responsibilities in Malaya until they are satisfied that Communist terrorism has been defeated and that partnership of all communities, which alone can lead to true and stable self-government, has been firmly established.

One of Templer's first acts was to issue a thirty-four-word circular to his Government officers saying, " Any idea that the business of normal civil Government and the business of the Emergency are two separate entities must be killed for good and all. The two activities are completely and utterly interrelated." This obvious fact he also emphasized to the people when he said in a speech, " There is no one who is not affected in his daily life by the Emergency. There is not one person who has not a personal responsibility for contributing something to its suppression. The Emergency is a thread that runs through the pattern of all our lives, whether we are employed in the Government, in commerce, in industry, in our own business, or in winning a livelihood from the soil."

In these two statements Templer indicated how he intended to fight the Emergency. The people would be called on to play a greater part than they had done.

General Templer's success in Malaya was based on a plan of campaign which had for its objectives the seven points contained in his directive from the Secretary of State. His approach to these objectives was twofold—a military campaign aimed at the defeat of militant Communism in Malaya, and a social and political campaign which would destroy Communism at its source, and would prepare the country for self-government within the Commonwealth. In both these fields his lines of action were as clearly defined as any order in an Army textbook. When he issued his first thirty-four-word circular to his officers he was not only under-scoring a fact, he was laying down a plan of campaign with a military precision which he was to follow for the next two years.

In his first year he reiterated again and again that the terrorists must be defeated before Malaya could even talk of self-government, let alone get it. He set about reorganizing and reconditioning the military machine which he had found on his arrival to be almost completely run to a standstill. Within days he had changed the whole structure of his High Command. General Sir Rob Lockhart, who had succeeded General Briggs as Director of Operations, accepted the change without murmur, although he found himself almost overnight in the subordinate post of Chief of Staff to Templer, who himself took on the task of Director of Operations.

From King's House, his office and residence, Templer was in direct communication with his new operational headquarters on a hill overlooking Kuala Lumpur. Here the complete military and civil planning of the war was centred.

Templer went on to streamline the forces of war and of Government and the people. Because he considered it impossible to divorce the 'Emergency side' of government from the normal peacetime processes, he abolished the Federal War Council, which had existed since Briggs established it in 1949, and merged it with the Federal Executive Council. Both had been separate policy-making bodies, the one on the conduct of the war, the other on the conduct of government. Amalgamating them, Templer decreed, "There can be but one instrument of policy at the Federation level." He wanted no Government with a split personality guided by two separate councils. Through this new and enlarged Council Templer hoped to evolve plans for the absolute defeat of Communism and for the creation in its stead of "a way of life"—"not necessarily the British way of life, nor the American way; it must be the Malayan way of life."

Templer based his blueprint for a united Malayan nation on some of the ideas propounded by his predecessor, Gurney. It called for a well-trained and efficient police force "which has the admiration and friendship and trust of all the law-abiding people in the land," the establishment of a Federation Regiment (apart from the Malay Regiment) formed of all communities, up-to-date medical and health facilities in towns and villages, a national education system, land tenure for peasant farmers, the encouragement of non-racial youth movements through which boys and girls would be taught to realize their future responsibilities to the land of their birth, the introduction of a common form of citizenship, and elections among rural communities up to Municipal Council level as a first step leading eventually to elections to the various legislatures and finally the Federal Legislative Council.

Templer reiterated in his own inimitable manner what Gurney had said before him, " I could win this war within three months if I could get two-thirds of the people on my side." So he began trying to win those two-thirds. He went about the country exhorting villagers to defend themselves, to inform the Government about their enemies, and to try and run their own villages as a first step towards self-government. Then occurred an incident which was to have a profound effect on Templer himself, on his reputation, and on his future conduct of the Emergency.

On March 25, 1952, occurred an ambush which by its calculated coldbloodedness horrified a Malaya which had apparently grown hardened to tales of successful Communist ambuscades. The scene was the town of Tanjong Malim, which stands on the Selangor-Perak border and is fifty-one miles north of Kuala Lumpur.

Tanjong Malim, a town of about 20,000 Chinese and Malays, straddles the north trunk road. It is the centre of a vast rubber-growing district, and it possesses an important training college for teachers. Tucked in the hills is a reservoir from which Tanjong Malim gets its water supply. The two-mile-long pipe-line ran through good bandit country. Since June 1948 terrorists had sabotaged that line five times. On each occasion the line had been repaired, and none of the repair parties had been ambushed. On the night of Monday, March 24, terrorists smashed the pipe for the sixth time.

At seven o'clock the next morning a repair party set out to restore the town's water supply. With this technical group went fifteen men of a police jungle squad, Mr R. M. C. Codner (the Assistant District Officer of Tanjong Malim), and Mr W. H. Fourniss (the Executive Engineer of Public Works in charge of South Perak).

Michael Codner had become world-famous during World War II when he and two others had escaped from a German prisoner-of-war camp by using a wooden horse. In the best-selling book *The Wooden Horse* Eric Williams, the author, described Codner as a man who had won the respect of his fellow-prisoners because of " his fine intelligence and ready courage."

Codner had been born in Malaya thirty-two years before. After the War he had joined the Malayan Civil Service, and he had been sent to Tanjong Malim. He became the kind of District Officer who had been known and respected before the Japanese war, a man who immersed himself in the welfare and progress of the people of his district.

Resettlement had become one of Tanjong Malim's big problems, and the people were suspicious of it. Codner, I was told, worked incessantly to inform the people that the barbed-wire fence around them was for their protection rather than to fence them in. He was a capable, hard-working man who spent too few hours at home. As he went round his district building six resettlement areas he showed contempt for the terrorists.

Early that Tuesday morning Codner and his party followed the pipeline from the town looking for the break. Possibly they were not expecting any serious trouble despite the rather grim reputation of the district as a centre of Communist activity. Two miles from the town they walked straight into a planned ambush. The first burst of fire killed or seriously wounded most of the party. Codner, hit once, tried to crawl for cover, was shot at again, and was killed. His body was found later some yards off the track near undergrowth which he had tried to reach. Fourniss, too, was killed.

The first few minutes of the engagement were fierce as unwounded policemen fought back. Constable Lew Thai Lim, the only Chinese, who carried a bren-gun, had his arm shattered by a bullet in that opening hail of bullets. He handed his bren to another constable and fought with a rifle, firing it with one hand, the butt gripped between cheek and shoulder, until he was killed. The other police bren-gunner, Harun bin Ismail, was surrounded by bandits at very close range, but he fired two full magazines before he died.

The battle was heard in Tanjong Malim. Police-Lieutenant W. J. Jones in the station thought the terrorists were attacking the town. He and his squad scrambled into a truck, reached the perimeter fence round the town, jumped out, and ran a mile towards the firing, then found themselves in the zone of fire. Jones collected his men together and launched a counter-attack, charging up a hill in the face of the terrorists. As usual, the enemy were not anxious to stand up to reinforcements. They broke and fled.

Codner and Fourniss were among twelve dead men, who included seven policemen. Eight other policemen were wounded, but only three of them were fit enough to move unaided. Only one man, a Malay water overseer, escaped unhurt.

Two terrorists out of an estimated forty had been killed. Some of their positions were only two yards from the track, and it was from these that the terrorists had crept up to dead and seriously wounded men and grabbed their guns. They made off with a valuable haul of a bren-gun, several rifles, sten-guns, and pistols.

Three days later General Templer himself went to Tanjong Malim and pronounced collective punishment on the 20,000 people. He was using the Emergency regulation which had been used drastically on Tras, the village which was supposed to have bred the killers of Gurney. But the manner in which Templer imposed his punishment on Tanjong Malim staggered Malaya and brought him a good deal of criticism in the British Press and in Parliament. In Malaya, though, most people supported him.

Stalking angrily into the Training College hall into which 350 Malay, Chinese, and Indian community leaders from the district had been gathered, Templer plunged straight into a denunciation of their people. He said that the savage outrage could only have taken place with the knowledge of certain of the local inhabitants. " Of that I am certain," he added.

He reminded the men before him that Codner and eleven other men had been murdered as they were on their way to repair the water pipeline. " None of this would have happened if the inhabitants in this part of the country had had courage," he said. " You want everything done for you, but you are not prepared to assume the responsibility of citizenship.

" I want law and order, so that I can get on with many things which are good for this country. Why should it be impossible to do these good things? Because people like you are cowards? Do you think that under a Communist régime you will be able to live a happy family life? "

Suddenly he asked, "Are any of you Communists in this room? Put your hands up." Not one raised a hand. Templer went on, "All right. I shall have to take extremely unpleasant steps."

The leaders listened to the punishment in silence. The sentence,

The Main Street of Tanjong Malim Town during Daylight Curfew Hours

Photo "Straits Times"

A Typical Rural Village in the Federation of Malaya

General Sir Gerald Templer with Sir Cheng-lock Tan, Leader of the Chinese in Malaya

Photo "Straits Times"

Lady Templer

In her British Red Cross uniform.

Photo "Straits Times"

which affected every man, woman, and child for miles around, was a strict twenty-two-hour house curfew, the shops to open only two hours a day, no person to be allowed to leave the town, all schools to be closed, and the ordinary rice ration to be reduced for men and women to less than half the usual allowance.

Templer pointed out that the terrorists had only been able to operate in the district because they had received food from the population. He listed the terrorists' record in the district since January 1 that year. There had been five ambushes, ten attacks on military and police patrols, five lorries burnt, six thousand rubber-trees slashed, seven strikes due to intimidation of labour, three buses destroyed, five unsuccessful road ambushes, one train derailed, one attempted derailment, an attack on a Malay village, sixteen terrorist camps found, eight policemen killed and nine wounded, and seven civilians murdered and two wounded. On only three occasions had people come forward with information.

"This," he declared, "is going to stop. It does not amuse me to punish innocent people, but many of you are not innocent. You have information which you are too cowardly to give."

Finally he issued a warning to other towns in the Federation that he would not hesitate to impose similar punishment on them if it was obvious that they had allowed the Communists to thrive as they had been doing in Tanjong Malim.

Reaction to Templer's sentence on Tanjong Malim was immediate. In the House of Lords the Earl of Listowel (Labour) declared the restrictions were unnecessarily harsh. Lord Salisbury, Secretary for Commonwealth Relations, defended Templer, saying, "We have sent out Sir Gerald as the best man we could find to do a job of particularly difficult and delicate kind. Surely one must give him the proper chance to do it. Sir Gerald has the complete confidence of the Government; he has been given full discretion to deal with the Communist terrorists in Malaya."

Tanjong Malim suffered its curfew and its food restrictions for fourteen days, but during the first week of its punishment Templer initiated a new method of obtaining information, which he repeated with varying successes in other terrorist-infested areas of the country. Soldiers and policemen visited every house in the district and handed the occupants a sheet of paper with the invitation to write what they knew of Communist suspects and supporters. They were given the assurance that nobody but Templer would see their replies, to which they need not sign their names.

Twenty-four hours later each house was visited again and each householder was invited to place his sheet of paper, filled or unfilled, folded up into sealed boxes. Representatives from the communities accompanied the boxes to King's House in Kuala Lumpur, where they watched Templer unseal them, pour the contents on to a large table, and then go through some of them.

It has never been disclosed what proportion of the replies were blanks, and how many either authentic or vicious information. At any rate, before the punishment was lifted the police arrested about forty Chinese in Tanjong Malim who were suspected of being bandit couriers or food suppliers. Some were well-dressed Chinese of the shopkeeper and grocer type. Others looked like rubber-tappers.

Whether General Templer was right in imposing such a severe punishment on Tanjong Malim was a matter for discussion by arm-chair critics for weeks. The criticism in London was, however, to slow Templer down considerably. He found himself in a situation in which every act of his was being watched in Parliament, and, therefore, he had to modify much of what he would have liked to have done or said in his first few months. He himself had a sneaking suspicion, I am told, that he had been too severe, but it had its effect in Tanjong Malim, where the district quickly built up a force of 3500 Home Guards.

No. 36 platoon of the Malayan Races Liberation Army, which killed Codner and his men, moved north and broke into small parties.

Four months later information from the people was officially described as " of a much better quality and in a far greater quantity " than had been received before. It was not all of immediate operational value, but it could be used by the police for building up their dossier of the terrorists in the area.

Tanjong Malim soon became one of the safest towns in Malaya. This could not be attributed solely to the new spirit among the people. It was rather owing to a belated effort by the Government to give the town the defences it had required long before. Two sets of wire fences, interspersed with fifteen high look-out towers now ringed the town, and the entire perimeter was lit up at night with one of the most effective lighting schemes in the country.

The Government's new-found determination was to try and end the Emergency by all means possible. It announced tremendous increases in the rewards for the capture or killing of every Communist in the country. The amounts excited the imagination of everybody, as they were undoubtedly intended to. The Government had taken the advice of the Chinese, who had always suggested that big money might tempt not only informants to talk but the lower orders of terrorists to surrender and turn police informer for cash. To-day a number of ex-terrorists have built small fortunes for themselves by cold-bloodedly guiding troops to their old camps and helping them to kill or capture ex-comrades. I know one ex-rubber-tapper-turned-bandit-turned-informer who has obtained at least £3000 in rewards locked up for the future. Chen Ping, the Secretary-General, naturally headed the new list. There was a reward of 250,000 dollars (about £30,000) for his capture alive. This represented a three-fold increase on the old figure of 80,000 dollars (about £10,000). Three-fold increases were also offered for the capture or killing of all Communist leaders above District Committee level.[1]

The announcement contained a sentence which was obviously directed to the relatives of many of the leading Communists; these people were known to be living in the New Villages and towns in the Federation. Using the significant phrase " bringing in alive," it said that this included " the positive arranging with the authorities of the surrender of a known terrorist now in the jungle."

Millions of leaflets announcing these rewards were air-dropped into known terrorist areas, where jungle discipline made it a serious offence for any terrorist to be caught picking them up or reading them. It took a long time, therefore, before any concrete results came from among the terrorists themselves. The most sensational surrender occurred in Perak when a terrorist gave himself up and disclosed that his platoon commander and many of his men were anxious to surrender. Negotiations were begun at once. In the end thirteen men and women emerged from the jungle. They immediately made long statements and then returned into the jungle with troops and police, directing them to camps and secret trails. Along the way they planned ambushes against former associates

[1] These rewards were withdrawn in 1953.

for which they raked in the half-rewards given to informers of their type.

The fourth year of the Emergency closed in a most optimistic atmosphere. Templer had proved a driving inspiration. He was going round to New Villages assembling their committees and their Home Guards, upbraiding those who had shown a lack of interest in their own defence, and congratulating those who had shown courage and a sense of responsibility. To all in the front line he repeated, " When you shoot at bandits shoot to kill." The Templer method seemed to be getting results. The Army had been reorganized and retrained and re-equipped with the best weapons for jungle warfare. It was in high fettle.

17

Communists Admit Defeat

EARLY in 1952 a Communist document fell into Government hands. Its contents were so remarkable that it was most closely scrutinized by Intelligence officers. All surrendered and captured terrorists were cross-examined about their knowledge of the document. Dated September 1951, a month before the assassination of Sir Henry Gurney, it had been issued by the Malayan " Politburo." Its detailed contents have been kept top-secret, but General Rob Lockhart, the Deputy Director of Operations, disclosed them in general terms in October 1952. A directive by the Central Executive Committee of the Party to all State and district committees, the document expressed neither defeat nor any intention of abandoning the original objective of establishing a Malayan Peoples' Republic. However, it declared that murder and intimidation had not been good tactics by which to gain the support of the people of Malaya. Therefore, said the Politburo, there must be a new approach to the campaign, an approach that had to surpass in its appeal the Imperial Government's resettlement and social progress policies.

The State and district committees were given the following new instructions:

Terrorism towards the civilian populace was to be curtailed. The guiding principle of all operations was that unnecessary " inconvenience " to the masses had to be avoided.

Attacks on the security forces to capture arms and ammunition should not be carried out if in their course members of the public were likely to be injured.

Food-collection was to be the primary task of the " self-protection " branches of the Min Yuen rather than sabotage and intimidation.

> Increased attention was to be paid to ensuring the security of the " Executives of the masses " [*i.e.*, the terrorist leaders and important State, district, and branch committee members]. More attention was to be paid to " urban organization."

This directive took months to reach all groups of the Malayan Communist Party, and it can only be assumed that the marked fall in the number of terrorist incidents and murders during the latter part of 1952 owed something to the new design in tactics.

However, it cannot and should not be assumed that the Communists would reduce their offensive to the mere capturing of weapons and ammunition. This was not the first time during the Malayan war that the Communists' central command decided to change the style of operations. Early in 1949 a similar situation arose after the Communists had realized that they had failed to achieve their immediate objectives of creating chaos and confusion among the peasants and rubber and tin labourers, and of driving the planters and miners off their estates and mines.

Police intelligence officers are certain that at that time the Communists must have considered calling off their war and beginning all over again with a new and really long-term plan of penetration into the trade unions.

As things turned out, they obviously threw out such a change of strategy, but they did withdraw their troops for retraining and they did recast their war policy in terms of a long-drawn-out military struggle, a decision that undoubtedly must have been affected by the progress of the war in Indo-China and the outbreak of the war in Korea. The Malayan Communists saw themselves as participating in a world-wide Communist struggle, despite the absence of direct orders from either Moscow or Peking.

The Communist forces were withdrawn for a short period, but at a time when the military and police could not take advantage of the opportunity to hit the enemy hard. The police themselves needed intensive training to make them a really aggressive force, and there were insufficient troops for thorough deployment in all bad areas of the country.

Therefore the terrorists were able to train without much interruption, and the Government's opportunity was lost. The Communists emerged again to begin an alarming and mounting series of successes against the armed forces, and of terrorist acts against civilians.

To-day, however, the situation is vastly different. The initiative has passed into the hands of the Government and its forces, and, with the great strength in Home Guards, coupled in addition with a rising confidence among the people, there does not appear to be any reason why the country should not seize the opening afforded by this Communist switch of policy and gather the strength for a knock-out blow.

The co-ordination between all arms of the fighting forces is the closest it has been in years, and, furthermore, the morale of all the troops is high—higher than it has ever been since the Communist revolt broke out. They all feel that at last they have the measure of enemies who are probably the world's best jungle fighters.

But the Communists still retain the advantage of surprise in attack and a disconcerting ability to keep up a steady flow of recruits to replace their casualties. They still have relatively enormous funds. For example, when the price of rubber was high, the Communists were reported to be collecting more than £1,150,000 a month selling stolen rubber to local dealers.

With all these advantages the Communists can prolong the fight in the field for a long time, perhaps indefinitely, because they are staking their future on a Chinese Communist advance into the country. They must also be aware that the end is in sight for their revolt if there is no outside assistance forthcoming. Their position cannot get better; it can only get worse. They have come to realize that they will be hit so hard and so often that a final knock-out has become a possibility. The Government's psychological warfare arm, which had been inept for four years, will have to play a great part in this stage of the campaign.

The Communists' new directive showed that the enemy had become as aware as the Government that it is the peasants, tappers, miners, shopkeepers, the ordinary people of Malaya, who must be wooed. The solicitude they expressed for " the masses " was something new and strange in their system.

They began to concentrate on a campaign of political subversion, and General Templer showed that he realized this when he said that such a campaign would be conducted " with even greater energy and stealth."

The question remains whether the tremendous propaganda machine that the Government built up in 1952 is not only ready but capable of combating the Communist propaganda corps, which has been remarkably effective despite the obvious drawbacks of having to work from the jungle.

The stress which the new directives put on food-collection and the need for improving organization in the urban areas confirmed that resettlement had broken the Communists' lines of communication.

Food to-day has become the greatest single problem for the terrorists. Enemy documents captured late in 1952 showed that it was only the state of foodstocks which determined whether men could be concentrated in numbers sufficiently large for an attack on a police station or rubber-estate, or whether only a small ambush could be laid. The Communists were finding it difficult to get supplies, shelter, clothing, tactical information, and other forms of support previously received from the Chinese squatters when they had lived in their scattered and isolated communities.

But Communist influence has not been entirely eradicated from the new villages. Communist cells have sprung up within them, food is smuggled out, admittedly not in large quantities, and young men suddenly disappear into the jungle to join the enemy.

There have been reasons for this continuing support, and the Communists have not been slow to exploit them. For example, compulsory resettlement developed mixed reactions among the squatters. Many felt undoubted relief in the comparative security of their wired-in villages, but this was offset by resentment over the undeniable irritations of constant or long curfews and certain restrictions over taking food or money out of a home. A man who leaves a New Village for a hard day's work in his vegetable-garden or on a rubber-estate is not permitted to carry any food for his mid-day meal except a bottle of coffee, tea, or water. He may not take even a biscuit. The official reasoning is that if, for instance, five men each take out a biscuit, their five biscuits can stem the hunger of one bandit for one day.

This is an undeniably harsh measure, and although villages agree it is the lesser of two evils, and that it has produced the expected results, it still rankles.

How effective the control of food can be where it is methodical and persistent is illustrated by the experience of Seremban, the capital of Negri Sembilan. An operation named " Mother Hubbard " was launched which called for a great co-operative effort by Government officers, Home Guards, Asian auxiliary police, civilians, and the police and the Army.

The heads of all Government departments, including the British Adviser and the Malay State Secretary, took turns to man roadblocks at the six main road exits from the town between 5.30 A.M. and 7 P.M. The auxiliary police took over as many road blocks as they could man from 7 P.M. to 6 A.M., when 200 Asian Auxiliary Policemen, who were still under training, volunteered to assist them, and the gaps were closed. The Home Guards patrolled the areas between the roads both by day and night.

In three months the supply of food from numerous shops and relatives and friends in Seremban was virtually cut off from the terrorists in the surrounding country. Their troops killed a courier just outside Seremban. On him they found a letter from a Communist district commander to his superior officer.

Part of it read: " Regarding the conditions here, the enemy are seen almost every two days. They lay ambushes at the place where we once camped. The controlling and checking of masses' [the peoples'] foodstuffs are still very strict and here nothing can be bought. This drastic measure applies to many places."

Information led to the arrest of people who had been regular food-suppliers to the Communists. More information unearthed food caches which showed how well the terrorists had lived. The dumps held hundreds of tins of British oats, meat, fish, milk, and cocoa. There were also great quantities of rice and sugar.

" Mother Hubbard " was a remarkable demonstration of co-operation and co-ordination, and it could have been repeated in other towns and villages in the country.

Unfortunately, food does not reach the terrorists from within the boundaries of the Federation only. The Colony of Singapore has always been a very important forward supply base for the Communists. Until a checking system was instituted on traffic on the Federation roads heavily loaded food-trucks drove over from Singapore and unloaded or ' accidentally ' dropped consignments along a planned route. When this became risky owing to movement-control measures supplies went over by boat across the Strait of

Johore. It was not until the end of 1952 that the Singapore Government deemed it necessary to co-operate with the Federation by taking anti-smuggling measures along the Strait. They placed searchlights at strategic points along the northern coast of Singapore island, and marine police patrolled the Strait every night. Belated though this co-operative effort was, it reduced the supplies of food, cloth for uniforms, and explosives to the terrorists.

Parallel with the war in the field ran the Federation Government's 'second front,' the battle to win the loyalty of the Chinese and other races, the ordinary people of Malaya, and build among them a sense of responsibility as citizens. This is the tougher of the two jobs, and Templer realized it as much as did his predecessor Sir Henry Gurney, the originator of the policy of capturing "the hearts and minds of the people." Gurney saw that one of the most important solutions to the problem created by the Emergency lay in creating a new loyalty among the 500,000 or more rural Chinese who had been resettled. They had to be made to feel a real allegiance to public authority and then support it fully in its anti-Communist struggle.

Gradually the policy gathered momentum, principally in the New Villages inhabited by the one-time squatters. Providing them with security has not been the only requirement. It was imperative that the lives of the New Villagers should be made more attractive than their old ones and that this should be done hand in hand with the operations to give them "freedom from fear." As a Government White Paper put it, "The foundations of a better life in the New Villages will be not only freedom from fear but also water supplies and sanitation, schools and dispensaries, the growth of civic sensibility, and pride in communal as well as individual achievements."

A very realistic Government officer, who has had years of experience with the Chinese and appreciates their forthright mentality, qualified this statement with a blunt, "The degree of co-operation we get from a New Village is in almost exact proportion to what we have put in it. In short, where the amenities are good the people are good."

Templer made the development of the New Villages into thriving communities with a civic pride a high priority in his work. So great was his emphasis on New Villages in the first months of his campaign that he was openly accused of being pro-Chinese and, inevitably, anti-Malay. His critics did not appreciate the singleness of purpose which was one of the man's chief qualities. Paradoxically, when he had dealt with the New Villages, and his policy changed, the Chinese called him anti-Chinese and pro-Malay. It is a stupendous task, and Templer's determination is hampered only by the lack of trained men to push through the plans to give roads, drains, schools, clinics, community centres, playgrounds, and to bring adult education schemes and Boy Scout and Girl Guide movements to these villages.

The New Villages, now numbering 600, with 680,000 people living in them, are Malaya's new pioneering towns. They are bustling with activity, enterprising, expanding. Quite a number boast shops, markets, a laid-on water supply, and decent sanitation. Village committees are elected by popular vote, and each man on a committee is given responsibility for some phase of life in the community. Some of them have progressed so fast that they have been elevated to the dignity of Town Boards, with greater responsibilities of building up revenue and learning to spend economically.

At this stage a tribute must be paid to the New Village Supervisors, the Britons, Australians, and New Zealanders who have infected the people around them with their own faith in their work and its future. As I said in an earlier chapter, these men led lonely and dangerous lives, and the success of resettlement depended almost entirely upon their ability to win the confidence of an alien people, many of them frightened, many resentful at having been torn from their homes.

Side by side with them are British, Australian, and New Zealand Red Cross nurses, the women workers from St John's Ambulance Brigade, and the missionaries. They have all built up tremendous goodwill, not only by their work among the villagers but also by living among them and sharing their hardships and facing their dangers.

In nearly every village there is a team of one nurse and one welfare worker. Life is hard for the two women but it is a commentary on their success that they are asked for advice not only on matters of health but also on a great variety of personal and village problems.

Almost every village has a school, which the villagers maintain. The number of men and women joining adult education classes is growing. In many parts of the country the policy has begun to show the results originally hoped for. They are seen in the genuine enthusiasm shown by the people to manage their own affairs, to eradicate Communism from their midst, to display defiance to the terrorist groups which apply to them for help, and to defend themselves.

Essential to the defence of each New Village and Malay kampong are their Home Guards. For months they had been 'defended' by untrained groups of men who lacked purpose and resolution. It was not entirely their fault. The Government failed to take sufficient interest in them and did little to encourage enthusiasm.

At last it admitted the importance of Home Guards in the 'second front,' and money was swiftly set aside to recruit instructors. A retired British Army major-general was given the task of reorganizing the entire system. He had to build a staff to train a force of 420,000 men who could take on the defence of villages against terrorist aggression. When trained these Home Guards relieve hundreds of Regular police from static duties. For these duties, also, men have come from Commonwealth countries to be staff officers and instructors. They had fought against the Germans or the Japanese, and training the Home Guards and leading them on patrol against the Malayan Communists was their additional contribution to the cause of freedom.

Since they were thus taken in hand the Home Guards have shown considerably more interest and initiative in their duties. Their importance may be gauged by the fact that in 1953 the Federation Government spent £1,000,000 arming one in every three Home Guards, and also equipping them for the first time with armoured vehicles.

Parallel with the reorganization of this civilian defence arm is the great task of retraining 75,000 officers and men of the country's Regular police. This is in preparation for the day when, as Templer put it, the police in every village will be armed only with batons, working on purely police duties and acting as a reserve for the Home Guards who will be defending hearth and home.

If this ideal is achieved the Federation police will have a phenomenal achievement to their credit. It is appropriate here to pay a tribute to all those pre-war police officers and the post-war new-comers for their herculean labours.

What has been achieved already, particularly in 1952 and 1953, is remarkable enough when we consider that rather less than one in seven police officers had no previous experience of Malaya, and also the more important fact that the police have never had time to consolidate since the Emergency began.

The police will not be used wholly on static duties. Four hundred operational sections have been formed to move out with the Army in jungle patrols.

Colonel A. E. Young, then Commissioner of Police, who came from the City of London Police to succeed Gray and to reorganize the Force, acknowledged the task of the Federation police in Malaya's Emergency to be " the most difficult in the world." Young, a tremendous organizer, full of tact and a policeman to the hilt, succeeded in the fourteen months he was in Malaya in welding the Force into a closely knit organization.

In only one directon has the attempt of the Federation Government to build a truly national police force failed. Chinese have refused to join its ranks despite the appeals of Templer and of their own leaders. Sir Cheng-lock Tan has told his community that the Government was right in demanding that Chinese should form a reasonable proportion of the armed forces, considering that they form more than half the population.

He said, " If out of a population of three million Chinese we cannot recruit between two thousand and three thousand into the police then we deserve to have conscription placed on us."

A form of conscription had been introduced by Gurney, and had proved a failure. It led to wholesale ' dodging ' by Chinese who preferred the risks of life in the jungle, or in Communist China, to serving in the police force. After two years of trial the experiment was dropped. Chinese leaders in Malaya, surprisingly, still prefer conscription to a system of volunteering for the defence of the country. But although the legal machinery for conscription now exists, lack of finance precludes its use.

18

Decline in Terrorism

GENERAL Templer's military brilliance and his dynamic personality produced wonders in the two years he served in Malaya. In the administrative and political fields he showed qualities which few expected from a military career man. He called for action all the time; where it had not existed, or did not exist, he created it in his inimitable and forcing manner.

Templer wooed and won the co-operation of most of the men and women in the New Villages and the kampongs. Once they were surly and sullen. After a little more than a year of seeing and hearing from Templer they changed their attitude. They smiled and waved at him when he visited them again and again in his famous fact-finding tours round the country.

They accepted his bluntness, the bluntness that told them they could have done more in the past and would be required to do more in the future, otherwise there was only one place for them—and that was China. He poured scorn on them, and they looked at him in a new light, a light that made them respect him and what he stood for more than they feared the Communists.

So as 1953 followed 1952 the change in the situation became marked. The main roads hummed again to traffic which sped even by night. Travellers found they had lost that fear which had painfully contracted their stomachs whenever they drove along certain stretches and took bends in desolate country. The railway service came into its own again as it became clear that the line was no longer under constant attack. The night trains, suspended for many months, were resumed, and soon reported capacity custom as travellers gained confidence. The terrorists, it seemed, were being pushed farther into the jungle, away from the roads and the railways and the towns. The security forces were thrusting themselves deeper and deeper into the jungle after their enemy. The intensive food control measures were reducing daily supplies to terrorists. This was affecting their stock-piles.

Occasionally gaunt and emaciated Reds, men and women, green uniforms in tatters, staggered out to surrender, and, according to the releases of the Government's information service, told harrowing tales of insufficient food, " a cigarette-tin of rice a day," " eating leaves," " haven't been in a rubber-estate for months."

Home Guards and special constables showed greater pluck in fighting it out with marauders, and the Chinese among them committed themselves to anti-Communism. The great majority upheld the trust placed in them. There were, inevitably, some lapses when the shot-guns in the armouries of a very few New Villages were raced triumphantly into the jungle by Communist pillaging parties. It was impossible to prove that these successes had been inspired by traitors within the wires.

The time came when Templer decided to place responsibility for local defence wholly on village Home Guards. It was a risk, but Templer never baulked at taking risks. His new move became popular, lifted morale still higher, and developed an *esprit de corps* among the people whose villages had been chosen for the honour. The Regular police were moved from their old static duty to more important work elsewhere.

Then in the autumn of 1953 Templer suddenly announced the policy of instituting what he called " White Areas." Places which had been free from Communist incidents over a long period of time and whose inhabitants had proved themselves anti-Communist by helping the police were given their freedom. Food control and other irksome restrictions were lifted. Shops could open day and night instead of for limited hours. Curfews were cancelled. Hawkers could set themselves up again. Goods, once tagged " restricted," could be moved freely within the boundaries of the ' white ' area.

The people could live normally again. They could take a full midday meal to their tapping, or their padi-fields, or their vegetable-gardens, instead of no food at all. Lovers could walk up a lane again without thinking of the hour, or being sharply challenged by prowling patrols for being out during curfew hours. The coffee-shops and eating-shops could be noisy with nightly gossip. Children could run about wild at night instead of being cooped up in a hot room from sundown to sunrise. Life in 'white' areas was no longer to be all work during the day and no play in the evenings.

For his first 'white' area Templer chose 221 square miles along the pleasant coast of Malacca. With a flourish of ceremony and speech he declared it so one sunny morning in September 1953. This freedom affected 160,000 people, well over half the population of Malacca. Templer told the 400 representatives from all parts of the territory gathered before him that the Communists might try to return to get the food being denied them elsewhere. "That," he said, "is a risk I am prepared to take.

"It is the job of every one to keep the Communists out. Refuse them supplies. Report their presence at once to the police if they do come back."

As the weeks passed Templer's faith seemed justified. It was not until five months later that a Communist foraging expedition was reported in the area and successfully ambushed. After this other areas were declared 'white.'

All in all the Communists seemed to be taking a sound beating in the field. Reports showed they were being harried, killed, or starved. A new word was used by the Government to describe victories. It was "elimination," which meant terrorists killed, captured, or surrendered; it also meant kills by traitors in the jungle. The graph of Communist-inspired incidents took a downward plunge. The figures spoke for themselves. In 1951 there were over 6100 incidents. In 1952 they had dropped to 4700. By the end of 1953 they totalled 1100.

Even more gratifying was the fact that the security forces were making an increasing number of contacts. They were finding and killing terrorists, particularly important members of district, branch, or State committees. These were the Reds with experience, with knowledge, imbued with fanaticism to the militant cause. They would never have surrendered. They were therefore almost irreplaceable in the Communist command.

There were exciting moments when tired-looking terrorists surrendered and reported having killed their leaders in order to "free" themselves. There was the section leader who shot Yong Hoi, the Terror of South Perak, who boasted he had personally murdered a hundred people. Yong Hoi was one of the toughest

General Templer unlocks a Box of Secret Information

This information came from the residents of the punished town of Tanjong Malim, some of whose representatives watch him.

Photo "Straits Times"

Two Characteristic Photographs of General Templer

Left: He discusses the problems of resettlement with a Malay at Seminyih in Selangor
Right: He listens to a British planter in Pahang.

Photos "Straits Times"

SIR DONALD CHARLES MACGILLIVRAY, K.G.M.G., M.B.E.

High Commissioner of the Federation of Malaya.

Photo Central Office of Information

and most cunning fighters in the Red command. His own gangsters feared him.

There was also the bodyguard who killed Ah Kuk, a member of the Central Executive Committee, decapitated him, and then on surrender produced the gruesome proof of his act.

These were isolated instances but they seemed indicative of the change of mind that was affecting the weaker of the enemy. Psychological warfare was improving, but very slowly. Millions of leaflets were dropped into the jungle calling on terrorists to surrender. These painted a pleasant picture of life outside the jungle. They bore photographs of terrorists showing them " at time of " and " after " surrender. The contrast between the gaunt, ribbed figures before capitulation and their smiling, well-fed, well-dressed appearance some weeks later must have spoken volumes to the men in the jungle.

The leaflets had some effect, but the psychological warfare experts wryly admitted that the rate of surrenders was very slow. Discipline in the jungle was still rigid enough to force waverers to withstand the Government's appeals to " forsake the jungle " and its offers of " freedom to start a new life," and of an attractive reward for bringing " five or more of your comrades with you."

Templer was prepared to try anything in the psychological warfare field if it might have an effect. He even went to the length of mastering a message in Mandarin to broadcast via that new psychological weapon, the Voice Aircraft, which flies low over the jungle and amplifies messages to individual terrorists or groups.

Templer said in Mandarin, " This is General Templer speaking to all armed members of the Malayan Communist Party. You needn't be afraid and can surrender. This is my personal pledge to you. You will not be ill-treated."

Templer paced up and down King's House for three days mastering his Mandarin. Time will tell what effect it had on the Communists.

While life outside the jungle appeared to be easing for people who had lived in fear since 1948, what was happening within the enemy's territory? It took nearly a year for the 1951 directive to penetrate to the State Committees and then filter down to the districts. As it was promulgated locally, so terrorist attacks slowed down. Thus, the beautifully kept charts in the outside world began to reflect this militant inactivity. The Communists reached a state of suspended animation. With only a limited number of targets left for them to attack under the terms of the directive—security forces, police posts, and convoys—their fighting men round the towns and villages were split into small units, whose main task was to collect food. The majority of the fighting men were withdrawn into deep jungle along the central mountain range in Kelantan, Pahang, and Perak.

The situation in this vast and dark territory to-day presents a serious long-term threat, unless the Communists can be isolated and their leaders killed or captured. The Communists dominate that territory. They have found they can live in it, and they have as valuable supporters, whether voluntary or forced, the nomadic aborigines whom they have dominated since, as the M.P.A.J.A., they fled into the jungle from the vengeance of the Japanese in 1942.

Once upon a time security force commanders cried, "Win over the New Villagers, and the terrorists are beaten." To-day their cry is, "Win the aborigines and we win the war."

They stress that whoever controls the aborigines controls the deep jungle, and whoever controls the deep jungle wins the Emergency. It will therefore be necessary to winkle the Communists from every hole and corner in the deep jungle into which they have thrust themselves.

In one and a half years, from the date of the directive, the Communists cultivated hundreds of little vegetable-gardens in the deep recesses of the mountain range and in the forests of every State. It was a formidable accomplishment, despite the reported lack of relish with which platoon commanders and superior bren-gunners and killer squads dropped their weapons and handled hoes to dig for a Communist victory. Many of these gardens could be seen from the air. They were plotted. In the course of time they were destroyed, either by ground forces or by chemicals sprayed by aircraft. More disturbing became the fact that hundreds more gardens are hidden from the lenses of aircraft cameras. In the early days of their digging campaign the Communists had laid their vegetable-plots with traditonal Chinese rectangular neatness. The bombers and the ground forces were attracted to them, and their attacks forced the cultivators to camouflage their gardens.

As they had once learned that rubber-estates were never bombed and they could therefore find refuge in them from attacking aircraft, so, as they worked with the aborigines, they realized that unkempt, haphazard native plots were also free from aerial attack.

It was not the policy of the Government to destroy the holdings of the indigenous people unless there was absolute proof they were for the use of the enemy. To-day the difficulty is to discover which untidy plots are bona fide aborigine, and this becomes a distinct problem when it is remembered that there are 100,000 aborigines with the wanderlust. The Communists are also using these timid people as spies and as a highly sensitive human radar screen around their jungle hideouts.

Gurkhas possess an uncanny jungle sense, and they have reported " feeling," but not seeing, the eyes of aborigines in front and behind them as they moved cautiously forward to Communist camps, which were deserted when they reached them.

Deep in the jungle, too, the Communists have built bases. These were part and parcel of the 1951 plan of the Central Committee. Their intention is to hole up in these bases and in the course of time to launch " major " operations from them against the Government, a rather ambitious plan considering their extremely limited resources. Yet they can continue to exist as a menace from these bases, which represent another reason why the jungle has to be controlled by the security forces.

The Central Committee drew up a three-year programme to construct at least two deep-jungle bases in every State and Settlement of the Federation. In the first year they planned to send their less useful members and suspected waverers to lay the foundations of these ' forts.' This labour force also had to plant vegetable-gardens. In the second year the independent platoons of the fighting forces were to withdraw into these sites and complete the fortifications, In the third year the armed units would move into them and there be retrained, reindoctrinated, and held in reserve.

Several bases already exist. They are difficult to find. Templer once sent five battalions into deep jungle in Kelantan after some vague information about the existence of such a base. The troops thrashed around for six weeks without finding their target.

Towards the end of 1953 a new Central Committee directive made its appearance. It was issued after an internal battle about future policy. The rapid decline in terrorist acts had raised the morale of the public but lowered that of the Communists. In addition, many supporters, once driven by fear, had ceased to assist the Communists. The flow of money and food decreased considerably.

At the Central Committee meeting the military representatives demanded the re-exploitation of the troops. They declared these had been neglected. The powerful political men were against renewing terrorist attacks, principally on the grounds that the Party could not support large military groups and terrorism would hamper the work of building subversive organizations in towns and villages. Indeed, they wanted to cut the armed forces to the minimum.

It became interesting to learn, and the Government's Intelligence had their sources of information, that Chen Ping, the Secretary-General, favoured resumption of armed aggression, and that he was strongly supported by two men who lost their lives soon afterwards, Chan Poon, of Pahang, and Ah Kuk, the supreme military commander for South Malaya. Chan Poon was killed by security forces, and Ah Kuk was decapitated by his bodyguard. A new directive calling for renewed aggression was issued. The question is: Will it come?

Are the Communist units still well-armed?

At the height of their campaign in 1950 and 1951 they won a considerable armoury from the security forces, but during a certain period in 1953 they were losing an average of sixty weapons and 3000 rounds of ammunition a month. The Communists have resourceful armourers who are accustomed to improvise when faced with munition shortages. They extract cordite from unexploded shells or bombs. They dry old cordite. They retrieve empty cartridge cases and refill them with the cordite. The same resource is shown in the manufacture of guns. Some new weapons come in via the Siamese frontier, but the Government asserts that this supply is negligible.

Communist recruiting is the really serious problem. General Templer was "passionately concerned" about it. A scientific analysis of statements by surrendered terrorists showed that where previously fear had fed them with recruits, now it was dread of police action threatened by treacherous Communist agents which sent young men into the jungle.

A separate investigation by the psychological warfare department produced different results. They reported that it was a combination of the two which kept up the Communists' numbers, although their quantity was unknown.

Whatever the reasons, recruiting is a problem that does not appear to have a solution.

Perhaps the most alarming feature created in Malaya by the lull in terrorism was the dangerous complacency which developed among the public. They believed the shooting war to be almost over.

Planters lost their lives because they ceased to observe the normal security rules. Many allowed their high-frequency radio sets to run down. These were installed to give them alternative communication with the police should their telephone lines be cut. Formerly they tested these sets every night. As the months of reduced terrorist activity passed they foolishly omitted to take this precaution. Indeed, the United Planting Association of Malaya was forced to remind all planters to maintain the elementary safety rules on their estates. Even V.I.P.'s were reminded by the Government to maintain their usual escorts, even though they might be travelling in clear areas.

The Communists are likely to remain a force to be reckoned with for a long time. Their latest policy to renew aggression makes them more dangerous. They know that time is on their side, and they do not forget to remind their comrades on the lower levels that this is so. They maintain that the China Communist Party will come to the aid of the Malayan Communist Party either via Indo-China or by direct assault on Malaya.

The comrades are also reminded that Mao Tse-tung and his men lived " in the Chinese jungle " for thirty years before they rolled the Nationalist Government out of China. " What he did," they say, " we can do."

The Central Executive Committee is aware of the fact that in the near future Malaya will be given its independence.

Can the Party be eradicated before this day comes?

19

Malaya's Problems

CAN Malaya win this war against armed Communism? Police and Army officers express the hope that the backbone of terrorist violence will be broken by the end of 1954 if terrorist losses continue at the 1952 and 1953 rate. In that sense the war can be won, but it will still take a long time, and much will depend upon the external situation.

Can Malaya fulfil the more important immediate requirement, which is to disrupt the Communist Party so completely that it will be unable to prosecute its war or plan subversion with any sort of discipline and cohesion?

The answer does not lie in field measures alone. To win the war the Government must win the hearts of the masses, the majority of the population, below the social strata represented by the businessmen, the planters, the miners, and the middle-classes. That mass must be won over to be actively anti-Communist.

In particular the Chinese must be won over quickly because time is not on the side of the Federation Government. The uncertain factors affecting the morale of the Chinese in Malaya are world Communism in general, and Chinese Communism in particular.

If Communist China continues to show little interest in the Malayan affair beyond its usual fulminations via Peking Radio the Malayan situation will not be affected considerably. There remains Indo-China, in which Communist China shows tremendous interest.

Indo-China is the key to the entire situation in South-east Asia. If the Communist Viet Minh forces succeed in that country the Communist road of advance runs into Thailand, down through Malaya, into Indonesia, and then points southward to Australia.

Sino-Soviet expansionist policies are already well-known, and in Malaya it is imperative that the great Chinese population should be staunchly on the side of the Government before Red China begins moving southward with her enormous manpower, as many feel she will one day.

This threat from Communist China overshadows the minds of the Chinese in Malaya. They remember the fate of Chinese who were pro-British or anti-Japanese when the Japanese walked into the country. These men were the first to be singled out by the Japanese for torture and execution. Thousands were killed.

To-day the Chinese want to be certain that they will not jeopardize their own safety by taking a stand against Communist China. The successes of the security forces have impelled many Chinese to jump off the fence they had been straddling, but too many still remain on that fence.

I remember very well the conversation I had with a friend in the Government who is an authority on the Chinese in Malaya. He said that early in the Emergency the Chinese would have liked to help the Government to quash it overnight, but they were to a great degree powerless because they were not a community at all but a " collection of individuals paralysed by fear—fear of the present and fear of the future." Such a state was traditional with them, and many accepted it, but there was no discipline among them, and consequently no automatic obedience. Every Government decree or order was weighed in the balance against Communist displeasure, which itself was very real considering the number of Chinese who had been murdered, always brutally.

My friend went on, " To try and handle a community in this state is, some say, an impossible task. It is often said that the only way to deal with the Chinese is to make them fear Government more than they fear the Communists. Now, that's most attractive in theory, but what threat are we to use which is more effective than the threat of death? How are we to make our threats effective against more than two million individuals?

" It's highly dangerous in a war of ideas to plump for the much advocated ' strong line with the Chinese ' without the implications.

" The answer must be to try and build up a community or groups capable of internal discipline and susceptible as a body to external control and guidance. We must concentrate on those Chinese who have been described as law-abiding. Bring them completely over to our side and make full use of them."

He felt that the Chinese who had known the control of the Communists since 1945, the labourers, tappers, miners, skilled craftsmen, were not "all fools." Give them protection and encouragement and they will resist the Communists.

"If this Emergency is to end," said my friend finally, "the Chinese must be controlled, disciplined, and from time to time severely punished. If they fail to accept responsibility they should be dealt with firmly."

Templer's tactics proved my friend right. But military successes are not the only assurances the Chinese want. They demand a stake in the land and the rights of Malayan citizenship.

The Malay State Governments finally recognized this. They agreed to some highly important and controversial reforms being launched in the Federation in order to win over the Chinese. These reforms were intended to run hand in hand with the military measures. Some go back to the policy of Sir Henry Gurney, others have been initiated since Templer's broom got to work, but all have been introduced since the Emergency broke out. Indeed, they might have been delayed another decade but for the Emergency. Whatever its damaging effects, therefore, the Emergency did Malaya a good turn. It gave the impetus needed to break down the barriers of prejudice, tradition, and vested interests.

The theme in the country to-day is "Malayanization"—the Malayanization of Chinese, Europeans, Indians, Eurasians, and other races, who look upon the Federation as their real home and the object of their loyalty. This was the most complex of all Templer's problems, and will be the most complex for his successor.

Malayanization, it is hoped, will overcome the communal differences and prejudices existing principally between Malays and Chinese, who suspect and distrust each other, and whose suspicion and distrust threaten to turn the Federation into a second Palestine.

Throughout the country, therefore, the peoples of the two races are being urged to co-operate with each other. In every New Village, in every Malay kampong, there is the entreaty, "Co-operate. Be brothers."

Government officers make it, Templer emphasized it, Chinese and Malay leaders repeat it.

Legislation to create a common Malayan citizenship has been adopted in the Federation as a necessary first step in the evolution of the Malayan nation of the future. To-day more than a million Chinese are Malayan citizens by law and the way is open for many Chinese, Indian, Ceylonese, and other residents from beyond the Federation to become citizens by registration.

Although the law has not gone far enough to satisfy the Chinese and has gone too far to please the Malays, it is generally accepted as a great step forward.

There is also a new education policy. Free primary education has never been given in Malaya. Chinese and Indians and Malays were educated in communal schools and in their own languages. They had therefore no common tongue and they lived exclusively within their own communities when they reached adult years. This made the development of national unity in a plural society impossible until reform began at the bottom and at the beginning, in the schools. National schools are one solution, and a policy to establish them has been approved.

Land reform was the first of the great concessions to aliens by the Malay Sultans on representations made first by Gurney and then by Templer. Agreement on land reform would have been inconceivable in the days before the Emergency when the Malays would have demanded adherence to old promises, which acknowledged the complete rights of the Malays.

The Sultans and their Governments accepted the fact that the Chinese had to be regarded as integral members of the permanent population and that many thousands of them were anxious to remain in the Federation. This decision in many instances was influenced by events in Red China. Rather grudgingly, though, the Sultans agreed to the grant of land to the Chinese inhabitants of New Villages.

The Chinese agriculturist can now get a title to his patch of good earth in Malaya. The land will be on lease rather than freehold, but this does not detract from the fact that the Malay Governments have made a great departure from traditional policy and racial privilege.

Another Malay break with tradition was opening the Malayan Civil Service to Chinese, Indians, and other non-Malay Asians who are Federal citizens. This administrative service has always been regarded as a British and Malay preserve. Domiciled Chinese and others who wanted professional openings for their sons objected.

Templer in announcing the reform emphasized the need to retain " the special position of the Malays " in the Civil Service. A ratio of one to four was to be maintained, he said, between non-Malays and Malay recruits. Presented with this opening, non-Malays have not rushed to apply for places. In one year only two Chinese and three Indians applied for admission to the Service. Only three of the five had the necessary qualifications. Chinese are still suspicious of the implications of working under the Malays in this service and fear that advancement for them will be slow.

A national Federation Regiment was created as another move towards inter-racial co-operation. This force is intended to be the " younger brother " of the Malay Regiment, which is purely Malay, now seven battalions strong. Here, as with the attempt to form a national police force, few Chinese enlisted. Conscription may yet have to be used to fill the ranks.

The political front has become active. Malaya has never known the franchise and elections, and a start has been made with local government as the best training for taking on larger voting responsibilities in the State and Federal Councils.

An elected majority exists in Municipal Councils and also in the Town Councils of the larger towns of the Federation. Elected councils in the New Villages are increasing rapidly. Templer has said that in 1954 the first move will be made towards elections for State Settlement Councils. By the middle of 1955 will come elections on a national basis for the Federal Legislative Council, thus setting the gate open to Parliament in a self-governing country.

In honesty, it must be admitted that the demand for democratic reform seems at present to come only from a small articulate minority. The large majority in all races remains uninterested. This apathy and indifference is confirmed by the small percentage of eligible voters who have turned up for Town Council and Municipal Council elections. The Malay is content if he is governed fairly. So is the average Chinese, except that he wants the necessary elbow-room in which to carry out his business. He also prefers comparatively peaceful conditions in which to do it. The theory of political advancement may be said to be unintelligible to at least 95 per cent. of the entire Malayan population.

It can hardly be said that there are political parties in the British sense operating in the Federation. The two main political organizations up to the end of 1953 were the United Malays National Organization and the Malayan Chinese Association. Both are communal in character. Both, however, opened their membership to other races but only as "associates," which means they cannot participate in the affairs of the party. In large towns U.M.N.O. and the M.C.A have declared an "alliance" to contest local elections, but the cynical declare that this alliance exists on the surface only; underneath, the dangerous antipathy between the two races continues strongly. The cynics add that each party is making use of the other for political ends. Only time will tell whether the alliance will prove the cynics right, or whether it is leading to a firmer and more enduring partnership in political life.

The Independence of Malaya Party, an admirable effort to found a party on a multi-racial basis, has had a very small following confined to what might be called the intelligentsia of the Asian population.

Dato Sir Onn bin Ja'afar, its founder, who resigned from the presidency of U.M.N.O. because he was convinced its purely Malay character was bad for the country, has admitted that the founding of I.M.P. was premature.

In the beginning of 1954 he and his followers established a new non-communal Party named "Party Negara" (*negara* is a Malay word meaning country), which they hope will be the first party in power when the Federal Legislative Council receives its first elected majority.

There is a strong fear in Malaya to-day that unless a united Malayan nation is achieved before the British Government hands self-government to the country a "much more terrible Emergency" of racial strife may break out.

Tension exists between the Malays and the Chinese, and it will require a great deal of mutual friendship, trust, and understanding to kill this growing dislike.

In 1952 Dato Sir Onn himself startled Malaya by some remarkably candid comments on racial relations. He declared flatly that racial tension was on the increase. He described the horrors of Sino-Malay clashes in 1945 when, he said, he saw Malays and Chinese "killing each other for no reason whatever except that they were driven by a blind hatred." He added:

> I should hate to see another period like that in Malaya, either to-day or in years to come.
>
> As one who has spent a considerable part of my life in trying to bring together the different communities in this country to work as friends, I feel that the present position is one about which there can be no complacency. I speak with some feeling on this particular aspect of Malayan politics, because there have been allegations that there is nothing to fear as between community and community.

Of course, Dato Sir Onn's declarations brought vehement denials the next day from the political parties. One admitted that " some communal differences and prejudices " existed but added that " these are only to be expected in a plural society."

There is the fear that any premature transference of power would precipitate chaos and strife in Malaya—and would inevitably lead to Communist domination.

The problems that lie ahead are, indeed, most serious and complex. It is literally the British Government's last chance in Malaya to prove its ability to rid this vital protectorate of its Communist enemies and clear the road for a free but united nation, in fulfilment of its promises. Malaya is valuable to the British Commonwealth. It is valuable for its raw materials and for its prestige and position in world strategy.

During the first three years the handling of the fight against the Communists was slow, but the fresh impetus and resolve that came with the dispatch of General Templer to be High Commissioner and supreme commander, with the sweeping powers that Sir Henry Gurney and General Briggs lacked, gave promise that Britain's immediate mission in Malaya would not fail.

In January 1954 came the news that Templer was not to remain in Malaya. He had fulfilled most of his tasks; there was not only considerable improvement in the anti-Communist war, but plans for social and political development were advancing on the " second front " despite the Emergency. Templer's ambitions lay, not in Malaya, or in politics, but in his Army career. He was given command of the British Army on the Rhine, the biggest Army job outside Chief of the Imperial General Staff. When he was leaving Malaya, however, the War Office cancelled his new post, and said that it would shortly announce an important military appointment for him.

The British Cabinet announced that Sir Donald MacGillivray, Templer's Deputy High Commissioner, would succeed him in Malaya as High Commissioner. However, operational command of the security forces engaged against the Communists would be placed in the hands of a military Director of Operations. This was a switch-back to the days before Templer, and thinking people feared that dual control would seriously affect forceful continuation of the field offensive. Many people also felt that the termination of the Emergency should be paramount above political and social development, even though the country was in the stage when the emphasis was quite definitely on social and political progress rather than on the Emergency itself.

To some of the fears expressed about the future conduct of the Emergency, it could be replied that the new Director of Operations was promised all the powers of a fighting commander that Templer possessed. Also, Sir Donald MacGillivray had already served two years in the onerous job as Templer's administrative and political head, and knew only too well the dangers that could develop from lessening the offensive at a critical turn with the Communists on the defensive. Thus, with his experience and brilliance as an administrator, and his ability to get on with Asians, his promotion found general acceptance in London and Malaya.

As High Commissioner, however, he was to be faced with political and social problems that would not only be difficult but also aggravated by a most serious financial crisis which, long before Templer had left Malaya in June 1954, had begun to slow down plans for developing the country, and, a more serious thing, to affect the anti-Communist campaign. Templer had been forced, for instance, to order a serious reduction in the strengths of the police force and the special constabulary. No country without money can fight a war and progress in social and economic spheres at the same time. This lack of money came about when the prices of rubber and tin, which had reached record heights in 1950 and 1951, bringing riches to State and people, had slumped in the succeeding years. Templer had several times warned Britain and America of the military and financial dangers to Malaya if they did not support the Malayan rubber industry. In 1954 the Federation Government worked on a budget deficit of nearly £30,000,000—a lot of money for a small country engaged in a long anti-Communist war.

So, with very little money behind him, MacGillivray took on a Malaya which was restless for speedy political development. He faced the unenviable task of developing a united Malayan nation. He was, however, given a country which was high in morale and confident about the eventual outcome of the war against the Communists, provided there were no complications created by the Communist world outside Malaya.

The people had heeded Templer's continuous warnings that there was no short cut in the fight against Communism. He said several times that it was " a ruthless war against ruthless men," and that there was " a long way to go yet." The situation to-day might be aptly described in the words of one of Templer's most trusted advisers, who, in private conversation, said, " Just as aircraft pioneers have reached the sound barrier and have not conquered it because they do not know what is beyond it, so have we, in this war in Malaya, reached our ' sound barrier.' We must stall around until we find out what the Communists on the other side intend to do—and we can remain in this ' sound barrier ' stage for years."

The Communist high command is not expected to surrender, or even contemplate asking for conditions of surrender. It is fanatically intent on its determination to create a soviet republic in Malaya—however long it may have to wait for a suitable opportunity. That is the picture on the Emergency side.

Socially and economically, Malaya has also reached the stalling stage. The lack of finance will hold up for some time the massive schemes for social and economic development which Templer put into motion when Malaya was riding the high crest of big money. Politically, there is great danger of lack of unity. Templer never minced his words when he spoke of the political dangers confronting Malaya and when he asked for closer understanding to develop between the Malays and the Chinese. He said once, " We have a wonderful chance in Malaya to see that the transfer of power, when it comes, is achieved in an orderly way and without bloodshed and suffering." Can this be achieved in spite of the background of the Emergency?

Glossary of Words not explained in the Text

Bahru: new
Blukar: secondary jungle, scrub
Bukit: a hill, small mountain
Kampong: a village, cluster of houses
Kota: a fort
Kuala: an estuary or a point of junction with a river of its tributary stream, or the source of a river
Kubu: stockade
Ladang: a plantation on dry ground (in contradistinction to one on swampy ground), a description applied to aboriginal holdings
Lumpur: mud
Mukim: a parish
Padi: rice (a general term)
Parang: a chopper, knife used in felling
Pulau: an island
Rotan: a generic name for rattans (plants belonging to genera Calamus and Dæmonorops) especially when these plants are of economic value.
Sakai: aborigines
Siput: A generic name for snail
Sungei: river, stream
Trishaw: (a mixture of the words rickshaw and tricycle) a mechanical rickshaw
Ulu: a remote place, back of beyond hinterland

Many names of towns are made up of words in current usage, thus Sungei Siput means Snail River, Kuala Kubu Bahru is The New Stockade (Fort) at the Source of a River, and Kota Bahru the New Fort or New Town. Translations are not given in this glossary for all towns, but the reader who is interested may readily find the significance of these names in a good Malay dictionary.

Index